Claws of the Crab

Stephen Brook is the author of many acclaimed travel books including *New York Days, New York Nights, Honkytonk Gelato, Maple Leaf Rag, The Double Eagle, Winner Takes All* and, most recently, *L.A. Lore*. He also wrote the bestseller, *The Club: The Jews of Modern Britain*. He contributes a regular column on wine to *Vogue*.

Claws of the Crab:
Georgia and Armenia in Crisis

STEPHEN BROOK

PUBLISHED BY PAN BOOKS

First published 1992 by Sinclair-Stevenson, London

This Picador edition published 1993 by Pan Books Ltd
a division of Pan Macmillan Publishers Limited
Cavaye Place London SW10 9PG
and Basingstoke

Associated companies throughout the world

ISBN 0 330 32638 4

9 8 7 6 5 4 3 2 1

A CIP catalogue record for this book is available from
the British Library

Typeset by Deltatype Ltd, Ellesmere Port
Printed in England by Clays Ltd, St Ives plc

To Penelope Hoare

Contents

Acknowledgments

Travelling to the Caucasus during the troubled months of 1991 and 1992 was not easily organised, and I am greatly indebted to the many people who made it possible for me to visit both Georgia and Armenia. Michele Burlington-Green of Intourist put me in touch with Pnina Deadman, who arranged for invitations to be sent to me from both republics. Svetlana Chudaneli and her late husband Soso Kheladze looked after me splendidly in Georgia, and I am particularly grateful to Erekle, Demo, and Zeinab Grigolia, and to Levan Butkhuzi and Giuli Ebralidze for taking me into their home in Tbilisi. I also wish to thank Sandro Taktakishvili, Teimuraz Buachidze, Nunu Gabunia, Academician Jumber G. Lominadze, Dr Otar Darakhvelidze, Mzekala Shanidze, and Dr Gerald Mars.

In Armenia I was kindly invited by Kevork V. Zakoyan and Arman Maroukhyan of the Armenian Society for Friendship and Cultural Relations with Foreign Countries. George Hintlian and Rita Balayan also helped to arrange my visits to Armenia. I also wish to thank, in London, Reverend Vrej Nersessian, Reverend Onnig Kiremidjian, Misak Ohanian, Baroness Cox, the Armenian National Committee of Great

Britain and Andrew Kevorkian. In Yerevan I owe much to the help given me by Vladimir and Armine Ossipov, Aram Vayroumian, Ashot Mkrtchyan, Armen Petrossian, Kamo Tanielian, Dr Gerard J. Libaridian, and Arman Grigorian. Particular thanks go to Jennifer Gurahian. Jane Hargreaves of Chapter Travel coped heroically with coaxing information and reservations from Aeroflot. Gunnar Wiebalck of Christian Solidarity International kindly allowed me to use photographs taken by his team in Nagorno-Karabakh.

All pictures were taken by the author unless otherwise stated.

List of Maps

PART ONE

1 Advanced Denial

They were blots on the map, pimples on the backs of Turkey and Iran. They were represented in the Western mind by equally scrappy images: genocide and earthquake in the case of Armenia, wild horsemen and smiling centenarians in the case of Georgia. If Armenia registers more strongly on our consciousness, it is because murderous neighbours forced the survivors into a worldwide diaspora. The Georgians stayed home, too rooted in their culture to find life comfortable beyond their borders. Squeezed between the Slavic mass of Russia to the north, and the proselytising fervour of Islam to the south, both nations have come close to extinction. The total inhabitants of both do not surpass the population of London. Yet their cultures reach back further than those of most European nations. They were Christian nations by the fifth century, and solving complex architectural problems a century or two before Carolingian and Romanesque architects achieved comparable mastery. Both nations have not only their own language, but their own alphabet.

In the rush to independence that followed the slow dismemberment of the Soviet Union, both Armenia and Georgia asserted strong claims to free and separate existence. In the pursuit of that goal, both republics became the prisoners of their histories and cultures.

Mesmerised, like all the world, by the changes taking place in the Soviet Union, I wanted to be a spectator. In an earlier book, *The Double Eagle*, I had observed parts of central Europe on the brink of decisive change. I could see how economic and thus political

GEORGIA

Kirovabad

Grozny

Orjonikidze

KHEV-
SURETI
TUSHETI

MTIU-
LETI
PYAVI
ZRTSO-
TIANETI

KAKHETI

Telavi

Rustavi

KHEVI

Alaverdi

SOUTH
OSSETIA

Tskhinvali

Gori

Mtskheta

TBILISI

LOWER
KARTLI

Stepanavan

Khashuri

INNER KARTLI

C A U C A S U S   M T S

RACHA

Kutaisi

Zestafoni

Borjomi

TRIALETI

TORI

DZHAVA-
KHETI

A R M E N I A

R U S S I A

LOWER
SVANETI

UPPER
SVANETI

Mestia

LECH-
KHUMI

MEGRELIA

Zugdidi

Samtredia

IMERETI

MESKHETI

Akhaltsikhe

T U R K E Y

ABKHAZIA

SUKHUMI

Mikha Tskhakaya

Poti

GURIA

Kobuleti

ADJARA

BATUMI

Black Sea

N

National boundaries ▪▪▪▪
Present-day provincial boundaries ▪–▪–▪
Historic provincial boundaries ⋯⋯⋯

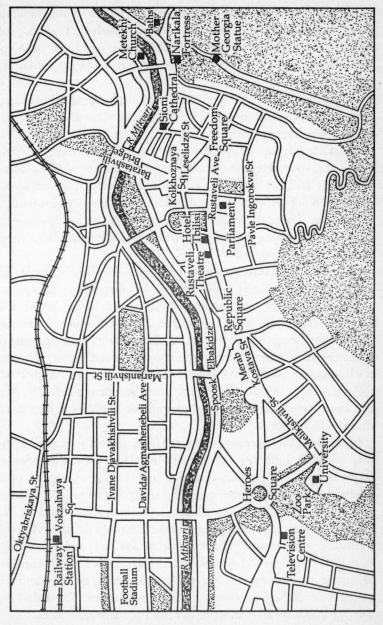

TBILISI

Baths
Metekhi Church
Narikala Fortress
Mother Georgia Statue
R. Mtkvari
Sioni Cathedral
Kolkhoznaya Sq
Leselidze St
Freedom Square
Rustaveli Ave
Baratashvili Bridge
Pavle Ingorokva St
Hotel Tbilisi
Rustaveli Theatre
Parliament
Republic Square
Elbakidze
Spoosk
Marjanishvili St
Merab Kostava St
Melikishvili St
University
Ivane Djavakhishvili St
Davida Agmashenebeli Ave
Heroes Square
Zoo Park
Oktyabriskaya St
Railway Station
Vokzalnaya Sq
R. Mtkvari
Television Centre
Football Stadium

pluralism were developing in Hungary but, like everyone else at that time, had no inkling that the Velvet Revolution would soon transform the cynical neo-Stalinist Czechoslovakia I visited in 1987 into perhaps the most prosperous of the former Soviet satellites in eastern Europe.

By the time I left for Georgia and Armenia in the autumn of 1991, both republics had declared their independence. Events were moving swiftly, especially in Georgia, where the president, Zviad Gamsakhurdia, was acting in ways that were, in the most charitable view, eccentric. He was accused by his opponents of autocratic behaviour and his extreme nationalist rhetoric prompted serious worries among Georgia's many ethnic minorities as well as among its neighbours. Gamsakhurdia could maintain that he had been elected by an overwhelming majority and thus enjoyed a mandate to pursue the policies he espoused.

In Armenia the turmoil was not domestic, but international. The uprising within Nagorno-Karabakh, an Armenian enclave surrounded by Azerbaijan, had severely strained relations between the two new republics. The war within Karabakh and the constant skirmishing along the borders of the two countries were straining the resources of a poor country already pulverised by a calamitous earthquake in 1988. As I set off for Armenia, the republic was seeking to cope with the latest and most severe of a series of Azeri blockades, which had reduced the supplies of building materials and energy to a trickle.

My trips to this part of the Soviet Union were intended as a jaunt that would include visits to the dazzling High Caucasus, leisurely inspections of early medieval churches, a thorough sampling of the celebrated local gastronomies, and a study of the problems inevitably encountered by two small nations seeking independence from the disintegrating Soviet Union. I would be overtaken by events. As Georgia's polity crumbled towards civil war, and as fuel shortages worsened in blockaded Armenia, travelling around both countries became more and more difficult. Tourism would be supplanted by political developments that were hard to monitor. Rumours, lies, bias, propaganda all combined to keep the situation volatile.

*

Anyone travelling in the Soviet Union knows that something will always go wrong. There's rarely any point in asking why: you just mutter 'Aeroflot' and give a bitter laugh. On landing at St Petersburg, I learnt that back at Heathrow British Airways had neglected to load fifty pieces of luggage on to the plane, and mine was one of them. At the Lost and Found office, I filled out forms so that my suitcase could eventually be forwarded to me in Tbilisi. Since there wouldn't be a British Airways flight to St Petersburg for another week, I could look forward to a long wait.

I wandered over to the bank to purchase some roubles, which the teller doled out in fives and tens. The wads bulged embarrassingly from my jacket like a transvestite's padding until I could stash them more discreetly. Before going to the other terminal for my flight to Tbilisi, I looked in at the Lost and Found one last time. In the corridor stood a trolley, from which my suitcase was being unloaded. I reclaimed it with glee, but no one could explain its sudden appearance after I had been doggedly assured that every item of luggage had been unloaded an hour earlier.

It was only a few kilometres to the domestic terminal, but the taxi driver wanted ten dollars. We settled on three, so he earned a week's wages for five minutes' work and a demi-tasse of petrol. He left me at the Intourist section of the terminal. All large Soviet airports have separate facilities for foreign visitors, who are given preferential treatment. At museums foreigners are expected to jump the queues, and it was no different at the airport. A minibus took me and an American passenger to the parked plane. A couple of hundred Soviet citizens were cooling their heels on the tarmac, while we were led directly up the steps. I sat next to a Georgian woman, who insisted on handing me some toffees she was bringing back from Moscow to the sugar-free zone called Transcaucasia.

Svetlana and her husband Soso were at the airport to meet me. It was Svetlana who had invited me to Georgia under the auspices of the organisation she had recently founded to promote cultural contacts with Great Britain. It would soon become apparent, with painful irony, that just as the frontiers were opening to her and other

Georgians, a more impenetrable barrier was descending in the form of a plummeting rouble, thus multiplying the costs for Georgians visiting the West, while political instability was deterring all but the most intrepid Westerners from visiting Georgia.

She seemed relieved that I had actually arrived. There had been rumours of more violence in Tbilisi that morning, and some flights had been cancelled. She had booked me into the Hotel Tbilisi, an old-fashioned pile, Edwardian in its gestural grandeur, splendidly located on Rustaveli Avenue, the main street of the city. My room was small but comfortable and a balcony overlooked the central courtyard.

After a cold supper in my room I took a stroll down Rustaveli towards the Parliament. For some months there had been political disturbances in Tbilisi. Despite an overwhelming victory in the presidential elections, the new president Zviad Gamsakhurdia soon antagonised an influential segment of the population. There had been frequent demonstrations against him, to which the response had sometimes been violent. Rustaveli was quiet, but only because buses barricaded the street near the Parliament buildings, preventing traffic from getting through. A broad flight of steps led from Rustaveli up to the main courtyard of the Parliament, and tents had been pitched on the steps. Despite the late hour there were loudspeaker vans in the street broadcasting slow Georgian chorales as well as fiery speeches from the podium at the top of the steps. Small groups of men were parading with flags, while others stood about in small knots arguing among themselves. I returned to my room, to which the breeze carried fragments of the speeches that continued to blare out late into the night.

In the morning there was still a small crowd outside the Parliament, but some of the demonstrators now lay snoring on camp beds beneath the portico. If these were angry demonstrators, they were behaving in a very good-natured way. I continued down Rustaveli towards the former Lenin Square. Its centrepiece, a statue of Lenin, had gone, and the space had been renamed Freedom Square. Nearby stood the largest department store of Tbilisi. Independence had not brought abundance. There was a reasonable stock of records and shampoos and lotions, of tawdry clothing and of toys unlikely to survive an infant's half-hour attack. Some sections, emptied of goods, had simply been closed off. Half the escalators didn't work, neither did most of the fluorescent lighting.

Back at the Parliament the demonstrators were folding up their camp beds and preparing for another day of speeches. On the pavement opposite, where bread was being sold from behind makeshift stands, a crazed woman scurried past, her face a mask of white paint, with half-inch bands of mascara above and below her eyes, and a splash of scarlet lipstick twice the area of her mouth. She looked terrifying and terrified. The men behind the stalls called out to her, but she paid no attention.

I returned to the hotel. At the far end of the lobby a desk impounded passports and dispensed keys. In the left corner a switchboard would, in exchange for the dollar equivalent of over three months' average wages, attempt to make connections with the West. Journalists with laptop computers waited behind the counter for their calls to come through. A much larger counter claimed to be the Intourist Service Bureau, but the woman who sat patiently behind it was working for a private tourist agency. She needed patience because there were hardly any tourists in Georgia. Travel posters urged us in English and German to visit Soviet Georgia but the word 'Soviet' had been taped over in every case. In the front of the lobby, which was maintained in a state of permanent gloom, there was a news stand and chairs for the hotel staff. The lobby staff consisted of a few old men who did nothing except sit on the chairs and gossip among themselves. Immediately outside the entrance was a shoeshine stand.

The dining room was at its best at lunchtime. In the evenings, a reluctance to turn on more than the minimum of bulbs kept lighting and spirits low, but during the day light streamed in from the courtyard. The decor of this large neoclassical salon was ornate in the extreme. Three huge chandeliers shaped like inverted phalluses flopped down from the ceiling, but only once, and then by accident, were they switched on, giving a theatrical explosion of light. Lunch was also more copious than dinner. After a range of cold dishes –

tomatoes, salty cheese, bunches of parsley and other herbs, mashed beetroot with garlic, sliced aubergine in a cold walnut sauce, and variations on the theme of cold cabbage – we were brought soup, sometimes a borscht or more often *kharcho*, a spicy broth with rice, vegetables and chunks of beef. The main course might be plump pork shashlik, the fat and gristle content varying according to availability and budget. There was no fruit and no coffee, although such items were easily available elsewhere.

Many Soviet cities are studies in orderly blandness, but not Tbilisi, which grew up along the twisting valley of the River Mtkvari, overlooked by mountainous slopes too steep to be built upon. Along the more gentle escarpments are tiers of wooden houses on stone foundations, tricked out with carved balconies. Built at various angles, depending on the stance of the rocks which anchor them, these balconied houses, often cheerfully painted in blue or white, are Tbilisi's most striking feature. The antiquity of the town is evident not so much from the essentially nineteenth-century houses and institutions near the centre but from its surviving churches.

Sioni Cathedral, close to the river, is the seat of the revered patriarch of Georgia, Ilya II, who inhabits a pleasant round-arched villa, its porch smothered in ivy, which stands in a pretty garden within the compound. Founded in the sixth century, Sioni has been destroyed and rebuilt on many occasions, a frequent victim of fires and invasions by Moslem neighbours. Sioni is typically Georgian in style: a cupolaed church roughly in the shape of a Greek cross. As in so many Georgian churches, the interior seems unexpectedly large, since the compact proportions of the exterior keep the volumes tightly packed. Inside, the eye soars to the height of the cupola, hemmed in by hefty tufa walls darkened by gloomy nineteenth-century frescoes. To the left of the iconostasis is the Cross of St Nino, the Cappadocian saint who brought Christianity to Georgia in the fourth century. Legend proclaims that she created the distinctive national cross of Georgia, with its sloping arms, by binding vine branches with her own hair.

Even older than Sioni is the other riverbank church, the Anchiskhati basilica, which was founded in the early sixth century.

It too has been much rebuilt but its three-bay arcades preserve its early design. Behind the church stands a delightful belfry of 1675 capped with a delicate little cupola, and a tiny café, renowned for oriental sweetmeats that I never found available.

Beyond Sioni the river narrows and turns beneath untamed cliffs. On the tip of this rocky outcrop stands the Metekhi church, while on the riverbank opposite are carefully preserved vestiges of old Tbilisi. In a basement bakery fresh dough is slapped on to the sides of deep conical ovens, issuing as delicious long thin loaves that are warm and chewy but extremely heavy. Nearby a large irregular square is bubbled by the breastlike domes of the subterranean baths, tipped with glass nipples that allow the sulphur-scented steam to escape. There have been baths here since the twelfth century, and some are still in use, although the tiled walls and marble floors give the interior a more clinical appearance than the curvacious masonry of the shallow domes. The brightly tiled entrance to the Orbeliani baths is the most overtly Islamic design in the city, originally constructed in the seventeenth century and subsequently restored. Behind the square and its jumble of balconied houses rise the hefty minaret of the nineteenth-century mosque and the looming eighth-century ruins of the Narikala fortress.

The Metekhi church is now open for worship again, after decades of misuse, first as a tsarist prison and then as a theatre. A church has stood here since the fifth century, for the site was always of strategic importance. In 1235 the Mongols destroyed the church and palace which dominated this outcrop, and the present replacement with its fine stone carvings was built between 1278 and 1289. As at Sioni, the interior seems unexpectedly tall, with thick piers rising to support the lofty cupola. From the terrace alongside the church I looked down on to the old city and the walls of the Sachino Palace. I stood in the shadow of one of the many examples of modern monumental sculpture in Tbilisi, the powerfully stylised equestrian statue of the city's founder, Vakhtang Gorgasali. From this height it becomes apparent that the Tbilisi of broad avenues and squares is a nineteenth-century creation superimposed on a more haphazard urban pattern of slopes and ramps and terraces.

Between Sioni Cathedral and Freedom Square a section of the old town is still partly inhabited by Jews and Armenians. Along Leselidze Street, the Armenian church was always closed, unlike the synagogue. Seated on benches within the small garden in front of the synagogue were a number of elderly Jews, one of whom was happy to show me around. The gloomy lower synagogue is used only for sparsely attended daily services. The main synagogue upstairs is a noble hall decorated with bright painted designs, as merry as carnival. Large chandeliers contributed to the grandeur, but were outdone by the radiant light pouring through the clear glass windows.

The Jewish community in Tbilisi accounts for about half of the 25,000 Jews still living in Georgia; most of the remainder live in western Georgia. Many emigrated to Israel, where they remained a cohesive group clinging to the traditions of their native land, notably their legendary ability to hold their drink. Georgians are proud that Jews thrived without harassment here for 2600 years. Georgia, unlike Russia, has no tradition of antisemitism.

Before Vakhtang founded Tbilisi, the Georgian capital had, for eight centuries, been Mtskheta, some twelve miles upstream where the River Mtkvari meets the Aragvi. The road to Mtskheta follows the river, passing one of the few striking modern buildings in Georgia: the highways department, assembled on a hillside site from towers and horizontal bands of offices which interlock. Just before Mtskheta a side road twists up through rocky scrubby slopes to a high promontory overlooking the confluence of the two rivers. Perched here is the monastery of Dzhvari, of which only the ravishing sixth-century church survives, alongside the ruins of an even earlier chapel. For almost two centuries the church was closed, but candles once again burn in front of the holy images. The church is well preserved, as are the exterior reliefs portraying the founders. The interior is wonderfully lofty, a marvellously sophisticated construction, considerably in advance of most European ecclesiastical architecture of that period.

The Mtkvari valley has been despoiled by highways and industrial development, but Mtskheta, its shady streets dappled with light, stands slightly to one side, at the base of tall conical hills. Dominating the former capital is the cathedral of Sveti-Tskhoveli, which was founded shortly after the conversion to Christianity of King Mirian in 337. The cathedral, which in its third and present form dates from the eleventh century, stands within a walled compound, and embedded in the gatehouse are two carvings of bulls' heads, heathen fertility symbols coopted into Christian service.

The church, built of multicoloured tufa blocks, confronts those who approach with a wonderful stepped façade. Carved bunches of grapes, common imagery on many mediaeval Georgian churches, and ornamental designs enrich the windows and eaves. A famous relief of an arm with a bevel is identified in the inscription as the chopped-off hand of the architect, Arsukidze. According to legend, Arsukidze was deliberately maimed to prevent him from repeating such splendours in stone.

Inside, a bizarre stone structure from the fourteenth century is tucked against the south wall; this miniature domed church is supposedly modelled on the chapel of the Sepulchre in Holy Sepulchre, Jerusalem. Nearby is the massive patriarch's throne and a high-sided seventeenth-century pavilion which is the tomb of Sidonia. She was the sister of Elias, a Georgian convert who, it's said, returned to Mtskheta with a portion of the robe Jesus had been wearing just before his crucifixion. Sidonia, reaching out to touch the robe, was overcome with emotion and died on the spot, clutching the cloth so tightly that it had to be buried with her. Sidonia was rewarded with instant veneration, and King Mirian chose her grave as the site of Georgia's first cathedral. A cedar which had grown out of her grave was chopped down and used to supply the wooden foundations. An additional branch became a pillar from which miracle-inducing, disease-curing sap flowed at the behest of St Nino, and a famous icon in the nave depicts the saint and the miraculous pillar.

King Mirian is buried in another part of Mtskheta at the monastery complex of Samtavro. The older of its two churches, allegedly from the fourth century, is a mere doll's house of a chapel, but the main church is decorated with splendidly carved windows. Inside the eleventh-century church there are remains of old frescoes, but most of the walls retain the blank whitewash daubed over most of the ancient frescoes in Georgian churches by the country's Russian masters in the nineteenth century. One of the elderly black-swathed nuns who look after the church directed me to the tombs of King Mirian and Queen Nana, both of whom were converted by St Nino; they rest inappropriately beneath a nineteenth-century Italianate marble canopy.

Svetlana often entrusted me to the care of Erekle. A graduate of the Institute of Foreign Languages, he worked part-time for her, and his duties could not have been especially arduous. He had an awkward look about him: stocky, thick-set, inscrutable, with little of the Georgian volatility. Nor did he have the Georgian darkness of complexion; he was fair-haired, thin-mopped. On our first meeting we took a walk together, and I suggested a stroll around the old town. At the riverbank, Erekle wanted to cross the road and walk to one of the bridges. Georgians may be used to strolling across six-lane highways thick with Ladas and lorries, but I was not, and after a few false starts I retreated to the edge and refused to venture out again. We tramped back to the bridge, where we could cross more easily to the cobbled ramps that led up to districts of sturdy brick houses, stuccoed and prettily balconied, their arches carved with renaissance or oriental motifs.

This walk was not an auspicious start to our association: traffic noise, and the need to walk in single file along the edge of the highway, had made it impossible to talk, and later, among the lanes of the old town, the steepness of the terrain and the fumes produced by cars pumping out exhaust from low-grade fuel left me tired and disgruntled. Turning back, I mentioned that I wanted to buy a few bottles of Georgia's famous wines. There was a wine shop halfway up Rustaveli, but the doors were locked and the shelves empty. Erekle did not give up; we visited three wine shops in different parts of the town: all locked up. President Gamsakhurdia, we eventually learnt, had decreed that no wine or other intoxicating substance was to be sold in the capital, a temporary act of prohibition intended to prevent the populace from becoming over-excited. And so it remained throughout my visit.

That evening I dined alone at the hotel. The waiter asked what I wanted to eat. What was there? He handed me a menu, the one and only time I encountered such a document. I flicked through the volume; only a few prices were marked, suggesting that most dishes were unavailable. I asked for soup. He shook his head: no soup. I asked for borscht. He laughed: no borscht. (I had forgotten that soup is served only at lunchtime in the Soviet Union.) The waiter offered me salad and shashlik, which I had already eaten once that day, but it seemed I had no choice. I asked for beer or wine. *Nyet*. Prohibition extended to hotels too. Two drinks were available: sweetish *limonata* and the heavy and strongly flavoured mineral water from Borjomi.

The waiter, I later learnt, had graduated with honours from the Soviet Dining Room Arts School in Moscow. Demand is keen to gain admission to the school, as graduation is equivalent to early retirement on full pay. Introductory courses teach elementary disciplines, such as how to avoid any sign that you recognise even the most regular of customers, and how to make foreigners feel like idiots. Table management teaches students to ensure that no table is completely set; something is always missing, whether napkins or a salt cellar or a spoon. One of the most popular courses is Denial, where you learn how to tell customers that what they want is not available; in Advanced Denial you learn to dismiss the client's requests despite ample evidence that what he has asked for is in abundant supply. There are postgraduate courses in Restaurant Management, where students learn how to sit at a desk just inside the entrance and read the newspapers all day. Restaurant service is a thoroughly enjoyable career, as is immediately evident to customers ignored while the waiters and waitresses sit around their own table sharing out cigarettes and sipping tea. ('Tea? No tea. Tea finish.')

After dinner I walked up Rustaveli. The barricades had opened the broad avenue to pedestrians. Since everything was firmly shut for the night by eight or nine, walking was the only entertainment on offer, other than listening to speeches in front of the Parliament. The Rustaveli Theatre and the opera house were both closed. Indeed, all cultural institutions were shut. Svetlana was bitterly disappointed, as she had wanted me to enjoy the concerts and theatrical productions for which Tbilisi was renowned. The universities were closed too, as were the schools. Nobody had the remotest idea when life would return to normal.

Beyond the opera house I came to a large tufa building, the former Institute of Marxism-Leninism. This building, vacated when its function evaporated with the collapse of Communist rule, had been used by Opposition parties, but they had been ousted by the government and the doors were now plastered with pro-government posters. I watched as an immense truck with a mechanical arm and elbow hoisted two men equipped with power drills to the plaster frieze which ran along the top of the building. It illustrated ideologically stirring themes such as Georgian Labour and incorporated portraits of the Communist pantheon.

I was just in time to see the profile of Engels tumbling down in two large chunks of white plaster. The handful of spectators, including myself, rushed up to pocket souvenirs, while the men in their mechanical basket got to work on Lenin, showering the pavement with plaster dust as the thudding, shuddering drills did their work. They pried Lenin loose in one piece and I photographed the triumphal moment. For some days Engels's nose stood on my desk, until it occurred to me that without special knowledge of its provenance it resembled any other grubby white plaster I might have picked up on the street. I threw it into the bin.

2 Civil War or Ice-Cream

Each morning buses would roll in and park near the Metro station close to the Parliament. Each bus carried a fresh platoon of demonstrators who marched towards the Parliament steps to the applause of those already encamped there. The bus windows were taped over with portraits of Gamsakhurdia, so I deduced that the demonstrators were not calling for the president's resignation but were voicing their support for the government. It was a peculiar state of affairs. In most countries political dissenters gather around the seat of government, yell their heads off, then go home. But not in Georgia, where the demonstrators were in some sense *guarding* the Parliament, despite the absence of any visible threat to the building or its occupants.

I had my hair cut at the barber shop in Freedom Square. This scissor dance which left my hair in complete disarray cost only three roubles, so I couldn't really complain. I wandered into the fish shop a few doors away, where I found white-capped women sitting behind the counters reading the newspapers. As there was no fish to sell, what else was there to do? On the edges of the square, however, stalls were offering fruit and vegetables of reasonable quality.

Despite the wholesale closure of most of Georgia's cultural and educational institutions, the Art Museum, also on Freedom Square, was open. I strolled in. The European collection, crammed into two large rooms on the ground floor, was arranged in no discernible order. After a cursory inspection of a Bernardo Daddi, a half-wrecked polyptych by Paolo Veneziano, a portrait by Winterhalter, a grotesque *Procuress* by Cranach the Elder (haven't I seen this before somewhere?), and a Metsu, I walked upstairs. Here I found more interesting exhibits, stone carvings and fine mosaics from the fifth century onwards. The quality was variable, but the best carvings were of deeply incised geometric designs.

The rooms devoted to modern Georgian painting proved remarkably interesting. The most revered of these painters is Pirosmani, whose statue stands close to the bathhouses in old Tbilisi. Pirosmani is regarded as a primitive, but the term does him an injustice. Born in 1862 as Niko Pirosmanashvili, he survived as a self-taught itinerant painter by decorating taverns and shops. Gradually a wider circle became aware of his singular gifts as a painter who could capture the unique Georgian atmosphere in an unaffected but atmospheric way. But growing appreciation wasn't translated into widespread recognition, and Pirosmani died a pauper. He painted dark-toned portraits and cheerful scenes of rural life: harvest, feasts, a dancing bear, a laden donkey, a bemused gazelle, a dignified family of pigs, hunting scenes, a mother giving suck, a wild boar. Pirosmani's Georgia is a bucolic place populated by peasant women in kerchiefs, moustachioed men with thick dark eyebrows clad in fur caps and boots with curly toes and jackets with diagonal bullet pouches crawling up the chest. They emerge from the darkness, static and timeless, fixed within the natural order.

Paintings by other nineteenth-century artists portray the Georgian middle classes, assimilated into the European bourgeoisie, the men in Russian uniform or western frock-coats, their wives and daughters more traditionally clad in embroidered caps with lacy veils. The leading twentieth-century artists are represented by angular allegories and bloated historical paintings by the inconsistent Lado Gudiashvili, and more inventive works by the gifted Shalva Kikodze, who had spent his formative years in Paris before a premature death.

A special wing houses the treasury of ecclesiastical art, which may only be visited in the company of an official guide. Mine spoke English, incomprehensibly. She had no notion of phrasing and punctuation and ran clauses together without regard for sense. By the time I had managed to dismantle her speech and reconstruct it, it was time to move on to the next showcase. To make matters worse, her singsong delivery often ran contrary to the sense of what she was trying to say. It was like being given a guided tour by the mechanical doll Olympia in *The Tales of Hoffmann*. What I managed to see of the exhibits was of outstanding quality. Early mediaeval Georgian metalwork is quite remarkable, a cornucopia of superbly wrought silver icons and crosses, often adorned with *cloisonné* enamels, all crafted before the eleventh century. The astounding chalice of Bagrat III, dated 999, is still in impeccable condition; it is fashioned from 24-carat gold studded with figures of the Virgin and saints. A small crucifix set with rubies, emeralds and pearls formed the pectoral cross of Queen Tamar, and the travelling case in which she cosseted this exquisite masterpiece is preserved by its side. The Khakhuli Triptych is more monumental; the twelfth-century metalwork is superb, but what makes this item exceptional is that the icon itself is an encaustic wax painting depicting the head of Christ. Dating from the sixth century, it is an incredibly precious survival.

The collection of enamels is astonishing too. Some are twelve centuries old, but the twelfth-century examples are particularly brilliant in their colouring, the dense blue swirl of the draperies glowing against the gold background. The museum owns the largest piece of *cloisonné* enamel in the world: the hands and face of the Virgin preserved within the Khakhuli Triptych. King David the Builder encased this precious tenth-century image, which was regarded as miracle-working, in an especially splendid case incorporating 115 enamel panels, crosses, filigree panels, and precious stones. The triptych is as lavish an example of secular homage to ecclesiastical values as one could ever encounter.

After the twelfth century the Georgian craftsmen seemed to lose their touch. There are exceptions, such as a fifteenth-century panel of St George at prayer with not a dragon in sight, and a sixteenth-century golden chalice in which the dignified austerity of Georgian metalwork is softened by oriental decorative forms bequeathed by waves of Islamic invasion. By the eighteenth century the emphasis was on outward display rather than inward intensity, and one bishop's mitre, composed of a kilogram of 24-carat gold and precious stones, is topped, gratuitously, with a diamond-studded cross. The tribute of the secular to the spiritual has been supplanted by mere ostentation.

I emerged from these dungeon-like halls glowing with silver and jewels into the relatively colourless expanses of Freedom Square, the air soupy with the coarse fumes of bus exhaust and flashing with glints from plate-glass windows protecting nonexistent goods from nonexistent shoppers. Back at the hotel I joined Svetlana, who was waiting for Nunu Gabunia, a well-known opera singer who was today adopting a lesser role as our driver to the Tbilisi brandy cellars.

Georgian brandy was no longer on sale in Tbilisi – except at grossly inflated prices in the hard currency shop on Rustaveli – but it was still being produced in cellars established in the 1880s. There is not a great deal to see in a brandy cellar; the distillation takes place elsewhere, and the cellars are simply used to age the spirits for up to twenty-five years in large oak casks. The white-coated technical director opened the tap on a cask of their oldest brandy and handed me the glass. My reluctance to knock back a double brandy at noon was construed as very bad manners.

From the cellars Nunu drove us up into the hills overlooking the city. A hillside has been designated as Georgia's ethnographic museum, essentially a collection of nineteenth-century houses, reconstructed and placed within authentic farmstead settings. Most of the houses are wooden, with huge verandahs, their roofs supported on carved posts. Enclosed within wattle fences, the gardens are planted with a profusion of trees – apricot, quince, walnut – and large earthenware amphorae which would once have been filled with wine and half-buried in the earth.

Where do they find these guides? She came from nowhere, a small dumpy woman who never smiled and whose delivery was as automated as that of her counterpart at the art museum. She wasn't much fun but she knew her stuff, and pointed out a wealth of architectural and domestic features as she showed me around. A particularly grand cabin was ornamented with classical motifs to denote its sophistication, and filled with fine walnut furniture. From a peg hung two typical Georgian garments: the *nabadi* felt coat with chunky square shoulders, ideal for shepherds on wintry nights, and an *abalakhi* coat with bullet pouches, identical to those painted by Pirosmani a century ago. Today they are worn only by folk troupes. I looked around for the kitchen, and found it in a separate building a few yards away.

The Imereti region in central Georgia developed a log cabin which rested on a stone base and was entered by steps placed along the walls. The open space within focused around a central hearth on an earthen floor; the sleeping area was simply a raised and rug-strewn section along one side of the room. Kakheti, in eastern Georgia, contributed a stone house which had been partly burrowed into the hillside. Over the hearth there rose a brilliantly carpentered angular structure underpinning the dome visible from the path outside; the top of the cupola was left open to the elements, providing ventilation and lighting for the half-submerged house. I remarked on the ornamental stone columns which supported the cupola.

'They are called the mother columns,' my mirthless guide informed me instantly, 'and the ornamentation is connected with astral phases.' She knew everything, this Gradgrind of the ethnographical museum, but wouldn't let me enjoy what I was seeing.

A hand-scrawled note on the hotel's Intourist noticeboard informed anyone who cared to know that Gamsakhurdia was giving a press conference in an hour's time. I decided to attend. On Rustaveli the noise of speechmaking was more frantic than usual, and I realised that loudspeakers had been rigged along the length of the avenue, making it impossible to escape the blare from the Parliament steps. I had hoped this kind of thing had gone out with Brezhnev, but in Georgia it was still compulsory for shoppers and strollers to listen to uplifting pro-government sentiments.

I pushed my way through the crowds towards the portico. Somebody clutched my arm and jabbered at me in Georgian; I jabbered back in English. The soldier guarding the entrance to the courtyard responded positively to my cry of 'Press!' and let me through. A door on the right led into the main building. 'Press conference!' I yelled, and was stopped by a skinny old man with a cigarette grafted between his fingers. He told me the press conference had been postponed until eight that evening, and I wouldn't be allowed in without proper accreditation. I asked where I could obtain accreditation, and he directed me to the foreign ministry.

I hauled myself up a steep street to the hideous red-brick ministry. I found the office of Mr Gabashvili, the deputy minister who authorised accreditations, on the fourth floor, and his secretary told me to walk in. Behind a desk I found a huge man speaking very good Italian, and around the conference table were a few scruffy people in jeans immediately identifiable as journalists. Nobody, including the minister, paid the slightest attention to me, so I took a seat and kept quiet.

Mr Gabashvili, sweat evenly coating his large red face, was bawling out the correspondent of the *Corriere della Sera*, who had come to renew his accreditation. His offence, in Gabashvili's eyes, was biased reporting. Gabashvili had, he informed us, made a special study of Italian mass communications, and he wasn't going to have the wool pulled over his eyes by this particular journalist.

'Your articles,' he said sternly but politely, 'are inciting civil war, when all we want is for the people to stroll about and eat ice-cream.'

The Italian correspondent smiled weakly at the minister's charming vision, and gave a shrug indicating that he wasn't going to argue. If the Georgian government didn't want him at the presidential press conference, it was no skin off his nose, and he would spend his evening elsewhere. The phone rang, and while Gabashvili took the call, we asked the Italian what he had done to incur such displeasure. He had interviewed various Opposition leaders, notably the former prime minister Tengiz Sigua, and his newspaper had printed the outcome. Since every journalist in town had interviewed Sigua, the offence did not strike us as heinous.

His call over, Gabashvili leaned forward and addressed us all. He wanted us to know that accreditation would be granted, but it was important for us to understand that any unrest in Tbilisi was being instigated by Moscow, indeed by Mikhail Gorbachev himself. Yes, there were those who were accusing Gamsakhurdia of acting like a dictator, but what kind of dictator could he be, with no army at his disposal and without forces that could act against his political opponents? We had to understand that seventy years of Soviet oppression had left Georgia without democratic institutions and a liberalised economy, yet the West was expecting the country to be instantly democratic. Georgia, he went on, was being denied the opportunity to make the reforms which would lead to greater democracy, though who was doing the denying he did not say. Opposition demands for the president's resignation were equally undemocratic, and the defection of large parts of Georgia's National Guard was in effect a *coup d'état*, but he hadn't heard any protests from the West about their volte-face.

'So,' he concluded, 'I ask you only to be more responsible and not to be manipulated by Russian imperialists.'

'So you're not allowing me to attend the press conference,' said the Italian, ignoring everything else the minister had been saying.

'What you have written in your paper,' replied the soft-spoken Gabashvili, 'has greatly offended the president.'

'If I understand all this correctly,' interposed Robert Parsons of the BBC World Service, 'what you're doing is interfering with the right of the press to gather information.'

'You have the right to gather information, but not to instigate civil war.'

'But he's writing in Italian for Italian readers!' replied the exasperated Parsons. 'His articles can't possibly have any effect on what is happening here!'

'Anyway,' added a dark-haired French photographer with granny glasses, 'we're here for accreditation, not for an hour-long class in politics.'

'All these lectures from the minister,' said the Italian, 'only confirm what he wants to deny, namely that we are being pressured to give only the government's point of view.'

Gabashvili rose to his feet, like a hot-air balloon unsteadily beginning its ascent, and said he was placing us in the hands of his assistant, a weak-chinned young man who proved more cooperative than he looked. The minister shuffled out, and we took advantage of his absence to introduce ourselves. The French photographer had just arrived from Yerevan where, she told me, conditions were far worse than in Tbilisi. Like some of the others in the room, she was a veteran of Kurdistan, Romania and Yugoslavia. Georgia was one more news resort on the international circuit.

The assistant asked us for our cards, from which he made laborious longhand transcriptions. He turned to Parsons. 'You have been to Georgia before?'

'*Diakh*,' said Parsons, and gave the rest of his reply in fluent Georgian. Sometimes you have to hand it to the BBC. He later told me that he had studied in Moscow and written a doctoral dissertation on the Georgian social democratic movement.

Some of the journalists were staying at the Hotel Iveria, a skyscraper at the other end of Rustaveli in Republic Square, which was commended for its location. Situated halfway between Parliament and the Opposition headquarters at the Television Centre, it was perfectly placed for hearing trouble during the night.

'I heard gunfire last night,' said an American staying at the Iveria, 'but we couldn't tell whether it was fighting or an accident or a domestic squabble.'

'Or a party,' I added.

'Or a party,' he conceded.

The photographers had run into problems near the Parliament, where some of the president's supporters had little patience with representatives of the Western press who, as constant speeches no doubt informed them, were inciting civil war.

'I am tired,' said the Frenchwoman, 'of having my camera smashed, and having my head beaten with wooden sticks.'

The weak-chinned one told us to go away for half an hour, and when we returned our papers would be ready. I was now suffering from severe caffeine deprivation. The Hotel Tbilisi was still refusing to serve coffee, and morning tea was not doing the trick. I found a café on a corner of Freedom Square where the coffee, although served in ancient cracked cups, was at least thick and sweet and strong. It worked wonders. After collecting my letter of accreditation from the ministry, I returned to the hotel for an early dinner. At a table near mine three Georgians were dining sumptuously and a waitress arrived with a paper bag stuffed with a bottle of cognac, which they polished off. Prohibition in Georgia was selective. At 7.30 I hurried off to the Parliament building.

Zviad Gamsakhurdia had not always excited such controversy. There had been a time when he was as popular as any politician could hope to be. In his youth his protests against the Soviet system had been rewarded with spells in prison. Gamsakhurdia was passionately, sometimes intolerantly, nationalist, but despite his populist rhetoric his background was sophisticated. His father, Konstantin Gamsakhurdia, was a celebrated Georgian writer, and had brought up his son in a thoroughly literary household. Zviad had lectured at the university and translated poetry from English and French. In 1976 he had co-founded Georgia's monitoring group for the Helsinki agreements on human rights. Soon after this he was jailed, and spent a year in solitary confinement. But there was a blot on his copybook which opponents were not slow to exploit. Sentenced to a five-year term, Gamsakhurdia had recanted two years later, denouncing some of his fellow dissidents on television, and been released. He claimed that this had happened with the agreement of the other imprisoned dissidents so that one of their number would be free to continue the struggle, but others cast doubt on the story.

In the late 1980s Georgia was just one of many Soviet republics in which nationalist independence movements were growing. Yet the Soviet authorities treated Georgia with exceptional harshness. On 9 April 1989, a large rally in the capital called for independence. The rally, ironically, was called in response to demands from a group living in northwest Georgia, the Abkhazians, for *their* independence from Georgia. The Abkhazians were an ancient Moslem community, long discriminated against, who believed they would be more secure within the Russian Federation than within an independent Georgia. The Georgians, with some justification, believed such demands were instigated by the Soviet authorities as part of their divide-and-rule policy in the republics. The response of the Soviet troops in Tbilisi on 9 April, however, was one of unbelievable savagery. Using tear gas and sharpened shovels, the soldiers weighed in, and when the clouds of gas had dissipated twenty-one Georgians lay dead, and many more injured.

Such brutality inevitably brought the Georgian struggle for independence to the attention of the world. The Soviet troops, in suppressing a demonstration, had created martyrs. By 1990 just about every political faction in Georgia favoured independence. Zviad Gamsakhurdia led the Round Table grouping, a loose coalition of seven parties, and expressed one of the more intense and intolerant versions of Georgian nationalism. By August 1990 he was proposing to limit the franchise to speakers of the Georgian language, and further restrictive proposals soon followed, alarming the many non-Georgians who inhabit the republic. Exact figures are hard to come by, but a fair guess puts the figure of ethnic Georgians within the republic's borders at about 70 per cent. About 7 per cent are Armenian, and a similar figure accounts for the Russian population. There are pockets of Moslems – Azerbaijanis at just under 5 per cent and Abkhazians at 1.8 per cent. And there were the Ossetians, who accounted for 3 per cent.

The dispute with the Ossetians was to prove the most intractable. The Autonomous Region of South Ossetia, northwest of Tbilisi, was created by Stalin in 1922 as part of his nationalities policy; it injected a few 'foreign' enclaves into the Soviet republics as a farsighted means of nipping any nationalist movements in the bud. Posthumously, the policy has proved a great success. Georgian nationalists assert that South Ossetia has historically always been Georgian land and that until the early years of this century Ossetians were virtually nonexistent in the area. The Ossetian population, however, feel they have little in common with their Georgian neighbours and would rather unite with neighbouring North Ossetia, which is part of the Russian Federation. The Georgians have always resisted any moves by the Ossetians to incorporate into Russia what the Georgians consider their lands.

For Gamsakhurdia and the other nationalists, the dispute was a godsend, especially since there was evidence to support Georgian claims that the unrest was being encouraged by the Soviet authorities. 35–40 per cent of the population of South Ossetia was Georgian, so this was fruitful ground for conflict. And conflict there has been. By January 1991 the capital, Tskhinvali, had become a divided city, and the clashes between the two groups had been exacerbated by South Ossetia's declaration of independence the previous month. Nor did the dispatch of Soviet troops into the region calm the noisier Georgian nationalists.

In August 1990 the statue of Lenin was toppled. Multi-party elections were held in October, and the Supreme Soviet, hitherto a packed house of Communists, became an elected forum. Within the Supreme Soviet, Gamsakhurdia's Round Table coalition won 155 of the 250 seats. The coalition was often supported by the Communists, which led to accusations that he had made some kind of deal with them. On 14 November, Gamsakhurdia was elected president of the new Parliament (still widely known as the Supreme Soviet), and changes were rapid. On 30 January 1991, Parliament established the National Guard, Georgia's own military force, and in the spring approved the replacement of the old system of local soviets with a dual system of municipal councils and ninety appointed prefects.

Not everybody was happy with this move. Nodar Natadze, a professor of philosophy who led the Popular Front, and an opponent of Gamsakhurdia's, argued that the prefects were being given too much power, and that the system was an exercise in personal patronage. By now Gamsakhurdia was beginning to exhibit the extreme intolerance which was to blight his presidency. He could not acknowledge that political opponents such as Natadze might have genuine, indeed patriotic, reasons for disagreeing with the policies being pushed through Parliament by Gamsakhurdia's bloc. Instead he branded them as criminals and madmen. Insulting the president was made an offence that could land the perpetrator in jail. It was not a formula likely to promote political harmony in the months ahead. Gamsakhurdia ordered political arrests and tightened his grip over the media, keeping the airwaves and newspapers under government control. By mid-1991 there were some seventy political prisoners in Georgia. Gamsakhurdia did not deny that those named as prisoners had been arrested, but he did deny that they were arrested without cause. Few of those detained were charged and brought to trial.

On 9 April 1991, there was an almost unanimous vote for independence, and the Supreme Soviet issued a formal declaration of independence. On 26 May Zviad Gamsakhurdia was elected president with an astonishing 87 per cent of the vote; the Communist vote was reduced to a trickle. Many had misgivings about Gamsakhurdia, but the large majority opted to give him the benefit of the doubt. This overwhelming victory, instead of imbuing the new president with confidence, prompted more extremist rhetoric: among other ethnic groups which met with his disfavour were the Armenians, who had lived peaceably, for the most part, within Georgia for hundreds of years. Rumours were circulated about ties between Ossetian nationalists and Soviet interior ministry troops (OMON), and South Ossetia was virtually sealed off. The death toll rose on both sides, and so did the numbers of refugees fleeing from the violence. It became illegal for Georgians to join the Soviet Army, and the National Guard was used to siphon off young men of conscription age into an all-Georgian force. Moscow denounced the Guard as unconstitutional, but the Georgians were unmoved. Gamsakhurdia justified its formation as a legitimate response to armed bands of Ossetian nationalists. Originally 3000 strong, the National Guard grew to about 15,000 by the late summer.

Despite growing criticisms of Gamsakhurdia's authoritarian style and of his failure to implement the reforms promised during the election campaign, he continued to enjoy widespread support, especially among less educated Georgians who lapped up his populist rhetoric. Then came the attempted coup against Gorbachev on 19 August 1991, and though this had little direct impact on distant Georgia, it would have devastating consequences for the Gamsakhurdia régime.

After the attempt foundered, the triumphant democrats made it clear that in the post-coup reckoning silence counted for much the same as active support. The Soviet foreign minister, who had remained silent to see which way the wind was blowing, was sacked, and nobody seemed to think any great injustice was done. Zviad Gamsakhurdia had impeccable credentials as a nationalist, but during the coup his attachment to democracy seemed less fervent. As opposition to the coup focused around Yeltsin's stubborn resistance, broadcasts of these crucial events were not shown on Georgian television, which was instead devoted to light entertainment. Gamsakhurdia urged Georgians not to demonstrate against the coup. Even worse, he was prepared to give in to the putschists' demand that the National Guard should be disbanded. He insisted that his apparent willingness to do so was mere prudence under the circumstances, but the response of the Guard itself was to split. Many officers, disgusted at what they perceived as the president's betrayal, moved their forces out of the capital and away from Gamsakhurdia's control. Moreover, the prime minister, Tengiz Sigua, resigned in protest against the growing abuse of power by the president. He also claimed that Georgian government officials had flown to Moscow to strike deals with the coup leaders, suggesting the president's support for the coup had been active rather than merely passive. Sigua, an urbane professor of engineering, threw in his lot with Tengiz Kitovani, the commander of the rebellious National Guard.

Gamsakhurdia's response to these defections was to denounce his opponents as criminals and agents of the Kremlin. Their opposition, he insisted, was instigated by Moscow as a means of undermining Georgian independence. If the Georgian people followed the siren voices of the Opposition, it would only be a matter of time before the republic fell once again under Soviet control. Of course Gamsakhurdia himself, by colluding with the leaders of the coup, had laid himself open to similar charges, but for the president the best defence would always be offence.

The situation continued to deteriorate. There was more fighting in South Ossetia, with both sides maintaining a propaganda war which obscured the truth about what was happening there. None the less, Georgia's sole policy in South Ossetia seemed to be military force. Meanwhile thousands of rebellious National Guardsmen rallied to Tengiz Kitovani, a sculptor with a murky past who had, like so many Opposition leaders, once been an ardent supporter of Gamsakhurdia. He set up headquarters in Shavnabada, ten miles from Tbilisi, warning that he would employ his troops if the president attempted to suppress the Opposition. Kitovani claimed the support of 10,000 men; clearly an exaggeration, but nobody knew the true number. Despite the factionalism of Georgian politics, dozens of Opposition groups managed to team up with the paramount aim of unseating the president. The moderate Popular Front under Natadze joined hands with the principal Opposition group, the National Democratic Party led by Georgi Chanturia, another former associate of Gamsakhurdia's. A mere four months after his landslide victory, there were regular demonstrations against his rule.

He threatened force and on 2 September he kept his word. OMON troops opened fire to break up an Opposition demonstration outside the Parliament. Nobody was killed but there were injuries. Gamsakhurdia called on his supporters to rally round, to guard the Parliament with their bodies day and night. From the provinces they came, and set up their armed encampment on the Parliament steps. Censorship tightened, as television programmes out of Moscow, and Moscow-based newspapers such as *Pravda*, were banned, as were some Opposition news sheets.

The role of Parliament in the new Georgia became increasingly fuzzy. Gamsakhurdia's refusal to allow the proceedings to be televised was interpreted by some Opposition deputies as a wish to stifle public debate, and there were walkouts. Land reform was stalled, and the president blamed the Parliament, which he effectively controlled, for the lack of action. The government's failure to introduce other measures to stimulate a free-market economy was blamed by cynical Opposition deputies on the pressure still exerted by former Communists on the president. The economy faltered. Georgia had always been prosperous: the fertility of its soil and considerable mineral reserves had underpinned a high standard of living. Now there were shortages, and inefficiencies in the industrial sector were worsening.

The arrests continued, and government spokesmen appeared on television to denounce Opposition figures, many of them elected deputies, as enemies of Georgia. On 16 September the plane taking Giorgi Chanturia to Moscow for a meeting with the American ambassador was ordered to turn back, and when the plane landed Chanturia and his wife Irena Sarashvili were arrested and held without charge. She was later released, and promptly set off for Parliament where she sat down to begin a hunger strike. She was beaten up.

The next day I arrived in Tbilisi, and now I was about to have my first glimpse of the president. I found myself crammed into a small room, my view blocked by a battery of cameras, with the largest camera and the most central spot occupied by the man from CNN. Gamsakhurdia entered, followed by a rifleman who stayed in position by the door. The president was a stocky figure, well-groomed, intense, watchful. His sad eyes and deathbed pallor were alarming, as though the man hadn't seen sunlight in years. He sat behind a long desk, his interpreter beside him, and spoke in a slow monotone. This didn't prevent the interpreter getting into frequent muddles, and Gamsakhurdia often intervened to correct her English.

He interpreted the events of recent days as an attempted coup: Sigua, Kitovani and others had been combining to form an illegal junta. They had occupied buildings illegally, such as the Television Centre, and had twice attempted to seize other government buildings. This attempted coup, he told us, was being directed by Moscow. Indeed, Sigua had just returned from Moscow where he had received instructions from his masters, who included Eduard Shevardnadze. The daily rallies at the Parliament were being misreported as anti-government demonstrations, when the truth was the very opposite. The foreign press were partly to blame for this, since it was referring to the junta as the Opposition. 'They are not the Opposition, but the directors of an anti-constitutional coup.' He spoke derisively of what he called the 'street opposition' who had been building barricades in the city. Those demonstrating against his régime consisted mostly of former Communist mafiosi who had lost their privileges in the new Georgia. Among them were criminal elements who had been supplied with weapons by Moscow.

None of this was new, and most of it was nonsense. But Gamsakhurdia was also declaring a state of emergency in Tbilisi, to take effect the next day. There would be no curfew, but there would be an unspecified tightening of controls. There would be no action against peaceful demonstrations, but there would be action against illegal armed groups. It all seemed too ill thought out to be taken seriously, and in the days that followed nothing much was heard of the state of emergency.

Somebody asked why he didn't respond to calls for the reopening of Parliament. Gamsakhurdia disingenuously replied that it wasn't up to him, but up to the chairman of the Parliament, Akaki Asatiani. (Technically, Gamsakhurdia was correct in saying that only Asatiani had the authority to summon Parliament into session, but everyone knew that Asatiani could usually be relied upon to support the president.) What credence should we give to rumours that the president was considering dissolving Parliament? The reply was that this would only happen if certain deputies didn't stop supporting the 'coup', and in such a situation new deputies would be appointed and presidential rule instituted.

The president was asked why he didn't release the political prisoners and free the press. He replied that the press was free, and denied that he had signed any orders for arrests. Any arrests had been made by the prosecutor's office. This too was plainly disingenuous.

Would he send the busloads back to the provinces from which they had been summoned? This he couldn't do, he replied, since his supporters had come here of their own free will.

Would he negotiate with the Opposition? He certainly wanted to avoid bloodshed or even arrests, but 'the junta is not the Opposition. You can't negotiate with criminals.' What was the evidence for his claim that Shevardnadze was actively supporting the 'junta'? 'This is well known throughout Georgia.'

The press conference lasted about one hour. Gamsakhurdia's responses had been a predictable mixture of denials and stonewalling, and the new measures he had announced were muddled and indecisive. But a Dutch journalist with whom I strolled back to the hotel was anxious. He interpreted Gamsakhurdia's references to mobilising public opinion to defeat his opponents as an invitation to his more violently inclined supporters to take matters into their hands. Indeed, later that night shooting broke out at the Television Centre, where the Opposition had established their headquarters, and at a power plant where five soldiers were killed. The next morning the government claimed that Kitovani's Guardsmen had been trying to take over the power plant, while the Opposition claimed that the shootings had followed the arrest of a National Guard soldier who was being taken to hospital.

3 Your Question is Wrong

Svetlana produced a new driver to conduct us through eastern Georgia. He was the novelist and translator Givi Nizhavadze. Since I had brought a shortwave radio to Georgia, while they heard only the occasional government news bulletin, I knew more about what had happened overnight than they did. Everybody feared further bloodshed in the capital.

Driving out of Tbilisi, we were soon among farmlands and orchards filled with apricot trees. The foothills were dotted with the summer houses with which dutiful servants of the state had been rewarded. In a village a drunk lay sprawled and motionless in the road, but nobody stopped. Hills and crumbling cliffs separated the Kartli region from the eastern province of Kakheti. Deciduous trees covered the slopes like wool on a sheep. Pigs rooted among the chestnuts. In the villages stood spacious older houses of stone, some with their original wooden verandahs, others with less attractive but more functional aluminium props. All were enclosed in gardens and orchards and grape arbours. Whenever Givi was unsure of the way he would pull up next to a car as he was overtaking it, honk, lower the window, shout for directions, and then, after instructions had been shouted back, continue on his way.

We made straight for Tsinindali, the site of a country estate and, since 1884, a famous winery. We sought out the director, with whom Svetlana had made an appointment, but he had been summoned unexpectedly to Tbilisi – 'because of the situation' – and we were greeted instead, and without enthusiasm, by the technical director.

There were only two methods of making wine, he informed me:

the classical French method and the Kakhetian method. In Kakheti winemakers ferment red wines on the skins.

'All red wines are fermented on the skins. Otherwise they wouldn't be red,' I responded.

'But we ferment and age our wines in earthenware amphorae for three years.'

'Really? Then how come all I can see here are huge concrete tanks?'

'That's because this is where we make white wines, which we make by the classical method. The winery for the red wines is a few kilometres away and that's where we use the jars.'

He didn't seem inclined to show me these jars, which would have interested me more than a battery of tanks. I'd only seen amphorae used to ferment red wines in one other wine region, in Alentejo in southern Portugal, and I was keen to see how the Georgians employed them. But it was not to be. The technical director was also confusing me. What is peculiar about traditional Kakhetian wine is that the *white* wine is fermented on the skins and left to macerate for weeks, giving the wine a strong tannic flavour which is very much an acquired taste.

'Our wines,' he said proudly, 'are stronger and more manly than most other wines.'

'How strong?'

'Ten to thirteen degrees.'

'That's an average range anywhere.'

'Well,' he said mysteriously, 'it all depends on the concentration of sugar.'

In the tasting room he offered me first 'a very old wine'.

'How old?'

'Two years.'

I took a sip (there was nowhere to spit) and made a few notes.

Svetlana looked at me in horror. 'What's the matter? You don't like it?'

I looked around me. All the other men had drained their glasses. I had come to taste, but the notion was alien to Georgians. My judicious sip had been interpreted as disdain.

'No, no,' I hurried to explain, 'the wine is very good, but I'm just not used to the Georgian custom of downing a whole glass in one go.'

'This is not only the Georgian way,' she rebuked me. So I knocked back the rest of the glass, and lied about its excellence. Then I drank the 1990 which, being younger, was slightly fresher and more palatable.

'How long is the white wine aged before being bottled?' I asked the technical director.

'Your question is wrong,' he replied. I asked him to answer it anyway. The wine, he told me, was aged for two years in tanks before being sent to Tbilisi for bottling. It is a characteristic of most Georgian wineries that they are not equipped with bottling lines.

The tasting over, we were shown around the immense brick cellars, empty except for a few storage tanks. The winery was a depressing place, ramshackle, with ancient tanks, a tangle of overhead pipes, antediluvian crushers, all crammed into barrack-like buildings of stone and brick. The technical director admitted that it would be nice to return to the practice of barrel-ageing their wines, but it was simply too expensive. The Tsinindali winery is famous for a collection of bottles dating back to the early nineteenth century, but nobody thought of showing it to me.

I asked whether there were plans to privatise the winery. Not here, he said, as the enterprise was so large and the debts to the state so enormous. 'No private buyers would want to take on this place.'

'But you told me earlier that the winery is expanding?'

'That is correct.'

Not far from the winery, gates led into the Chavchavadze estate. A modern avenue with awful metal lamps, a design more appropriate for a community sports centre driveway, led through the park towards the house. Alexander Chavchavadze was born in 1786 and became a leading Georgian Romantic poet. The front of the house has spacious rooms kept cool in summer by the large and elaborate verandahs surrounding them. Towards the back, smaller bedrooms and halls display exhibits relating to the Chavchavadze family history. The glory of the estate, though, is the park, which was based on English models and planted with hundreds of trees, now mature and majestic, and many of them very rare.

Svetlana hoped we could lunch at the restaurant near the park entrance, but it was not operating because the electricity had failed. So we went instead to the Intourist hotel in Telavi, where a basement bar serves *khinkali*, little moneybags of dough stuffed with minced meat. The bar was dreary, its walls painted a reformatory green; the furnishings were plastic and in a poor state of repair. It took the staff almost an hour to prepare the *khinkali*, even though there was nobody else eating there, but it was worth the wait. We were served a huge portion, which we ate with our bare hands. You grip a dumpling by the little knot at the top, sprinkle it generously with black pepper, then chew into it, slurping noisily to suck in the juices released by your teeth.

We drove on to the village of Ikhalto, which has a church and the remains of an academy where the most celebrated of Georgian poets, Shota Rustaveli, is believed to have studied in the twelfth century. The church is older, and dates from the ninth century. The interior, whitewashed during the last century, is of little interest, but the ruinous walls of the ancient academy are romantic in the extreme. The main building, the refectory, lost its roof long ago, but the stately arched windows and the rough stone walls remain. The ruins are shaded by tall cypresses, and the only sound was the rustle of leaves. Tombs scattered among the tall wild grasses gave the enclosure a quiet melancholy. Here, in the depths of the Kakheti countryside, the antiquity of Georgia was far more perceptible than among the bustle of Tbilisi.

The history of Georgia stretches back into a time when truth and myth can't be differentiated. Western Georgia has been identified with the land of Colchis, where Jason found the Golden Fleece – and Medea. Although Georgia was spared by Alexander the Great as his armies swept eastwards, the region did fall under the sway of the Romans, yet managed to salvage a degree of independence by exchanging loyalty to the Romans for the empire's protection. There was conflict between the Romans and the various dynasties of Persia, but Georgia, unlike Armenia, stayed out of the worst of the fighting. When the Sassanid dynasty signed a peace treaty with the Romans in 298, Mirian III was recognised as king of eastern Georgia – the same Mirian who followed the Armenian lead by adopting Christianity as the state religion.

Thereafter the history of Georgia is one of tangled instability. Sandwiched between two ranges of the Caucasus, it formed a trade route between Asia Minor and the Orient. Over the following centuries it was troubled by invasions of varying degrees of severity. The Arabs who conquered Georgia in the seventh century were content to leave the native kings in power so long as they recognised (as they did) the supremacy of the caliph. The Arabs maintained their hold over Georgia for about three centuries, then their grip weakened and, despite the threat of an expanding Byzantine empire, it became possible for King Bagrat III to consolidate his control over both the eastern and western lands of Georgia, although Tbilisi was outside his otherwise extensive domains.

A new threat to the region's stability arose when the Seljuk Turks advanced through Persia and Armenia and into the Georgian heartland of Kartli in 1068, wreaking havoc as they went. The Georgian rulers managed to keep their throne, and in 1089 sixteen-year-old David the Builder became king. David had the good fortune to share the same enemies as the Crusaders, but he was a powerful military leader in his own right. He defeated the Seljuk Turks and expanded the Georgian domains far to the south and to the east, annexing Kakheti in 1105. Defeating the Turks was not accomplished overnight, and only in 1121 was his victory complete. He captured Tbilisi the following year and died in 1125.

The dominant figure of twelfth-century Georgia was Queen Tamar, who was born in 1154 and reigned first jointly with her father Giorgi III and then alone from 1184 to 1213. She inherited from her grandfather, David the Builder, a strong feudal structure which underwrote monarchical power in exchange for strong local powers for the fiefdoms. Culture thrived, and churches and academies such as the one in Ikhalto were founded throughout the land. Poetry and the pictorial arts flourished. At the same time she expanded the Georgian empire far into present-day Armenia and Turkey and eastwards to the Caspian Sea.

The legacy she left to her son Giorgi IV proved short-lived. In 1220 the Mongols came charging through Armenia and into Georgia. Only during the reign of Giorgi V, who ruled from 1314 to 1346, were they driven out. But this did not end Georgia's problems. The next wave of invasion began with Tamburlaine in 1386, compounding the suffering already afflicted on the country by the Black Death, from which the Caucasus was not immune. True to his reputation, Tamburlaine was a destructive force, reducing Tbilisi to ruins and capturing the reigning king, Bagrat V, and by the mid-fifteenth century, once powerful and resplendent Georgia had disintegrated. Any recovery was likely to be impeded by the fall of Constantinople a few years later to the Ottoman Turks. Georgia was now squeezed between the Turks to the west and the Persians to the east; fragmented between various princes and unable to organise a coherent national defence, Georgia again succumbed to repeated invasions.

In 1555 the Safavid Persians and the Ottomans carved it up, with the Persians dominating Kartli, although Georgian kings were tolerated on the throne. Any nationalist stirrings were swiftly crushed. The academy at Ikhalto was one of the buildings destroyed when in 1616 the Persian Shah Abbas punished one uprising with a wave of slaughter, deportations and razings. The cycles of invasion and terror may have seemed unending to the long-suffering Georgians, but by the eighteenth century a kind of stability had returned to the region, and with it a modest cultural and intellectual renaissance. King Vakhtang VI endowed the country with a badly needed infrastructure in the form of canals and new institutions, but in 1723 even this progressive monarch was ejected and exiled to Russia.

Towards the end of the century it seemed that the only hope for stability lay in forging closer ties with Russia. Erekle II, like Vakhtang VI, tried to improve economic and social conditions, but these efforts were impeded by constant raids by Moslem tribesmen from the east. He could see little alternative to a treaty arrangement with Russia. The Treaty of Georgievsk of 1783 made Georgia a Russian protectorate by ceding its right to negotiate with foreign powers in exchange for guarantees that the Georgian monarchy would retain possession of its hereditary lands. Unfortunately the treaty proved worthless. When a new Persian ruler, Aga Muhammad Khan, signalled that he intended to recolonise Georgia, Erekle repeatedly requested help from Catherine the Great. She ignored him. The consequence was predictable: Aga Muhammad carried out his threats in the most brutal manner. In 1795 50,000 residents of Tbilisi were slaughtered, and Erekle only narrowly avoided capture.

After the death of Catherine in 1796, and the murder of Emperor Paul in 1801, Alexander I became tsar. In September that year he coolly proclaimed the annexation of eastern Georgia. Georgia could protest all it liked about this betrayal of a solemn treaty, but it made not the slightest difference, since the country was too weakened to continue an independent existence. Now that Kartli and Kakheti were part of Russia, it could only be a matter of time before the western kingdom suffered the same fate. In 1810 the last king of western Georgia, Solomon II, abdicated.

The subjugated nation would derive some benefits from its annexation. Russian institutions were established, especially schools and gardens and theatres, but other amenities, notably hospitals, were in pitifully short supply. New bridges and roads and a railway were constructed, but these benefits could not disguise the fact that Russia regarded Georgia as a colonial possession. By the late nineteenth century 58 per cent of the land was owned by Russians, especially by the Russian government itself, and they were also prominent as administrators, while many of the merchants in Tbilisi were Armenian. Tbilisi, half ruined by the end of the eighteenth century, had become a hundred years later a handsome cosmopolitan city with a population of 160,000.

At the same time the Georgians shared the political repression inflicted on the Russians. The secret police thrived, trade unions and strikes were outlawed; independent political activity had to be clandestine as more public activities invited appalling repression. A meeting of the Tbilisi social democrats in the town hall in August 1905 was used for target practice by a troop of Cossacks, who murdered sixty participants and injured hundreds more.

Georgia would benefit in some respects from the upheavals of 1917 and the ending of World War I. In April 1918 it became part of a federative republic embracing all of Transcaucasia, but this proved shortlived, and in May 1918 Georgia formally proclaimed its independence. It took a peculiar form, since the new-born republic almost immediately flung itself into the arms of Germany as a protectorate. This state of affairs didn't last long either, and the British replaced the Germans as guardians of the Georgians.

None the less, social democratic Menshevik rule over the fledgling Georgian republic must have come as a refreshing change after tsarist repression. Universal suffrage and health insurance were introduced, some enterprises were nationalised, strikes were legalised, and, more boldly, the great estates were broken up and redistributed. There were critics from right and left, inevitably, but the social democrats, under President Noe Zhordania, pursued a moderate and occasionally radical course in the face of considerable difficulties, notably the food shortages provoked by the economic blockade by Bolshevik Russia.

When in April 1920 Soviet troops entered Baku and proclaimed the republic of Azerbaijan, Georgia's days of independence were numbered, especially as Bolsheviks within Georgia had long been plotting to overthrow the Zhordania government, which had failed to revitalise the economy. A treaty of mutual recognition between Bolshevik Russia and Menshevik Georgia counted for as little as the Treaty of Georgievsk. Like the earlier treaty, this was born out of fear and expediency. The failure of the League of Nations to admit Georgia as a member in December 1920 must have given many a Georgian democrat a *frisson*. In January 1921 there was encouraging news: both the French and the British governments recognised Georgia's sovereign status. However, this didn't cut much ice with the Soviet authorities, and on February the Red Army crossed into Georgia and occupied Tbilisi. By the following month Zhordania was in exile and the Bolsheviks were in control. For the Mensheviks, there was no point looking to the British for help, since Britain had signed an agreement with Soviet Russia pledging that it would not support any anti-Soviet activities within the borders of greater Russia. The agreement in effect nullified the recognition of Georgia's independence, as the Bolsheviks were only too well aware.

As an old Intourist brochure put it: 'The Georgian people won full freedom and independence, however, only in 1921, when the Red Banner of the Soviets was hoisted over the Georgian capital, Tbilisi, and the working people of Georgia joined the mighty family of the peoples of the world's first socialist state.' The world's first socialist state inaugurated its rule by purging the Mensheviks. All the abuses perpetrated in Russia by the Soviet secret police, the Cheka, were paralleled in Georgia. When opponents of Soviet repression tried to protest, as they did in 1924, retribution was savage; at least 7000 were killed. Deportations followed, and non-Georgian groups such as the Kalmucks and the various German communities were shipped to Siberia, as were native Georgians who displeased the authorities. Forced collectivisation and the elimination of private enterprise caused further hardship, as they did in Russia. Nor did Georgia escape the horrors of the mid-1930s. Under the zealous direction of Beria and Stalin, thousands of Georgians, including many of the republic's intellectuals, vanished and perished. Repression and deportation continued after the war, ending only with Stalin's death.

Sitting quietly beneath a tree in the graveyard at Ikhalto, my mind was on an earlier period of devastation, Shah Abbas's invasion which had destroyed the buildings around me. Georgia's long history alternated periods of prosperity and cultural glory with decades of savagery and despoliation. There was no pattern to it, it was a geopolitical accident, a consequence of location. But it lent a constant drama to the landscape, where every field and every hill had been fought over. Usually there had been recovery of sorts, but the ruins of the academy had never been restored.

A few miles away there was another ecclesiastical site that was less melancholy. The old walls around the monastery at Shuamta must have offered limited protection against marauders, whose progress could be monitored from the immense belfry set into the walls. The precincts resembled a farmyard more than a monastery. Oaks and pines dispensed shade, and buildings far more recent than the church were slapped against the sides, providing quarters for a small number of monks and nuns. I wandered into the church, a tall shapely structure of no particular interest except for some surviving frescoes. I found a curious little nineteenth-century marble monument with a Latin inscription to a doctor of science called Meskief. Nothing remarkable about it except its unexpectedness in this rural spot.

Svetlana and I were approached by a dumpy nun with a white kerchief draped over voluminous black shawls. Behind her stood two shy teenagers, also in black. She wanted to know whether I was Orthodox. No, I wasn't. Protestant? No, I was Jewish. She beamed. She liked Jews, she had young relatives married to Jewish girls. But did I accept Jesus Christ? This is uncommon among Jews, but I didn't want to offend her, so I simply replied that I was not a believer. This answer was not welcome. She told me that she hoped I would be brought to religion. Then she went off at a tangent to discuss the political crisis in Georgia, which she regarded as the consequence of godlessness. In a battle between good and evil we must pray for good. We must trust to God, who would guide us. Quite so. Nice to meet you. Here are some roubles for the restoration fund. Goodbye. But she wouldn't stop talking and followed us out of the precincts to the car park, where Givi was waiting. I wanted to ask her about the young women in her wake – were they novices? – but Svetlana begged me not to, otherwise we would never get away.

Svetlana had hoped that in the course of our jaunt some rapport might develop between the two writers. But no spark flashed between Givi and me. I asked him a few questions about his work, which he dutifully answered, but there was no real exchange of information, let alone ideas. He was evidently in a lousy mood, and it showed as we drove back across the mountains. Georgian drivers are notoriously reckless, but I had been lucky so far. Now Givi put his foot down. The springs of the Lada are not supple at the best of times, and the ride, as we jolted at sixty miles an hour over potholed mountain roads, ranged from the uncomfortable to the terrifying. In Georgia, overtaking is a variation on the game of chicken, lane discipline is a form of womanish fastidiousness, braking a mere afterthought.

The axe murderer came for me at seven. He woke me with a thundering of fists against the door. It would be only a matter of time before the blade pierced the wood. I rushed to the door and yelled at him; he yelled back in Georgian, rattling the door handle. Svetlana had warned me to keep my door locked, as hooligans occasionally wandered into the hotel from the street. I yelled, he rattled and thudded. Well, if he was going to kill me, we might as well get it over with. I turned the key in the lock. He was a burly bugger all right, but he had hidden the axe. A little sign language established that he was a driver, responding to my request for car and chauffeur that morning. I made it clear that he must seek his employer elsewhere. Abashed and apologetic, he slunk away.

In the dining room twenty Canadian tourists were enjoying their final breakfast in Tbilisi. They had the distinction of being the last tourists in town. One woman sported an I LOVE MOSCOW baseball cap, which didn't seem the most tactful thing to do in Georgia, where the president devoted many of his waking hours to denouncing Moscow and all its works.

The sun was shining, but even so Rustaveli was looking terribly grey. It wasn't only that the historicist piles such as my hotel and the Rustaveli Theatre were built of begrimed dark stone. There was simply so little colour anywhere, and even the few shop signs which employed non-grey seemed dusted over into terminal dullness. The shops were dimly lit, and the plate-glass windows displayed little, sometimes nothing. At the souvenir shop halfway down the avenue, the only way to find out whether it was open was to push the door. It was possible to walk past my hotel's main entrance and assume it was closed for the season. At the café across from the hotel the coffee wasn't bad, but the shabby interior was as inviting as an undertaker's parlour. Only the parade of mature trees enlivened the avenue. Many institutional buildings were being used as barracks or for storage, and were guarded by dishevelled soldiers seated behind low barricades. Their windows had been broken and admitted the elements through ruffs of jagged glass. The former Institute of Marxism-Leninism was plastered with pro-government signs, including one in English, no doubt for the benefit of CNN film crews: 'Zugdidi, with 130,000 population, supports our elected President.'

Temuri, another of Svetlana's assistants, came to take me to Mount Mtatsminda, which overlooks the city. This was the first of many occasions when the Curse of Temuri operated: any arrangements made by this gentle young man would founder. Even I, with my limited knowledge of the city, could tell that the route he had chosen to reach the funicular up the mountainside was circuitous in the extreme. Temuri was an expert on Mycenae, largely self-taught. He was erudite, eager to please, delicate in his manners and unfailingly courteous. He also spoke so quietly that the merest rustle of leaves, let alone the traffic of Tbilisi, drowned him out.

Funiculars are designed to terrify by ascending vertical cliff faces very slowly, and the Mtatsminda vehicle gave the experience an extra turn of the screw by creaking, straining and groaning. Decelerating to the pace of a slug's promenade, the cabin crunched along its cables and into the shed at the top of the mountain. The summit, the best spot from which to see how the city has been tucked into the river valley below, has been laid out as a park, known until only a few years ago as Stalin Park. The Georgians were never in any hurry to condemn their local boy who done good, despite his tendency to take things to excess. Strolling through the pleasure grounds I saw the big wheel, the planetarium, the miniature train with its carriages lying on their sides – all deserted. But I could hear the industrial grind of the bumper cars rumbling for the amusement of three children. We walked over to the 900-foot television tower, lightly guarded by a handful of government soldiers at the gate, although an armoured car was parked in the forecourt. Temuri, ever the optimist, took this as a sign that the situation was less serious than alarmists maintained.

We reached the parking area, which was deserted. Temuri was looking for the bus. 'Or a car.' What car? There was something that might have been a bus stop, so I went and sat nearby under some fragrant pines. The Curse of Temuri took effect. There was no bus, nor were there any cars. True, one smartly dressed man had driven up and parked, but he and his moll had gone off into the woods, and I didn't think we'd be seeing them for a while. Temuri wandered off to ask somebody about the local transportation facilities (who was he going to ask?) but returned dejected. So we went back to the funicular, pausing at the stop halfway down to visit the pantheon devoted to Georgian heroes. Around the small church are the granite and marble tombs of artists, musicians and scientists, laid out on terraces. Only the great and good are given one of these graves with a view.

I followed Erekle along Rustaveli to Republic Square, dominated by huge loops of concrete which form the backdrop to a platform from which officials once watched May Day parades. The disrespectful Georgians immediately dubbed the loops 'Andropov's ears' in honour of the former head of the KGB. After Republic Square became the principal rallying place of the Opposition, Gamsakhurdia's men wrecked the platform. The president denied that he was trying to obstruct the Opposition – it was just that the platform urgently needed repairs that somehow were never completed.

From the square we continued towards the Philharmonic building – closed – and the university, also closed. Near the Philharmonic we encountered fresh barricades, where police were stopping cars and checking papers. We were not far from the Television Centre, which the Opposition had taken over as its headquarters.

Whenever I walked down Rustaveli towards Freedom Square I could see in the distance, rising from a hillside terrace, the immense statue known as Mother Georgia. Now we were on our way to dinner with Elgudzha Amashukeli, the sculptor of the statue and the designer of many other major monuments scattered about Georgia, including the fine equestrian statue of Vakhtang Gorgasali and the memorial to Pirosmani. Amashukeli was easily the best known sculptor in Georgia.

We crossed a tatty grass verge to the entrance to the tall apartment block where the sculptor lived. The block was as shabby as all such dwellings in the Soviet Union, a rat's nest of ill-fitting lintels and window-frames, accumulations of plaster and other debris in the hallways, no proper lighting (bulbs are easy to steal), and wheezing lifts vulnerable to electricity cuts. Inside the flat, all was different. I trod across a sea of parquet flooring, and was led from room to adjoining room. There was outward squalor but interior luxury, with fine antique furniture and the greatest luxury of all – space.

A slender man who looks younger than his years despite thinning and greying hair, Elgudzha Amashukeli had a breezy self-confidence. His jittery wife, Lia Shuria, is a poet, and she showed me a manuscript of an anthology of her work which had been translated into English. I offered to take it back with me to England, but she said she couldn't remember the publisher's address, which seemed rather odd. Elgudzha showed me round his flat, and I particularly admired some of his paintings, which, I said, reminded me of Henry Moore's drawings, though these had a submarine quality to them which gave them a different texture. Elgudzha was pleased, since he greatly admired Moore's work. He led me up some pitch-black steps to a top-floor flat, which served partly as a studio for his daughter, who painted, and partly as a private gallery for his work. He showed me a new project, a model for a seven-metre statue of David the Builder which he had been working on for years. Like all his work, it's characterised by monumentalism and stylisation and Michelangelesque muscularity. Elgudzha was keen for me to understand that although some people might deride monumental statuary as anachronistic, Georgia had always lacked such a tradition, as nineteenth-century Russification had stalled any commemoration of the nation's heroes. Thus Georgia had lagged behind other countries in establishing national consciousness through public art. Nor did he believe that his work was backward-looking. He was fully aware of modern developments in sculpture and made use of them in his work.

Meanwhile, in the flat downstairs, a low table had been laid with dishes. There were rolled crêpes filled with mincemeat, the doughy savoury cheese-filled pastries known as *khachapuri* and wildly popular throughout Georgia, sponge cakes with soft meringue, bowls of peach jam, and tumbling bunches of grapes. The doors kept opening to admit new guests: Erekle's mother Zeinab, smothering her rheum-afflicted nose with a handkerchief, and Erekle's cousin Levan. Zeinab, a florid motherly woman of great warmth and quick wits, spoke some English ('but slowly please'), as did Levan, a zoology student at the university. There was much anxiety about the latest political developments. Gamsakhurdia had given the forces loyal to the Opposition until eight that evening to surrender their arms. This they had refused to do, and the deadline had passed. Everybody wondered how the president would respond. Throughout the evening phone calls were made and received, but there was no information.

I asked Elgudzha whether independence would make any difference to the way he worked. After all, sculptors, more than most artists, are dependent on the state and its institutions for their commissions.

'It won't affect me at all. I've always been independent. I've never designed a statue of Lenin, or of Stalin, or anybody else, not to order. It made me unpopular with the Party bosses, and I was forbidden to travel for eight years. You've seen the Mother Georgia statue?'

'Of course.'

'Well, two attempts were made to get rid of it. As you know, Lenin Square was named after the large statue of Lenin there. The Party faithful claimed that when they were strolling down Rustaveli towards the square, the sword which Mother Georgia is holding appeared to be aimed at Lenin's neck. So they wanted my statue removed.'

'But in the end it was Lenin who was removed, not Mother Georgia.'

'Exactly!'

Georgian meals are formal occasions. Either the host or a distinguished guest will be chosen as *tamada*, or toastmaster. He choreographs the occasion, proposing many toasts himself and giving way to other guests in the course of the meal. Elgudzha began a whole series of toasts. The first was to women, the next to their guest from England, though this, as it burrowed through thickets of rhetoric, modulated into a meditation on the current political crisis. I asked Elgudzha whether he was optimistic about the future.

'When you consider the state of the world, only a madman is optimistic.'

He splashed more brandy into my glass, and then raised his own to propose a toast to Erekle, to the hope that rested with the new generation of Georgians, in which I was erroneously but generously included. By this time we had been joined at table by Erekle's father Demo, a bald tubby man, firm-jawed and eager-eyed, and rather intimidating in his presence and stare, an intensity which shattered whenever a huge beaming smile crossed his features. His arrival offered a pretext to Elgudzha to fetch more brandy, and Lia went out to fetch more food. At no time did any of the menfolk stir from the table to assist her. Lia may have been a famous poet, but at home her duties were more prosaic. Later in the evening she flopped on to a little French Empire sofa and attended to her nails; she was joined by Zeinab, a move reminiscent of Victorian ladies' withdrawal from the dining room.

'Dostoevsky,' Elgudzha began sonorously, 'said that beauty can save the world. I would like to add that poetry too can save the world.' This was the prologue to an elegant toast to his wife. She looked on pallidly from the sofa.

Demo's toast proved exceptionally long, but we remained attentive. The Georgian cult of woman, he explained to me, was not to be confused with the Islamic concept of womanhood. He reeled off the names of the major Georgian queens, and said that in modern times some of the most honoured women in Georgia were – yes – poetesses, of whom there were two shining examples. One I had not heard of, the other I most certainly had, as I happened to be clinking glasses with Lia, who had rejoined us to accept the honour Demo was offering.

When Elgudzha, not for the first time, went to refill my glass, I tried to stop him. 'You are not obliged to drain your glass with every toast,' he explained, 'but as *tamada* I am obliged to make sure it is always full.'

The toast to Lia was followed by Elgudzha's reflections on art and its audience. His oratory was interrupted by a tremendous thwack as Lia, wielding a plastic whisk, swotted a fly which had rashly landed on the table.

Talk turned to literature. Demo wanted to know what Shelagh Delaney and John Osborne were up to these days. Somebody else sought to know the latest dirt on the relationship between Laurence Olivier and Vivien Leigh. I couldn't enlighten them greatly but I was able to reassure them that John Gielgud and Paul Scofield were alive and well. All this served as a prelude to another toast from Demo. England, he began, is the land of Shakespeare and other great writers . . . At this point he was cruelly interrupted by the *tamada*, who had in mind another great and talented man: Meskhi, Georgia's most celebrated left forward. Elgudzha seemed inordinately proud that he had predicted the footballer's meteoric career when the lad was only fifteen. He dashed into another room to fetch a slide showing the tombstone he had designed for Meskhi. It was a simple slab, and on it there rested a bronze football. Demo now reclaimed his toast, and spoke of Georgia's cultural isolation under Stalin, and of the present political difficulties. But now, he declared, we were turning a new page, aided by Georgia's longstanding relationship with the British people, whom I represented. We once more clinked our brimming crystal glasses.

4 Guns and Knives

The next morning there was calamitous news on the World Service. Sixty National Guardsmen had been killed in a battle at Shavnabada. Half an hour later the news bulletin reduced the fatalities to five.

I awaited Svetlana at the hotel. Usually she was punctual, but there was no sign of her. Instead Temuri arrived, smiling his wan smile. My 'programme', he explained, had been postponed, because of the troubled situation. He had come to fill the gap.

I asked him to take me to the market not far from Freedom Square. Inside the functional two-storey structure I found an abundance of good-quality fruit and vegetables – for those who, on an average monthly wage of 400 roubles, could afford it. Carrots cost 2 to 6 roubles per kilo, onions 3, lemons 4, tomatoes from 1 to 3 depending on the quality, aubergines 3, pears and apples 5, raspberries 20, cucumbers from 8 to 10, and shelled walnuts were 50. I also found radishes and herbs, leeks and peppers, grapes and pomegranates, cheese for 35 roubles a kilo and a plentiful selection of chicken and beef for slightly less. Most of the farmwomen behind the counters were Azerbaijanis, stout women with a bronze sheen to their lined faces, their heads wrapped in brightly coloured kerchiefs, hennaed hair peeking out from the edges, and heavy gold or bronze jewellery tugging at the ears. Their brassiness made them an ideal sales force, blunt but approachable.

Later that morning I went off to the Television Centre. From the university, I walked down the avenue to Heroes Square. Beyond the square the merry rotunda of the circus rose up behind the trees. One exit from the square was barricaded and a crowd had gathered in the distance. I continued towards it, passing more barricades, a line of upended coal wagons, and an ancient piece of artillery in the middle of the road. To the left, the terraces of the television studios were piled with sandbags and old tyres. Soldiers crouched on top of armoured cars, though T-shirts with Western logos had replaced uniforms. A microphone had been set up at the top of the steps, mimicking the situation outside Parliament, and speeches poured forth, some provoking arguments among the crowd.

The crowd was quite different from the government supporters. There were exceptions, of course, but in general the loyalists were an uncouth lot, unshaven, boisterous, rough-edged. Here the crowd was more urban and urbane, packed with students and teachers and journalists. It was almost impossible to find an English or French speaker outside the Parliament but the Opposition seemed thick with accomplished linguists. A correspondent from *The Times*, Bruce Clark, later told me he even encountered a Latin speaker.

Upstairs in the improvised press office I found a French television crew, a handful of eager Japanese and downcast Russian journalists, and half a dozen overflowing ashtrays. A punky young woman from Bratislava told me that the speeches were debating the feasibility of organising some kind of human shield to counter any government attack on the Centre. There was a flurry of activity as a group of fast-moving figures, including numerous riflemen, emerged from a back office, crossed the landing and headed down the stairs. Down on the terrace the bodyguards fanned out to allow the former prime minister, Tengiz Sigua, to tell the crowd that he would be setting off for Parliament at two o'clock to present once again the Opposition's demands for the president's resignation. It was not clear whom he would hand these demands to. The Supreme Soviet was not in session, and it was not the kind of gesture that would go down well with the thuggish crowds near the Parliament.

I strolled back to Heroes Square to wait for any movement of the crowd. By 2.30 there was still none, so I returned to the Centre and the press office, and stayed put, largely for want of anything better to do. From this third-floor vantage point, a kind of lobby area with plate-glass windows, I had an excellent view on to the street. I seemed to be the only person in the building who wasn't carrying a Kalashnikov or a video camera. Where did all the weapons, and the equally formidable armoury carried by the pro-government militias, come from? Suddenly loud voices were raised in the corridor nearby, and a group of men, mostly soldiers, emerged. One of them, who was not armed, was immediately surrounded by journalists.

'Who's this?' I whispered to an interpreter standing near me.

'Kitovani.'

Good. I took out my notebook. He was wearing a blue suit and tie and a button-down shirt, and with his trim moustache and greying hair, he didn't look like a military man, but then Kitovani, sculptor and ex-con, was hardly a career soldier. He spoke in rapid Russian, answered a few questions, then headed down the stairs. An Australian reporter kindly put me in the picture: Kitovani had said that if Gamsakhurdia agreed to remove his troops from the Parliament, he would agree to remove his forces from the Television Centre. Some among the Opposition wished to proceed slowly, hoping to dislodge Gamsakhurdia by constitutional means; others wanted to force the issue. The march to Parliament, now an hour overdue, had been cancelled. It was fast becoming apparent that everything was improvised, that nobody knew from hour to hour what was happening. Hastily summoned councils proclaimed the tactics of the hour, which were often overtaken by events. The same was true of the government.

It was all very exciting, yet the ferment was ludicrously localised. Daily life, except on streets blocked by barricades, was carrying on as normal. It was possible, as the Canadian tourists had discovered, to visit Tbilisi undisturbed by the political situation. Yet within the orbit of each headquarters it was easy to be seduced by the constant drama stoked by both sides.

My hotel room was gradually revealing its deficiencies. The cupboard doors kept jamming on the runners, the thermometer on the wall was for decoration only, and the table lamp didn't work.

The telephone had stopped working days ago. The next morning the lights weren't working either, but the power was later restored.

When Svetlana arrived to take me on another outing, I was more than ready for it. There was little to do in Tbilisi except to monitor the minutiae of political developments, and a day off was welcome. Our driver was Sandro Taktakishvili. By training he was a physicist, although he comes from a family of distinguished musicians. Unable to support a growing family on an academic's salary of about 400 roubles a month, he had co-founded a small scientific company which planned to manufacture computer components. These were relatively inexpensive to produce and could be marketed internationally. That was the theory, but Sandro told me his efforts were being frustrated by the shortsightedness of the government.

'Instead of encouraging trade, they make it almost impossible for us. Whatever foreign currency we earn by our efforts, the government takes about 80 per cent of it. They call it a tax. But it's crazy. The root of the problem is that Gamsakhurdia has appointed his senior officials not because they are competent, but because they are loyal. All the competent people have already deserted him. The economic chief in Parliament was once a bookkeeper, so Gamsakhurdia thinks he knows something about economics. But he doesn't.

'We have to face the fact that Gamsakhurdia is crazy. He even talks of killing his enemies! I don't think anybody foresaw that he would be so awful. A number of people, myself included, were uneasy about him, but when it came to the elections we gave him the benefit of the doubt. A very few people warned that political power would change Gamsakhurdia, but nobody believed them, but now we can see that they were right. His father was a great writer but he brought up Zviad to believe that he would be a saviour of Georgia. Zviad really believes that's his role. His only strong card is nationalism, which can be a very destructive force. I'm disillusioned because all his promises have come to nothing. He was going to introduce land reform, but then he decided not to because that would mean giving land to Armenians and Azerbaijanis. But those people have lived here for hundreds of years, and there was no reason to deny them their share. Nor has there been any privatisation, and the economy here is in terrible shape, as you can see for yourself. Gamsakhurdia has done nothing to improve our trading relations, as I have discovered.

'Small companies like mine get no help. The older established companies, the state enterprises, the trading associations, are run by people who are incredibly unintelligent. They simply operate according to rules and structures that were laid down long ago. They have no flexibility. We have to take a more entrepreneurial approach if we are to succeed, but the new government is just as keen to control aspects of economic life as the Communists ever were. The result is higher prices and no improvements in the standard of living.'

Many prices had doubled or trebled in the past year; salaries had not. Salaries bore little relation to the importance or usefulness of the job. Ideology still dictated that 'workers' should be better rewarded than the intelligentsia. Sandro's salary, as a theoretical physicist, was the same as that of a Tbilisi bus driver, he estimated. He couldn't live on his salary alone, and many scientists had either accepted job offers in the West or abandoned their professions for more lucrative work.

I asked him whether administrators were well paid. For example, a winery director?

'He gets paid very well, perhaps 15,000 roubles a month. These jobs are so much sought after that people will pay a great deal to get them. There are other jobs that may not pay particularly well but they allow you to supplement your earnings in all kinds of ways. For instance, a city bus driver may not be well paid, but a driver on long-distance routes could earn up to 5000 roubles a month, usually by taking far more passengers than he is supposed to. That doesn't make them quite as rich as it may sound, as out of their earnings they have to maintain their bus and pay the dispatcher who assigns the routes. Nothing is straightforward here.'

I asked Sandro whether he could see any possibilities of change.

'At the moment Gamsakhurdia stays in power because he can appeal to the uninformed, especially in the regions. He goes on television and says, "My enemies are trying to kill me, please come and protect me." And his supporters come rushing to Tbilisi. But this cannot continue indefinitely. I think by the end of the winter he will have gone. Once the people realise they have no bread and no money, then things will change.'

Sandro was able to talk without losing control of the car, which is unusual among Georgians. We were now past Mtskheta, continuing westward on the highway. A car overtook us in the fast lane, and seemed to be tickling the rear bumpers of the car ahead of it. It then swerved on to the narrow verge between the highway and the central partition. With only inches to spare on either side, it overtook. Then we were overtaken by a Lada with an improvised roof rack on to which two crates had been tied. The car was about two hundred yards ahead when the crates fell off, but fortunately there was no vehicle immediately behind. The laden car was travelling so fast that the driver did not notice his loss, which was still causing the traffic to make frenzied twists and turns many hours later, when we returned along the same road.

We turned off to visit Gori. The town is overlooked by a splendid hilltop fortress, its crenellated walls climbing up and down the steep slopes. The mediaeval fortress, however, is a lesser attraction than the memorials to Stalin, who was born here in 1879. Instead of cringing in shame, the people of Gori were proud of their native son. The immense charcoal-grey statue of the tyrant still stands in the central square; it is the last surviving monument to the man. To see those odious features gazing steadily out from a great height was most peculiar, and I tried to imagine strolling through Vienna or Berlin and coming across a statue to Hitler. Nor is this the only memorial to the butcher in Gori. The Stalin Museum has been closed since 1989, but in a nearby park, tucked beneath a neo-Egyptian temple-like structure of yellow tufa, is his birthplace, a two-room brick cabin with a wooden verandah. On the temple roof medallions frame the hammer and sickle motif.

Sandro was convinced the whole place was bogus, that the authorities, back in 1939, had picked out any old cabin and transported it here. 'Like the ship, the *Aurora* in St Petersburg.

It was always a famous Communist icon, but it wasn't genuine at all.'

'That's because the symbol always mattered more than the truth.'

We were now in Inner Kartli, among the fertile lowlands of the Georgian heartland. Along the road were blue panelled fences and trim white screened houses and orchards. Soon we bore south, still following the River Mtkvari, and the road rose gently until we came to a land of steep wooded slopes and high meadows which was especially beautiful in the soft autumn sunlight. Here Sandro had spent his summers as a child and he spoke tenderly of woods where he had walked and streams where he had bathed. He knew of a restaurant not far from here – perhaps it was still there.

It was. It didn't look like a restaurant and there was no sign, it was simply a large house tucked into a hollow next to a railway line. The verandah where we sat was roofed with warped plastic coffering. Elderly women in kerchiefs, the grandmotherly preservers of traditional cuisine, served the food.

On learning that I was a foreign visitor, the oldest of the women handed me a bowl. She told me that it was a relic from the time of her great-grandfather, who had used it to toast Georgia. She hoped I would use it for the same purpose. It was beautifully shaped, about the size of a large French coffee cup, and it was half filled with good white wine. I thanked her and toasted her beautiful country and wished Georgia a prosperous future. At this the poor woman looked so pained that I thought she was about to burst into tears. With her hands clutched together, she replied that these were terrible times and she was desperately anxious about the future.

The food arrived: small dishes of beetroot, peppery cabbage salad, parsley and radishes, tomato salad. Then a pan of sizzling innards, which were rather tough, in a garlicky sauce, followed by trout sliced like cod steaks and fried, and fried chicken and fried potatoes. The restaurant was famous for its mushrooms, but the old woman told us that a wedding party had consumed the whole week's supply and there were none left.

Our lunch over, we drove into the spa town of Borjomi. Its streets wound along the contours of the valley and the banks of the river. A few houses had gingerbread balconies and bore traces of brightly coloured paint. We left the car outside the park where Borjomi's famous mineral springs bubble up. A narrow valley has been hollowed by the rushing stream after which the town is named. Wandering among the trees and formal flowerbeds, we almost had the place to ourselves, though on a warm Saturday afternoon in September one would have expected a park to be filled with visitors. The further we walked, the more empty and dilapidated the park became. Like other parks in Georgia it was cluttered with furniture, benches and lamps, children's playgrounds, arbours, huts and kiosks. Georgian parks are a haven of sociability rather than a taming and anthologising of nature. Nature lets rip on either side, where the mountain slopes, too steep to be subjugated, support a delicious mingling of pine and spruce and chestnut. Within the park most of the buildings, of Russian nineteenth-century design, were locked and deserted. So were the kiosks that once sold ice-cream, soft drinks and snacks. Not even the water fountains worked. In the distance Sandro spotted the swimming pool where he had often swum as a boy. He had not been here for sixteen years.

The change shocked him. The pool was empty, weeds scrabbled along the bottom, and the plaster along the sides had crumbled away. Around the poolside, benches were awry and some had been overturned. The decorative iron lamps lacked bulbs; where bulbs remained, they had been smashed. The changing rooms were filled with rubble. It was a melancholy scene.

I felt sorry for Svetlana as much as for Sandro. She was so anxious for me to see the good sides of Georgia and distressed that my visit coincided with political turmoil and social depression. She kept trying to prompt me into enthusiastic responses – 'Beautiful, yes?' – and I always tried to provide them. Here, among the wreckage, she tried again.

'It inspires you here. It inspires you.'

But it was no use. The deserted park, the neglected amenities and the unchecked disintegration, left us all dejected. We walked back to the large white building that houses the mineral spring. In the centre of the main hall was a polygonal counter, and behind this altar to intestinal cleansing a sour woman doled out brimming glasses from a fountain topped with two white putti. From the walls two stags' heads, gorgeously antlered, looked down on us. I took a sip. The water was warm and slightly salty, with a strong earthy mineral flavour.

Svetlana wanted me to be impressed: 'It's free of charge.'

'So it should be, considering how it tastes.'

'You must sip it. It is better so.' I drained the glass with difficulty. Sandro failed.

We drove a few miles farther up the valley to the resort park of Likani. This landscaped estate was once the exclusive haunt of senior Communist Party officials, but is now open to the general public. A fanciful turreted quasi-Tuscan villa of 1895, fringed with copies of Roman statues, dominates the formal gardens. From the terrace, steps lead down towards a pool, less structured gardens, and the river. These grounds seemed rather unkempt, but appropriately so, given the wildness of the landscape around us. Chestnuts lolled in their husks along the paths. I walked over a hideous rusting metal bridge that crosses the Mtkvari, here a dark olive in colour, and gazed back at the riverbank, where yellowing maples had been planted. The other buildings within the grounds are mostly rest houses. The Party bosses have gone from here, but even now only the élite can afford to come here for their twenty-four-day family holidays, a vacation only winery directors and long-distance bus drivers can afford.

We drove back towards Tbilisi, bunched in traffic most of the way. Mercifully, Sandro did not participate in the reckless scramble towards the head of the column. Georgians don't hesitate to overtake even if another car is speeding straight towards them. The three cars will somehow arrange themselves with seconds to spare and squeeze by. Or not. In addition to the heart-stopping drama of Ladas pushed to their limited limits, we had the foul black fumes emitted by buses and lorries. Find yourself stuck behind one of them for long and your lungs cry out for a transplant.

When a BMW overtook us, I asked Sandro how much a Georgian would have to pay for a smart German car.

'You can buy them in Moscow for about 300,000 roubles.'

'There are people here with that kind of money?'

'A few.'

'And what did you pay for this Lada?'

'New, it is priced at 9100 roubles. But I paid more. There is a ten-year waiting list, which is getting longer all the time. Under Gorbachev Lada was given much more freedom, and the company decided to export more, as the profits are so much greater if it sells its cars in the West. What does a Lada cost in England?'

'About five thousand pounds. And you have to put up with a lot of jokes.'

'Five thousand pounds is a lot of roubles. Lada has to sell many many cars on the domestic market to equal one export sale. Lada would like to sell its entire production abroad, but of course that would mean the supply of new cars here would dry up completely, so the government has had to retain some control over the company. Even so, the shortages are getting worse, so anybody who wants a car has to buy one on the black market. I could sell mine for about 60,000 roubles.'

There were new arrivals at the Hotel Tbilisi: two American journalists who looked like Mormon missionaries. They wore blazers and button-down shirts and ties, and carried identical customised journalist packs, cunningly stuffed with little pockets for pens and pencils, notebooks and calculators. In this town you needed to be nimble and light-footed, but this pair probably had to call an executive conference and check with mother before deciding what to do. I eavesdropped as they phoned their contacts, whom they preppily addressed as 'sir'.

I walked over to the Television Centre. Near the university, government soldiers were stopping cars and searching them, presumably looking for weapons. The area was plunged in darkness, as the electricity supply had been disconnected by the government the night before. In the apartment buildings across the street candles glowed dimly in the windows as residents were forced to share the Opposition's privations. At the entrance to the Centre I heard that a press conference was now taking place upstairs. I had just reached the landing when I heard the sound of rifle fire. Looking down from the large plate-glass windows overlooking the crowd-filled street, I could see people scattering for cover in all directions. I followed their example, taking cover behind a column, as anybody visible through the window was an easy target. In the darkness it was impossible to tell whether the shots were fired by a single provocateur or were part of a concerted attack.

The press conference had been taking place in a room off the nearby corridor, and no sooner had I ducked than the door was flung open. Reporters came pouring out. Some dashed for the stairs; others waited around. Kitovani was calmly lighting a cigarette. Nobody knew what was going on. Soon I was less scared of snipers in the darkened street than I was of young guardsmen whizzing around the building brandishing Kalashnikovs and pistols. The lights in the conference room were shut off. The press conference was history.

A Moscow-based reporter from Agence France Presse told me that earlier in the day the prime minister, Besso Gugushvili, had declared that the Opposition was split and would soon be leaving the Television Centre. When asked how this would be accomplished, he said vaguely that steps were in progress. Would there be a new session of Parliament? Not until Kitovani's forces left Tbilisi. Gugushvili went on to berate the press corps for their lack of understanding of Georgia.

At the Opposition press conference Kitovani had admitted that the National Guard had left Shavnabada, but said the move was of no significance. He minimised the Guard's losses, although abandoning three helicopters sounded more grave than a casual mislaying of armaments. He admitted that his estimate of sixty dead after the fighting had been an error; the correct figure was five. The French reporter thought that negotiations between the two sides would proceed, simply because there was no alternative. (She didn't know the Georgians.)

'Gamsakhurdia is crazy,' she remarked, 'but the Opposition, they are a little crazy too.'

I left the building. The shooting had been an isolated incident, probably the work of a lone provocateur. An Opposition armoured vehicle rumbled past reassuringly; the crowd returned to the steps, and speeches were resumed. I spotted a young man, a few yards down the slope from the microphone, inexplicably clutching a small Israeli flag. The spotlights beamed not on to the street but on to the trees above us, while we wandered below in a strange crepuscular half-light.

As I walked up the hill towards the university I heard more rifle fire. Two soldiers were setting up positions behind hides of fir branches which they were piling up near Heroes Square. The top of the street was now sealed off. It looked ominous, but no doubt such measures were intended to maintain psychological pressure on the Opposition.

I started to walk towards the Philharmonic. A little man with thinning hair, perhaps in his twenties, came up behind me, but I paid no attention until he grabbed my sleeve. He yapped at me in Georgian. I replied in English. He found this terribly funny, repeating 'English' in a curious booming voice and falling about as though I were a source of incomparable amusement. I marched on and he fell behind. Two minutes later I heard a padding behind me and looked back to see him running towards me. I walked faster, but he drew level, muttering to himself. The smirk on his face was worrying me, rightly so, since he rounded on me and again grabbed my sleeve. I shook him off angrily, and told him to leave me alone.

'Come here!' he roared.

I tried to dodge past him. But he kept bellowing 'Come here!' and mimicking my 'Go away!' Two youths shouted at him to leave me alone but he paid no attention and kept pestering me in a belligerent manner. Then I noticed he had something else up his sleeve: a four-inch kitchen knife, substantial enough to skewer me. The boys had by now moved off, and other people on the street were keeping their distance. I ran into the road and he pursued me, still clutching his knife.

'How are you?' he roared. If he was trying to make friends, it was a peculiar approach. Since shouting at him had proved counter-productive, I tried to calm him. I raised my hands to show I had no intention of harming him, and I said I was fine, I was very well, not that I knew whether he could understand a word I was saying.

Suddenly a red Lada pulled up, two burly men in sweaters in the front. They called the young man over, and to my surprise he obeyed. He leaned down towards the open front window and as he was doing so, a man ran up and pinned back the youth's arms. The two boys to whom I had appealed earlier came up and motioned to me to make a run for it. I thanked them for their intervention, and took their advice. After about two hundred yards I guessed that I was safe and slowed down. The red Lada, making a whirring sound like a muted siren, pulled up beside me, and the two men signalled to me to get in the back. I thought it probable that they were plainclothes militia who wanted to give me a lift, but since I wasn't sure I declined. They seemed to understand, and I reached the hotel without further incident.

5 Two Modiglianis

Sioni Cathedral was packed on Sunday morning. Old women in kerchiefs and younger couples in informal clothes crowded into the nave, candles couched in their palms. Priests emerged from behind the iconostasis and swung censers, lewdly anointing the congregation. Occasionally the Patriarch himself, resplendent in a red and yellow cope and a metal mitre, stepped from the throng of priests like a lead actor taking a curtain call, and stood before us solemnly, a crucifix in his hands. The congregation indulged in a frenzy of crossing, and one or two devout souls, including a young man who looked like Rasputin, genuflected so thoroughly that they could have touched the floor with their beards. Later in the service the expressionless Patriarch appeared carrying in one hand a double candlestick, looped like an elongated lyre at the lower end, and in the other a heavy crucifix. He crossed these accessories and held them up for our adoration.

The music was magnificent, a polyphony of the most astonishing complexity. The choir, invisible behind screens, was led by a bass with a deep rich chocolatey voice whom any international opera house would have longed to recruit. There was nothing oriental about the music, which combined Palestrinan polyphony with Orthodox sonority. Occasionally the rich treacly flow was stabbed by startling disharmonies, often repeatedly, and then the strands would resolve themselves again into a smoother harmonic flow. Some of these chorales date back to the tenth century, and I wondered whether this was as close as I would ever come to hearing the music of Byzantium.

At one particularly moving moment the choir sang *pianissimo*, and the whole congregation sank to its knees. One man surged forward and pressed his forehead to the flagstones, Islamic style. The new piety reflected the religious revival taking place throughout the former Soviet Union. In both Georgia and Armenia I was astonished to see how rapidly some acquaintances who had been observant Communists were transformed into observant Orthodox Christians who made a point, on entering a church, of buying and lighting a fistful of candles. In Georgia the Orthodox church had been doing its best to stay neutral, despite the eagerness of the government to exploit the revival of religious feeling in the country. In the old days officials and politicians used to place portraits of Lenin in their offices. Now they had icons of St George.

From Sioni Cathedral I walked back to Anchiskhati basilica, not for another dose of liturgy, but to refresh myself at the Oriental café behind the church. I sat down to admire the startling decor. On the wall behind me, cartouches of alabaster-like plastic – it was too light to the touch to be real alabaster – were decorated with floral motifs and lions' heads, one of which had a cigarette butt tucked irreverently between its jaws. Mirrors glittered between the dense ribbing of the wall panels, just as in a Moghul hall of audience. Unfortunately this splendour was not matched by the furnishings. We sat on rickety chairs at tables covered in cheap plastic. The managers presumably regarded any distinctive style, however kitschy, as an irrelevance. But to ignore style is to abhor style, and this contempt for shape and line, evident both in the blankness of Communist architecture and the wretchedness of most public spaces, was infinitely damning. City is theatre, but in the Soviet world such caprices had been regarded as contemptible. It would take a long time to recover the colour and trickery and quirkiness of a world where not everything serves an economic purpose.

There was coffee today, but no sugar, and thin slices of pastry with chocolate-flavoured topping. When I asked Erekle, who was with me, about these miserable offerings from a prosperous land, he replied that the shortages were probably the consequences of collectivisation. He neglected to add that corruption probably had much to do with it too. It was perfectly true that the collectivised system, which Gamsakhurdia had left in place, did not encourage productivity; nor was there any incentive for farmers to care for the land properly. People with assured jobs, whether on farms or in offices, didn't need to do much more than put in a daily appearance in order to collect their salaries.

'Remember the old Russian joke,' said Erekle. 'The government pretends to pay people, and the people pretend to work.'

We walked down to the riverside Rikhe Park, where each Sunday an art and book market is held. The paintings weren't up to much: many were lurid and weirdly lit townscapes and landscapes. Books used to be readily available in the former Soviet Union, although anything worth reading was usually published in small editions which went out of print the day after publication. The only way to find good books, especially translations, was either to queue up on the day of publication or to search for them at inflated prices on the black market. The prices here were certainly inflated, especially art books: a heavily illustrated American monograph on Dali had a price tag of 2000 roubles.

As we wandered round the park, we bumped into Erekle's cousin Levan. He was always brazenly self-confident, his English chatter gushing forth, any errors swamped by the rush of speech. We were all hungry, so we made our way to the riverbank branch of Lagidze's, a well-known haunt on Rustaveli which serves delicious soft drinks and *khachapuri*. We ate on the upstairs terrace, from which there were pleasant views on to the river and the prettily carved balconies of the clifftop houses opposite. The *khachapuri* were the variety known as *achma*, thin layers of dough interleaved with goat's cheese. I had to search hard for the taste of cheese.

Near the Lagidze restaurant I spotted a cellar which sold wines from the barrel. Despite the prohibition edict, the cellar was open and I was invited to taste the wine, which came from Kakheti. It was a full amber in colour, with an almost honeyed aroma of stewed apricots. On the palate the wine had the grapeskin asperity that surely derived from the Kakhetian method of fermenting white wines on the skins, which extracts a great deal of tannin. The grape variety was almost certainly Rkatsiteli. It's hardly a style of wine which matches modern tastes for something fresh and simple, but I liked it, as it was rich in flavour and full-bodied, making up for its very dry aftertaste. The cellar became my regular supplier of wine, at three roubles a bottle, until it was forced to close a week later.

Levan wanted to know all about the political situation in Britain, about which he had a rather confused idea, through no fault of his own. Margaret Thatcher had visited Transcaucasia and made a favourable impression. I had to point out to Levan that she had been foremost among those opposed to any break-up of the Soviet Union, though no doubt she had, like everybody else, modified her views subsequently. Levan, like every other Georgian I had met, thought that Mrs Thatcher had left office of her own free will, bowing out gracefully after a long and distinguished career. Again I had to point out that she had indeed resigned, but only because she faced defeat at the hands not of the fickle electorate but of her own former supporters. Of course it is not hard to see why Georgians have an exaggerated regard for the likes of Reagan and Thatcher. In their eyes, these were the politicians who kept up the pressure on Gorbachev, forcing the Soviet Union to enact the reforms which inadvertently made possible the republics' independence.

As for domestic politics, Levan feared that Gamsakhurdia would outsmart his opponents. He viewed Gamsakhurdia as a wily politician with no scruples who would not hesitate to play on the divisions among the Opposition. There was no shortage of those, since there were at least thirty political parties in Georgia, many reflecting minute subdivisions or personality clashes. Even the monarchists were split.

The royal house of Georgia has perpetuated itself, and the current Bagration in line for the throne is a young woman named Elisabeth. However, there is also, if I understand these niceties correctly, an ancillary line which was used to renew the dynasty by marriage whenever it was in danger of dying out. One of the monarchist parties argued that any new ruler should be derived from this ancillary branch. The current pretender, Jorge Bagration de

Mukhrani, was born in Italy in 1944 but now lives near Marbella in Spain. He speaks many European languages but no Georgian, and is best known as a rally driver. A Fiat executive, he had not shown much eagerness to take on his dynastic responsibilities. Nor was it clear what Elisabeth Bagration thought of the whole idea of a return to constitutional monarchy, especially since it might entail her marriage to the dashing Jorge. The idea ought to have been a non-starter, but it was taken with increasing seriousness after the overthrow of Gamsakhurdia.

We walked back into the town centre to visit the studio of Lado Gudiashvili. One worthwhile legacy of the Soviet system is the house museum, where the work of artists can be displayed in their former studios. Although these museums are theoretically open to the public, it is not always easy to gain admittance. Often some kind of introduction is required before an appointment is granted. Fortunately Levan was acquainted with Gudiashvili's daughter Chukurtma.

Chukurtma, a rather pretty but frail woman of about sixty, greeted us in the palatial first-floor drawing room of a town house behind my hotel. The enormous salon was furnished with handsome tables and dainty nineteenth-century neo-baroque chairs, mostly covered in gold brocade, as were the hefty tasselled pelmets over the numerous doors which led into other rooms. On one side of the room five tall windows overlooked the street, but the remaining walls were covered from floor to ceiling with her father's paintings.

Churkurtma spoke in French, which seemed appropriate, as she exuded an almost Parisian grace and *politesse*. Her father, who had died in 1980, had been one of a small group of Georgian artists sent to Paris in 1919, where he had flourished in its vibrant artistic ambiance. He married a Parisian woman and returned to Tbilisi in 1926, amazing his French friends by rejecting offers that promised him considerable worldly success. Even those close to him were puzzled by his determination to return to Bolshevik Russia, hardly the most comfortable environment in the mid-1920s, and the only plausible explanation is that he was homesick.

Gudiashvili's work falls into three distinct periods: the Parisian years, the dark Soviet years from 1926 to 1955, and the period after 1955. During the Stalinist years he adopted a heavy historicist style, but after Stalin's death the lines become more limpid and less grandiose, more colourful and less flabby. His most remarkable work consists of Goya-esque graphics – ink on paper with water-colour washes – which he produced during the most savage years of the terror, and no doubt kept concealed from all but his closest friends. One drawing simply called 'Censorship' shows people being squashed between books. In another grotesques dissect a naked woman to find the secret of her beauty; in 'Shashlik' animals skewer a man on a spit; in 'Division' a man saws a woman in half through her crotch; 'Composers' are portrayed as parrots; and 'Love' is a monstrous monkey embracing a woman. Civilisation is over whelmed by raw savagery.

In a bedroom crammed with drawings, Chukurtma showed me two precious Modigliani sketches of a woman. She told me how Modigliani and her father were seated one day in a Paris café. Strapped for cash, Modigliani sketched a Polish woman seated nearby in exchange for a cup of coffee. Since she disliked the sketches, Modigliani was about to destroy them, but his friend prevailed upon him to save them. Modigliani handed them over. Gudiashvili later sketched Modigliani, and this drawing also hangs here, together with a portrait of Mayakovsky. Back in the main salon, standing on an easel, is the last painting the Georgian worked on, a portrait of his granddaughter. He had a heart attack the evening after he started work on it; it stands where he left it.

Not long after his return to Tbilisi, Gudiashvili was ejected from the Tbilisi Academy of Arts for nonconformism; at no time, according to Chukurtma, did he ever paint political leaders. Even she was uncertain how he managed to survive the 1930s, but somehow he kept his head down. During that period he remarried, and his new wife supported him and took over all the practical aspects of his life, leaving him free to get on with his painting. Commissions had been scarce. Chukurtma wanted me to understand that these grand surroundings came to Gudiashvili very late in his life. Originally he occupied only a small part of the present-day flat, and in the 1950s the salon was still divided into three dwellings. Over the decades he was gradually able to expand his holdings, but it was only a few years before his death that he acquired the whole floor.

'This is his museum,' she told me, 'and he wanted it to be accessible to interested people. His spirit still lives here.'

The way back to the hotel from the Gudiashvili house crossed a small park with pretty fountains. A bulletin board carried hand-scrawled advertisements from people looking to sell or, more usually, exchange their flats. We came to a small open-air café, where I suggested that we refresh ourselves. This time, I said as we joined the short queue at the kiosk, I insisted on paying.

Levan protested at the very thought of it: 'We are Georgians and you are our guest.'

'But if you don't let me have my way once in a while, it means I can never again suggest anything like stopping for a cup of coffee. So I insist.'

'But if people discover you are a visitor and you are paying for our coffee, they will kill us.'

'Just tell them I'm a Georgian too, only I don't speak the language.'

I lost.

In the evening I returned to the Television Centre with Erekle. What else was there to do in this city which the government had closed and padlocked for the duration? There was considerable excitement in the building, as the Opposition, assisted by tech-nicians from the Baltic states, was trying to set up its own radio transmitter, which would provide the Georgian people, especially those outside Tbilisi, with accurate information. The attempt failed.

Near the press room I ran into the French AFP reporter again. She was excited: she was leaving for Moscow any minute.

'Won't you be sorry to be leaving Tbilisi?'

'I can't wait to get out of here. I have given all my information to my replacement, and look, I don't even have a pencil with me!'

Out on the terrace Erekle introduced me to Rusiko Beridze, the widow of Merab Kostava. Kostava, a classmate of Gamsakhurdia's decades before, was the great hero of the Georgian independence movement and had spent ten years in Siberian labour camps until his release in 1987. Two years later, on 13 October 1989, he was killed in a car accident. At about the same time his son committed suicide, so Rusiko had been doubly bereft. Kostava's memory lives on not only in the major street named after him in the capital but in the Merab Kostava Society. At this very moment the house of the society's present leader, Vaja Adamia, was surrounded by hundreds of his followers to ensure that the government would not succeed in laying their hands on him. Every day as I walked past the Rustaveli Metro station I would see the crowds watching over the steep street where he lived.

Whenever I met Rusiko she was dressed from head to toe in severest black, the folds gathered beneath her chin and secured with a cameo brooch. A mathematics lecturer at the university, she was a very striking woman, with deep dark eyes and a charming smile. There was nothing pompous or self-pitying about her, and her dignity linked arms with a quiet humour. She told me she was hopeful that the Opposition would eventually oust the president, although she admitted that most Georgians probably still backed Gamsakhurdia on the basis of the false propaganda he put out daily.

'If my husband were alive, he would be here. He was close to Gamsakhurdia but now Gamsakhurdia cheats the people, the simple people, and tells them that Merab would have been supporting him. The propaganda from the present government is worse than it was under the Communists. If Merab were living now and could see what has happened to Georgia' – she hesitated – 'he would have died twice.'

Erekle also introduced me to Guram Berishvili, a bearded mathematician who heads the Union of Free Democrats. I asked him about his policies.

'We are for maximum liberty and democracy. If Georgia ever becomes like Switzerland' – a terrible fate – 'we'll disband. We're essentially a liberal party.'

He was convinced that Gamsakhurdia's support would begin to diminish now that communications were improving, but it seemed a vain hope.

Shortly before ten I left with Erekle, and we walked up from Heroes Square to the trolley stop. As soon as we got there, we heard a tremendous explosion followed by an exchange of rifle fire. Some bystanders prudently began to run from the scene. We were joined by a red-haired woman whose son had just left home nearby for the Television Centre, and she was understandably worried. She spoke excellent English, although she had never left the Soviet Union.

'If this situation continues, and Gamsakhurdia remains as president, I think we will all die.'

Erekle insisted on walking me back to my hotel: 'I love to walk, it is my favourite thing, you know that by now.' He and his family were passionate supporters of the Opposition. Every day he would tell me of fresh outrages perpetrated by the government, though often I had only his word for it. Tonight he told me how the minister of health, herself a doctor, had ordered medical personnel to refuse to treat injured Opposition supporters. What was worse was that some doctors and nurses had said they would obey the minister's order, even though it contravened the Hippocratic oath.

He reiterated what many others had said at the Opposition rallies, that President Gamsakhurdia ought to resign.

'Why should he?' I asked. 'He's been elected with a huge majority in a free vote. He can claim that it's his duty to restore order to the republic. And he can also claim that, despite all the troubles, he still enjoys the support of the majority.'

'He should resign because he has lied and cheated his people.'

'I dare say, but that's not unusual among politicians.'

'But when the regions discover how he has called on them to defend him against a threat that doesn't exist, then they will stop supporting him.'

'Possibly, but until that happens I wouldn't count on Gamsakhurdia experiencing a crisis of conscience.'

The problem was that Erekle and many other principled Georgians saw democracy as a moral code rather than as conferral of power by a majority of the people. There was no guarantee in democracies that elected governments would be noble or disinterested or honest. It seemed to me that Gamsakhurdia was entirely within his rights to renege on his promises and appoint time-servers and idiots to his ruling circle, if that was what he chose to do. He was not entitled, however, to lock up his political opponents and stifle the media. There the Opposition was on firmer ground in maintaining their pressure on the president to resign.

Not that he was going to.

6 Bullets, Flowers and a Dead Dog

Temuri wanted to show me the famous botanical gardens, and he had even made an appointment with one of the directors. We stopped off at the café in Freedom Square, where he whispered incomprehensibly about ancient history. Then we took up positions along one of the streets leading out of the square. Temuri tried to hail a taxi or anyone else who might take us to the gardens. The Curse of Temuri came into effect instantly. Taxis stopped, but nobody was heading in that direction. After an hour we gave up and went to the Television Centre instead. There were rumours that a press conference was imminent. I took a seat next to a rather glum reporter from *Le Monde* and his interpreter.

Five minutes later a burly man with a cheerful rascally smile walked past, a bodyguard by his side, a holster on his belt. He waved us into an empty room. The interpreter said, 'You know who this is? This is the head of the Opposition forces.'

That was odd. I thought I had already met the man who played that role, the tall, elegant, moustachioed character who had been questioned by reporters a couple of days earlier. As the four of us sat down together, I recalled a description someone had given me of Tengiz Sigua, which matched very well the tall, elegant, moustachioed fellow. It dawned on me that I had not after all been eavesdropping that day on Tengiz Kitovani but on Tengiz Sigua. It had been Sigua and not Kitovani who had lit a cigarette after rifle fire curtailed his press conference. Tengiz Kitovani was the burly chap now seated about eighteen inches from me.

Oh well, so I made a mistake. It was not a preposterous

mistake, under the circumstances. With the Opposition being ignored by the Georgian media, there was no opportunity to see photographs or television shots of the major players. I had got it wrong, but so had the journalist who had given me the information. What's more, he had probably filed a story based on a muddled attribution. It was too late to do more than blush. I sat back and let the French correspondent do most of the talking, as he had requested this interview and I was just tagging along.

Kitovani told us that the explosion I'd heard last night had been a shell which had wrecked one of the buses being used as a barricade. I had walked past its smashed windows and twisted radiator as I approached the Centre that morning. Only one person had been injured. Kitovani also confirmed that negotiations with the government had broken down, and the situation had not been improved by these attacks on peaceful rallies. The hopes that the Opposition might be able to broadcast within Georgia had come to nothing.

The principal demand of the National Guard was for fresh elections, and he was content to allow the new Parliament to decide what to do with the Guard. When the Frenchman asked whether Gamsakhurdia's troops were trying to encircle the Television Centre, Kitovani laughed, showing a few gleaming gold teeth. It was impossible, he said firmly. He had men positioned on top of the circus building, and other guardsmen were helping to protect Adamia's house, so the Guard was dispersed and not simply bunched here at the Centre.

Would the president use force against the Opposition?

'Perhaps. He's a bandit,' replied Kitovani, borrowing an epithet Gamsakhurdia used to describe the Opposition. 'It wouldn't trouble him at all. Gamsakhurdia has no principles. He made many promises before the election and kept none of them. He is turning Georgia into an Albania.'

The Frenchman asked Kitovani why he had been chosen to head the National Guard. Kitovani laughed; he simply couldn't say. As he chuckled, I noticed that his watch was an hour fast, which seemed a worrying sign in a military commander.

*

That afternoon the prime minister, Besso Gugushvili, was scheduled to address the people in front of the Parliament. A large crowd had gathered, greeting with loud applause each new banner-waving contingent of supporters as it marched into the plaza. A Japanese news team was forcing a path up to the portico, and I simply followed in their wake. Flashing my credentials, I found a spot close to the microphone. At that moment a greasy-haired blue-cassocked priest began a series of prayers to establish which side God was on. A police line kept journalists, dignitaries and hangers-on at some distance from the microphone, but for some reason they ignored me. Prayers over, the priest came and stood beside me, and we both soaked up the adulation of the crowd. I turned to see if he was as repulsive close up as he had been from behind: worse, he had scabs on his nose.

An official read out a presidential declaration: if the Opposition surrendered their arms, no action would be taken against them. Tremendous applause. Suddenly Gamsakhurdia himself arrived, surrounded by an angelic choir in the form of eight bodyguards with Kalashnikovs. The president stood about four feet from me. On reaching the microphone, he greeted the crowd by raising his right arm towards them, and, as usual, he looked as though he had just been exhumed. His deepset, hooded eyes resembled dank pools. He spoke for only four minutes, but worked the crowd effectively and became quite agitated. He also made them laugh. During the graver moments, the priest kept crossing himself. I spotted a microphone being pushed forward, the letters BBC stencilled on the side. I craned my neck and spotted none other than Dr Parsons, listening attentively. As Gamsakhurdia reached his peroration and the crowd was roaring its approval, the president's grey head nodded steadily, like one of those wooden horses with necks on springs. It was a most peculiar gesture, expressing self-satisfaction at a job well done.

Parsons, despite his fluency in Georgian, couldn't hear clearly what Gamsakhurdia was saying, but he later passed me a translation. The core of the speech was: 'It is our moral duty to save the Opposition. We must not give up a single soul to the devils of the Kremlin. The whole nation must demand that the Opposition disarm. Power is morality, truth, not possession of weapons. We will defeat the putschists without weapons. We will defeat them with love. They shoot at us with bullets, we will respond with flowers.'

I hadn't seen many flowers that afternoon. Nor was there any truce in the propaganda war. The government press office had released a preposterous statement explaining that the explosion the previous night had been detonated by the Opposition. They also accused the National Guard of firing shells from the circus rotunda on to the nearby ministry of agriculture. Journalists had been driven there to inspect the damage, but the ones I spoke to said they could find no evidence to support the claims. They were, however, shown a dead dog.

Gamsakhurdia left the platform as swiftly as he had arrived, his carefully groomed battleship-grey hair cruising through a sea of uniforms and bayonets. I walked over to the foreign ministry to have my accreditation renewed. The weak-chinned official had abandoned his suit in favour of a check shirt and jeans and he hadn't shaved for a few days. The result was a great improvement. He took me upstairs at once to see Mr Gabashvili. Overflowing his chair, the obese, sweat-drenched deputy minister told me he was extremely busy, and then proceeded to question me for five minutes. The rebelliousness of his oversized body was at odds with the precision of his speech, and in both respects he reminded me of Sydney Greenstreet at his most disreputable. Gabashvili was puzzled by me because I didn't fit the usual categories, but he extended my accreditation.

I returned to the Parliament building for a scheduled press conference but was refused admission. Nothing personal. Parsons was cooling his heels too. Meanwhile some of the ferocious women who were the president's most ardent fans were explaining to another journalist that Opposition supporters were all drug addicts. Eventually the hacks were allowed up to the press office, where we learnt that the president had swept off in a motorcade to address a rally at the university.

The press conference had been indefinitely postponed, so I returned to the hotel for an early supper. I had been expanding my

Georgian vocabulary, and decided to dazzle the waiter. When he asked me whether I would like some *seer*, the Russian for cheese, I responded in Georgian.

'*Khveli?*'

'*Khveli,*' he affirmed.

'*Ara,*' I replied, realising I didn't fancy cheese after all.

The waiter nodded and walked off. Moments later I heard him addressing one of the blowsy waitresses in a torrent of Russian. The waiter hadn't been Georgian at all.

I was picking up a few of the simpler Georgian words, although some of them incorporate back-of-the-throat death rattles taxing to Europeans. These clusters of consonants, Robert Parsons told me, were the most difficult aspect of the language, since the clusters defy logic until one day the fog lifts and everything falls into place. The Georgian language was *sui generis*, though there were unexplained philological similarities with Basque. When I asked Parsons whether Georgian was hard to learn, he grinned and said: 'Try it and see.'

I had now mastered the dinner repertoire. The cold aubergine was reliable, but the shashlik was deteriorating daily, with bone and gristle growing at the expense of the pork. The other main courses were either 'rump steak', a sliver of tough beef fried in a frothy batter, or tough beef in an onion sauce. Both were garnished with rice, fried potatoes with soggy interiors, and soft chopped-up noodles which had been fried. In short, a wagonload of starch. As for drink, it was lemonade, Borjomi, or a wink and a nod and a tip. Waitresses brought lemonade bottles in paper bags to favoured parties of Georgians. These bottles were, of course, filled with brandy. Other diners arrived with bottles of wine which the waiter actually decanted for them, but when I asked for some wine I was told there wasn't any. I drew the obvious conclusion, and from now on smuggled my own supplies into the dining room and filled my glass from my very own bottle in my very own paper bag.

Back at the government press office nobody knew what was happening. Maybe there would be a press conference. Maybe not. I leaned out of the top-floor window to look down on the plaza. To my surprise I saw hundreds of government supporters streaming towards Rustaveli in the direction of Republic Square.

I asked one of the officials where they were going.

'They are going to the Television Centre.' He gave me a ghastly toothy grin.

'Why?'

His voice rose to a pitch of unrestrainable glee. 'To make friends with the Opposition!' And he laughed wildly at his wit.

This was not a good sign. The folk outside the Parliament were not gentle in their ways. Many were armed, others carried sticks. If they reached the Television Centre there could be trouble. I phoned Erekle and told him to meet me at the university. I ran up Rustaveli to overtake the marchers, whose numbers I estimated at 2000. Near Republic Square the militia were removing the barricades so that the marchers could pass through unobstructed. I met Erekle and we walked over to the Television Centre. His parents were already there.

Demo became quite possessive of me, grabbing my sleeve and hauling me about to meet various Opposition leaders. Our movements were restricted, since the National Guard had roped off the end of the terrace facing Heroes Square, as the soldiers didn't want civilians getting in their way. This outraged Demo, who argued furiously with the soldiers until they let me through. The first man Demo buttonholed was the head of intelligence of the National Guard. Like many of the other officers, he wasn't a professional soldier; he was an economist, militarised out of dismay at what he regarded as Gamsakhurdia's acquiescence in the August coup. He insisted to me that the Guard was protecting not just the Opposition but the entire Georgian nation. Zyrab Mamaladze, who led the union for the protection of the rights of Georgian Moslems, elaborated on what the officer had been telling me. Back in August, all the decrees issued from Moscow had been published in Georgian newspapers and the people had been urged to obey them. He had no doubt that Gamsakhurdia had been prepared to capitulate to the leaders of the coup against Gorbachev.

I had a fine view from the terrace as the government supporters poured into Heroes Square. It was an uneasy moment. In front of the Television Centre hundreds of people had lit candles, which they were holding cupped in their hands. Some were standing outside the barricades, a brave move. The Guard was on full alert, with soldiers posted along the terrace. But nothing happened. The government supporters remained in the square for half an hour, then began to disperse. The defence softened, the guard was relaxed, and we all breathed more freely.

Meanwhile Demo had pushed me towards a small gnomish man who was the chairman of the Christian Democratic Union, modelled on the German CDU. Its three main principles, he told me, were the freedom of the individual, the equality of rights, and solidarity – though with what he did not say. Despite its name, the party was not religious: 'Buddhists and Moslems are welcome to join too.' Their economic policy favoured a free market combined with social reponsibilities. He went into great detail about his party's proposals, which we discussed standing in a pond of broken glass which had not been swept up after the explosion of the previous night.

Demo went off to bag more prey: Valery Kvaratzkhelia, a celebrated television journalist.

'What I want to see,' he told me, 'is a system in which the government has no control over broadcasting other than the enforcement of the law. At present, if Gamsakhurdia doesn't like a broadcast, all he has to do is pick up the phone and it can be taken off the air. That doesn't happen with Mrs Thatcher and the BBC.'

'Oh yes it did,' I corrected him, 'though not in such a peremptory fashion.'

I then asked him how he thought the political crisis would develop.

'I have recently written an article in which I say that either Gamsakhurdia resigns or we will have civil war.'

'Why should he resign? I see no sign that he's going to.'

'He probably won't. But in fact he has no alternative, because otherwise there will be civil war.'

'But he seems to have the political advantage, if only because he controls the media.'

'Yes, but his strategy is to blame everything on the Opposition. And that is a mistake, because as president he is responsible for all political processes. The president's duty is to listen to the Opposition to achieve a more stable situation. If he is unable to do this, then he should resign. If he won't, then we will have an escalation of tension. In any case, for those of us in the Opposition there is no way back. If we give up our struggle, then Georgia is ruined.'

'Kitovani told me that if the Opposition fails, Georgia will become another Albania.'

'Exactly. And it is better to die than to have that.'

When I encountered Rusiko Beridze on the terrace, I asked her whether it was true, as the press was being told, that she and the rest of the Opposition were drug addicts.

'We are criminals too,' she reminded me, completing the litany. A smile flitted across her face. 'Do I look like a drug addict?'

'Well, it's possible. Maybe the government is right after all.'

Demo kidnapped me again and took me inside the building, where he had lined up the humorous writer Rezo Mishveladze. Humorist he may have been, but he gave the most vicious assessment of Gamsakhurdia I had yet heard.

'It took centuries to unite Georgia and Georgians. But Gamsakhurdia in a few months has divided the country, setting the regions against each other, and putting social and ethnic groups against each other. He has made the intelligentsia out to be the enemies of the people. At one thing only is he a master, and that is at playing on the psychology of the masses. As a result, he has become the true enemy of the Georgian people.'

Demo landed a bigger fish when he took me over to meet Nodar Natazde; if the Opposition had an elder statesman, it was he. A philosopher, Natazde is a stocky little man, bald, with strong black eyebrows and a neat little toothbrush moustache over a prim mouth. As chairman of the Popular Front and leader of the parliamentary opposition bloc called the Democratic Group, he was a senior spokesman for the Opposition, and with his dignified if somewhat ferocious demeanour he fitted the role admirably.

'You demand Gamsakhurdia's resignation,' I asked Natadze, 'but how can you secure it?'

'He is a pathological coward, so fear is the only thing that will force him to resign.'

'How will this impasse be broken?'

'The only way to save the situation is through the minds of the people. This whole crisis will be over within a month, and I think it's likely that he will resign. As his influence wanes, his crimes – and he is a man of many crimes – will come to light. He seems to have an advantage now because the occupation of the Television Centre has played into his hands, and he can blame the Opposition for food shortages and other problems. But that won't work in the long term.'

I wandered into a hall on the ground floor set up as a kind of field hospital. In a side room I found a white-haired Italian journalist in a smart white suit. Not for him the T-shirts and jeans of the rest of the press corps. We talked about some of the rumours coursing through the capital. He sighed.

'You know, I have hardly ever been to a place where there is so much bullshit. Remember that story a few days ago about sixty dead in a government attack? Bullshit. Yet for a few hours it misled the world. The whole place is seething with half-truths, stupid stories, exaggerations, plain lies. It makes you wonder to what extent we journalists are contributing to the crisis. The leaders on both sides are obviously getting such a kick out of the whole thing. They can phone up foreign correspondents at five in the morning and be sure of getting their attention. They can give press conferences and have cameras clicking for half an hour, they can issue press releases. They're having the time of their lives.

'Tbilisi is full of presidents, prime ministers, ex-ministers, military commanders, all swaggering about with bodyguards and with daggers in their belts. They're all play-acting. Georgia's been a backwater for decades, and now it's the centre of attention, and the Georgians can't get enough of it.

'I'm going to Armenia in the morning. Want to join me?'

'Can't, I'm afraid.'

'Pity. I hate driving alone.'

A handsome young man in a long white doctor's coat came and spoke to the Italian in German while he flung a few pills into a bottle, then walked out.

'Who's he?'

'That's Georgi. He's playing at being a surgeon.' I later got to know Georgi, who was a first-year medical student.

'They even have someone playing at being POW. Do you want to see him? Follow me.'

We crossed the hall and passed into a makeshift ward full of beds and screens. Two boys, perhaps fourteen, shouted at us to get out. We paid not the slightest attention.

'See over there? On the bed?'

In the far corner, a miserable looking runt of a man, his head bandaged as though for a sore tooth, sat on a bed and looked mournfully towards us.

'That's their POW. The only one. And these boys are guarding him.' He patted the more vociferous lad on the head.

'There, there. Isn't it time you went home to bed and stopped playing soldiers?'

I had told Svetlana that I wanted to drive up the Georgian Military Highway, and that I was prepared to rent a car or hire a taxi. In the event she and Soso decided to take me themselves.

For thousands of years the route followed by the highway has been the major link between Russia and Georgia across the High Caucasus ranges. A roadway was first constructed in the early nineteenth century by the Russians; at its highest point it reached 7805 feet at the Dhzvari Pass. As the name suggests, its primary purpose was military, but the route had always been used by traders.

Leaving Tbilisi we headed past Mtskheta and the statue of the writer Ilya Chavchavadze, who was murdered here in 1907 by the tsarist secret police. Heading north, we came to a broad valley and, at the head of it, a large dam only completed a few years ago. Soso told me that many people believed the dam to be dangerous. At the far end of the Shinvali reservoir stands the fortress of Ananuri. The Soviet authorities had wanted this outstanding and well-preserved example of military and ecclesiastical architecture to be submerged beneath the waters, but protesters mobilised enough support, even in those days when to campaign on environmental matters was hazardous, to stop the scheme.

Ananuri is embraced by compact crenellated walls, the fortress is built on a slope, at the top of which stands a tower with a single chamber on each floor. From the top there are lovely views on to the two church cupolas and, beyond, the reservoir and the wooded hills. From here the feudal rulers of the Aragvi valley controlled this crucial trading route.

There are two churches, one from the early seventeenth century, the other from 1689. A twelfth-century watchtower, a remnant from the earlier fortress, separates the two. The upper church is particularly interesting. Its loveliest feature is the cupola, with its diminishing circles of brick rising to the top, from which brilliant light pours in through the deeply recessed lancets around the drum. The outer walls are of stone, but inside, the two-bay arcades, the crossing piers, and the cupola are built of brick. The only furnishing remaining is a tomb canopy, its sides inscribed in flowing Georgian script and its roof frescoed. Alas, decades of graffiti, all in Russian, have obscured all but the very highest parts of the paintings. Scrawling your name in large clumsy letters is the most fatuous form of self-glorification, for graffiti destroy the object that other visitors have come to see. Graffiti writers arrogantly insist that their visit outranks the object visited.

The lower church is lavishly decorated with external carvings of crosses and of dragons and vines, lions and angels, and the purely ornamental carving is of much higher quality than the representational. The interior was damaged by fire in the eighteenth century, and the few frescoes that survived the flames are of good quality. The bare whitewashed walls have bleached the church of atmosphere, and the modest upper church is more intriguing by far.

At the lower end of the fortress stands a small seventeenth-century open-arcaded bell turret, from which I could look down on to the village below. Because of the threat of flooding, half the village has been abandoned and its brick church boarded up. It's a melancholy sight, a village that has died from fright.

From Ananuri the highway meanders up the valley between wooded slopes and high pastures dotted with conical hayricks. At strategic curves of the River Aragvi mediaeval watchtowers, now ruinous, keep guard. At a truck stop a spring in the form of a bronzed cow's head gushed water which was deliciously cool and fresh. We were joined by some Armenian lorry drivers and by two incredibly filthy pigs.

In the main street of Pasanauri schoolgirls were making their way home. Wearing brown dresses and white pinafores, they looked exactly like Edwardian parlourmaids. At least the children of the valley, unlike those of the capital, were able to attend their schools. We went in search of lunch. The Intourist restaurant had closed for lack of business; the outdoor restaurant had burnt down. A private restaurant had opened on the top floor of a lavish community centre, but customers warned Svetlana that the food was tinned and dreadful. We returned to the truck stop, where there was a private restaurant far less pretentious than the one in Pasanauri. It was just a shack, with the usual cheap formica and plastic furnishings, the kitchen visible behind the self-service counter. The food was good. We began with tasty *kharcho*, which we sipped while chewing on hot ovals of the heavy but delicious crusty cornbread called *mchadi*. Excellent veal shashlik was served with a sour plum sauce. Soso produced a bottle of his home-distilled honeycomb and beeswax spirit, a potion I found fiery but not stinging, warming but not reproving.

My main reason for wanting to make this trip was to glimpse the High Caucasus, and we were still among the foothills. So when we set forth after lunch, I hoped we would continue up the highway. But Soso turned the wheel southwards. Had we continued up the road, we would soon have encountered roadblocks, since the highway crosses South Ossetia. Ethnic conflicts had shrunk the country.

*

Back in Tbilisi I went for coffee in the little park behind the hotel. On hearing my clumsy attempts at Georgian, the friendly brassy woman in the kiosk not only refused payment for the coffee but handed me a large apricot to go with it.

Sipping my coffee at one of the outdoor tables, I could see a large crowd moving along Rustaveli. The men leading the procession were holding up portrait banners and behind them, borne on the shoulders of more young men, were two open coffins. I watched in some horror as they passed, for the blue-grey features of the corpses were plainly visible. Behind the coffins came the mourners: women in black, their arms linked, and men in sombre suits. The dead were apparently two of those killed at the power station some days earlier, but this was also a political demonstration some 2000 strong. The mourners were poor, the men unshaven, the women inconsolable. The procession crossed Republic Square and continued towards Heroes Square. A van glided ahead, bearing a coffin lid and a dozen wreaths. Women bystanders dabbed their eyes. Workers emerged from a ministry building and lowered the Georgian flag. At Heroes Square, buses moved into position to take the coffins and the principal mourners to the cemetery. Those who remained in the square participated in a brief demonstration, led by some of the men I had seen haranguing the crowd before Gamsakhurdia's speech. Although I couldn't understand what the speakers were saying, when the crowd turned and stared at the Television Centre the meaning was clear: the Opposition had been responsible for these deaths.

The crowd dispersed, and I walked up the slope to the university. The evening rush hour had begun, and the buses were jammed. Passengers clung to the metal bars of the doors, the tarmac rushing beneath their feet as the buses picked up speed. I walked to Rustaveli, where I found the barricades gone and the avenue open to traffic. I missed the freedom of the pedestrian, but it was good to see Rustaveli brought back to life, even if life did take the form of thunderous traffic.

Close to Republic Square a large pompous building houses the

Academy of Sciences. The universities in the former Soviet Union were primarily teaching institutions, while research was conducted at the Academy, which in Georgia was subdivided into forty-two institutes. The term 'science' embraces not only mathematics and the natural sciences but history, literature and the humanities. The Academy was an enormous institution, with a research staff of 7000. Jumber Lominadze, a distinguished theoretical physicist at the Academy, was also president of Svetlana's association and invited me to meet some of his colleagues. I recalled from my trip to Moscow in 1979 the Soviet passion for meetings. Luminaries would be summoned to meet visitors, who were supposed to strike up spontaneous and informative conversations with people whose exact position, role and importance were unknown. It was no different here, and though the intentions were the best, I found these occasions awkward.

The first contestant was Roin Metroveli, a burly man with a thin moustache who could easily have passed for a North Indian politician. A mediaeval historian, he told me that archaeological sites were still being excavated throughout Georgia, and some exceptionally important remains had just been dug up at Dmanisi. They were among the oldest human remains unearthed anywhere. I asked Metroveli how independence would affect Georgian academic life. He replied confidently that they would enjoy greater professional independence too. Georgian academics could now attend international congresses in their own right, not just as participants in Soviet delegations. But I knew it was not that simple. The Academy of Sciences, not only here but in other republics, had received considerable subsidies from Moscow. In the future, surely, there would be less money available from such sources for research and exchanges. Metroveli bypassed the question. 'Possibly. But the centre also took money out of Georgia. On balance I'd say they took more than they gave. They took manganese, tea, fruit, and wine. This is a problem we should be able to overcome.'

The next visitor, Giorgi Tsitsishvili, was a novelist and critic and former head of the Writers Union. His domed head was imposed upon a three-piece suit which stiffened his small dapper figure.

Under the Communists the Writers Union monitored and controlled literary production. Commissions were hard to come by and
publishers hard to find if you were not a member, but in return for
its favours the Union required a certain conformity. If you behaved
yourself, you were entitled to privileges such as spells in comfortable
rest houses in resorts such as Borjomi. I asked Tsitsishvili whether
the Writers Union would have any role in an independent Georgia.
Yes, he replied, primarily in the form of easier contacts with
comparable bodies elsewhere, without having to obtain the consent
of Moscow. The Georgian Writers Union publishes twenty literary
magazines, and the income generated from its publications and rest
houses is used to help unemployed writers, to offer writers free
medical care at special clinics, and to pay them pensions. It sounded
just like the old days.

In the hilly district behind the Television Centre stands the
Institute of Manuscripts. I was shown round by Mzekala Shanidze,
who spoke almost perfect English, acquired from her English
husband. Her father had been a curator here and she was continuing
his work of collating and editing the various translations into
Georgian of the Old Testament. She told me that the oldest of the
10,000 manuscripts at the institute dated back to the fifth century.
Of particular importance were the fifth-century translations of the
bible, since the texts themselves were considerably older than the
manuscripts in which they had been transcribed. Until the eleventh
century all the surviving manuscripts were theological or hagio-
graphical. During the eleventh and twelfth centuries, Georgia's
golden age, secular and literary manuscripts of outstanding quality
were produced, but this period was shortlived and the following four
or five centuries were, in cultural terms, mediocre.

In the archive room she showed me some of the most precious
items in the collection, beginning with a palimpsest. The faded text,
half obscured by a second text above it, probably dated from the
seventh century, and a colleague was now deciphering it using only
her own eyes, having tried an optic filter and found it wanting. She
opened a Four Gospels manuscript written in Old Georgian in 936.
No one knows who invented Old Georgian script, when it was

devised or what the models were on which it was based. Some scholars located its origins in the third century BC, but this has not been corroborated. Stone inscriptions from that time have been found only in Greek or Aramaic. Most researchers now believe either that Old Georgian was supplanted for some centuries by Greek and Aramaic and then revived, or that it was invented with the advent of Christianity in the third century. As for the model on which it was based, the prevalent view is that it was not modelled on Greek letter forms but that its sequences are related to those of ancient Greek.

In the tenth century Georgians adopted a more cursive script which was smaller and easier to read. In a lovely tenth-century example, the capitals and headings were still in Old Georgian, while the black-inked text was in cursive. Above the text abundant red marks indicated musical notation. It is from this kind of script that modern Georgian writing evolved. Mzekala Shanidze fetched illuminated manuscripts too and an astrological treatise of 1165 which incorporated beautiful naturalistic drawings of each sign of the zodiac. Other twelfth-century manuscripts contained marvellously realistic figure drawings, groups and postures handled with a vividness and brilliance that would be hard to match among contemporary European Romanesque manuscripts. A New Testament transcribed especially for Queen Tamar in Constantinople was even more florid, with exquisitely drawn birds. The most precious manuscripts had to be cosseted. Some are packed between magnificent bindings, employing repoussé work – silver poured over finely carved wood – and partitioned enamel, a technique which has been lost. This profusion of illuminated manuscripts brought Georgia's mediaeval past to life as vividly as the churches of the city.

Yet there had been an earlier Golden Age, and in the afternoon I went to the State Museum opposite the Parliament. A special collection displays artefacts from the third millennium BC to the third century AD. Infinitely precious are the tiny gold lion with a busily worked mane, dating from 2600BC, and a gold bowl encrusted with precious stones made in 1800BC by a soldering technique which has not proved recoverable. From excavations near Kutaisi come the contents of the grave of a rich woman and her servants. The haul includes a gold tiara and a stunning necklace hung with thirty-one tiny turtles – a symbol of longevity – each granulated with up to three hundred little dots; the eyes are filled with light blue paste. Another necklace is hung with tiny birds and yet another with small rams' heads. All this stupendous craftsmanship dates from the sixth century BC.

In 1908 ploughmen in central Georgia exposed a sixth-century grave of a woman and the six horses buried with her. The gold harness ornaments survive, with some astonishing pendants employing most of the known techniques of the goldsmith's art: the designs are chased, filigreed, granulated. These pendants depict paired horses in harness, with chains suspended from the platform on which they stand.

The third and second centuries were evidently even more luxurious. Excavated at Mtskheta were Hellenistic-style ornaments: a dagger and its gold sheath, amber scent bottles, jewellery adorned with turquoise and garnet. The most delectable item from the second-century AD Eastern Georgian grave of a young noblewoman is a necklace from which was suspended an amethyst ram's head which, when opened up, was found to contain her milk teeth. Archaeologists also unearthed a marvellous pendant depicting a hut with doves on the roof and two musicians at the entrance; beneath this domestic scene hang the usual golden chains and semi-precious stones.

The Romans left their mark, but could never match the wonderful delicacy of the earlier work. The most intriguing Roman contribution was an amethyst carved with the likeness of the Emperor Caracalla.

The Georgians' great pride in their history and culture is justified. From the very earliest times the country was highly sophisticated and technologically advanced. These early inhabitants were no barbarians, and their craftsmanship surpasses in quality some of the most acclaimed work of their European contemporaries.

7 The Laws of the Table

I followed Svetlana into the plane through a narrow passage beneath the tail, which was rather like taking a stroll up the anus of a cow. We were to spend a few days in Batumi on the Black Sea, and I was glad to be leaving the overcharged atmosphere of the capital. Aeroflot have never bothered with the nannying aspects of air travel: my seatbelt didn't work and luggage was piled up in the aisles. A glum stewardess came through with brown bowls of plastifizz, which I declined. I was more interested in the view to the north of the High Caucasus, its peaks now capped with snow.

Batumi felt distinctly soupy: warmer than Tbilisi and considerably more humid. Curving voluptuously along the shore, it ought to have been a jewel of a town, but most of its buildings were wretched in design and construction. Houses winked in the sunlight thanks to an inexplicable vogue for corrugated aluminium siding, hardly the loveliest of building materials. The standard twelve-storey apartment blocks, once whitewashed with balconies painted blue, were now stained and peeling. Damp washing, rugs and towels drooped over the balconies, but the colours were too muted to add gaiety to the picture.

The town's most attractive feature, which dates from tsarist days, is the wooded park which separates the beach from the town, stretching for a mile or so along the shore. Facing the park is the Intourist Hotel, a dull grey concrete block of 1939 where Svetlana had booked rooms. The managers had worked hard to depress the spirits of visiting holidaymakers – entire corridors were illuminated by a single bulb of record-breaking dimness, and the lobby was so gloomy that, especially after dusk, it was impossible to recognise anyone standing more than ten paces away.

My room was reasonably spacious – in a fit of extravagance Svetlana had ordered doubles – but threadbare. The curtains sagged and failed the primary test of covering the windows. The three-bulb ceiling lights, with only one lamp functioning, were barely sufficient to read by – but rather to my surprise, when I asked for a table lamp one was provided.

We lunched at the hotel with our host in Batumi, Ghia Bezhanidze, a local businessman who was developing trade connections in nearby Turkey and Greece. Svetlana noted disapprovingly that many of the other guests, and there weren't many of them, were Turks – the border was only ten miles to the south – hoping to have a bit of inexpensive fun with Russian molls. Since it must have been difficult for them to have comparable fun with Turkish girls, I found it hard to blame them.

We ate well, better than in Tbilisi. And there was drink. Over a bottle of passable demi-sec Georgian 'champagne', Ghia told me about his native town. Like many ports, its population is mixed; among the Georgians are distinct communities of Armenians, Russians and Greeks. A mosque still summons the faithful and in the mountains of Adjara, the province in which Batumi is situated, there is a large Moslem population. Ghia was a Moslem convert to Christianity. Adjara is fertile and populous, with about half a million inhabitants. It's blessed with minerals, copper and gold, and hot springs. A subtropical climate allows the cultivation of tea, citrus fruits and bamboo, and of course the Black Sea ports encourage trade – or used to.

The relaxed seaside atmosphere and the balmy climate only partly concealed Batumi's economic plight. The factories lack raw materials and many, such as the confectionery factory denied sugar and cocoa, have had to close. Private businessmen were also struggling. Like Sandro, Ghia complained of the government's confiscatory policy towards hard currency earnings. Just the other day 100,000 roubles had been removed from his bank account. Short of revenue, the government has resorted to more underhand methods to obtain funds. Complex rules, such as those permitting barter exchanges only with the personal permission of the prime minister, further hampered what little trade still existed.

'There's been no economic liberalisation at all,' said the frustrated Ghia, 'apart from some private shops and restaurants.'

After lunch we walked among the pines and palms and bamboo groves of the seafront park. Promenades led at either end to fairgrounds. The fountains were silent stagnant pools. Most of the benches had missing or broken slats, so there was a risk of impalement on rusty nails. Avid chess players worked their gambits beneath rustic canopies. I could hear the clatter of pingpong from a small clearing. Booths sold soft drinks and ice-cream, and at an outdoor café we had excellent Turkish coffee, ebony-black, but served in little plastic cups the colours of children's cheap tea sets. Tattered and stained umbrella fabric fitted inexactly over the metal frames above each table. Along the stony beach fleshy Russian matrons lay splayed on its inclines. Despite the pleasant sunshine, the mood was autumnal and desultory. Even the determinedly optimistic Svetlana observed, 'The people are not merry now.'

We came to one of the other hotels, a modern skyscraper called the Medea, which Ghia dismissed as mediocre. At night its windows gleamed with fluorescent lighting, and by day the tower, entirely aluminium-clad, seemed an act of homage to air-conditioning vents.

We turned inland. On Unity Street (formerly Lenin Street) houses with balconies attained a faded classical elegance with their Greek columns, entablatures and pediments. The oldest buildings were dusty pink structures in Russian neoclassical style, their dilapidation disguised by the flowering plants gambolling over their balconies and terraces. The gaunt State Theatre overlooks a small park where a statue honours Ilya Chavchavadze. Some art galleries nearby were open, and in one of them a party was celebrating the opening of an exhibition by two German photographers from Batumi's twin town of Saarbrücken. Ghia's company had sponsored this exhibition, so he wanted me to see it. After the speeches, prolonged by the need to translate each line into German, one of the photographers, Jürgen Kaiser, was presented with a large green vase; a bunch of roses, still wrapped in cellophane, was shoved inside it.

We continued our walk. Stalin Street had undergone an acrobatic ideological reversal and been born again as Freedom Street. A drunk lay flat on the pavement under a palm tree. The shopfronts were drab, but above there was an eclectic display of neoclassical motifs and a skittish panoply of pretty canopied iron balconies dripping with vines. On most corners old men and women were pursuing an uneven trade selling paper cones filled with sunflower seeds. One corner shop had tremendous decor: white and gilt plaster, a pale blue ceiling, mirrors on the walls behind the counter and on the piers, all within ornate rococo frames. The floors were marble, a sober black-and-white foil for the exuberant decoration above. But as a shop this splendid saloon was a failure; there was nothing for sale other than a few jars of jam and juice, and a slab of butter. In a bookshop nearby I found a map of Leipzig, but here, as in Tbilisi, no maps of Georgia or its capital were available.

In the evening a banquet was held in honour of Jürgen Kaiser, and I was incorporated into the celebrations as a subsidiary guest of honour. In the grounds of the beachside Salkhino restaurant are wattle huts known as *patzkha*, which are used for private parties. This one was roofed with bricks stamped with the name of the manufacturer in Marseilles.

The *tamada*, unusually, was a woman, and she intoned a series of long and ponderous toasts to the creative spirit, while Svetlana muttered conspiratorially next to me. A waitress appeared with *kefalia*, small fried trout, crisp and delicious, from the mountain streams of Adjara, and some platters of shashlik. From the adjoining *patzkha* I could hear the sounds of a particularly mournful Georgian folksong. The *tamada* turned to me to praise Britain, the land of Mrs Thatcher, and so forth. Another dish arrived, a kind of heavy cheese fondue, which I sampled happily during the toast to Woman the Life-Builder. The stream of toasts meant that the consumption of wine – white Furdjani and Tbilisi 'champagne' – proceeded at a serious pace. A doctor seated across from me assured me the local white wine was renowned as a cure for heart ailments, which he attributed to the vineyards' location midway between the sea and the mountains. A pity the wine we were guzzling came from Kakheti.

Our discussion was interrupted by a toast to all the little babies being born on this very day in Georgia, Germany, and Britain. Then a toast 'to tomorrow'. When my turn came, I proposed a toast to a long and prosperous future for an independent and democratic Georgia. The 'democratic' added a speck of political spice, but it was fairly safe, since the Opposition felt they had cornered democratic values, while the government enjoyed the popular mandate. Everybody was a democrat nowadays. The toast worked like a charm, and was greeted with a round of applause. Even Svetlana congratulated me on the apposite formulation.

At this point, the *tamada* stepped down, unleashing a free market in toasts. One sycophant rushed to toast the *tamada* herself for all the fine things she'd done in the past as a Communist Party official. By now the doctor was very drunk and required me to drink to brotherhood, which involved downing a whole glass with our arms entwined. Svetlana rescued me, and Ghia drove us back to the dingy hotel, where I tuned in to the World Service: the National Guard was moving out of Tbilisi, and the Opposition had left the Television Centre. The president was claiming a great victory.

After President Gamsakhurdia created the prefecture system in March 1991, ninety regional prefects were appointed throughout the country. Ghia had arranged for me to meet the prefect of Batumi, Tengiz Asanidze. Outside his office stood a dozen worried-looking people, mostly poor and elderly, and I was told they were claiming their new flats. I would have expected them to look more cheerful. Asanidze, wearing a grey jacket and ill-matched grey trousers, a faded green check shirt and a striped tie secured with a pin, seemed weary, with messy, thinning grey hair and a pallid complexion. He looked as though he needed a long spell at a Black Sea resort. But he was all smiles as he greeted me and took his place behind his desk. Facing him was the large blank screen of a television set; the walls were bare apart from a calendar; a conference table adjoined his desk.

I asked the prefect about the local economy. He plausibly extolled the shipping industry, but admitted that Georgia wasn't producing many goods worth shipping and couldn't afford to buy any goods to be shipped in. The economy's moribundity he attributed to the ideological straitjacket in which the republic's affairs had long been placed. He was vague about the best way forward, saying that the government should proceed 'step by step'. He hoped Western countries would give economic aid to Georgia, not out of charity but because it would be mutually profitable.

I asked Asanidze why Georgia had adopted the prefect system.

'Our national movement helped to destroy Communism, but the legislators, to avoid anarchy developing, introduced this system of prefects. It may not seem very democratic, but the goal is to organise the structure of our state. It's true that I have considerable powers, but they are regulated by law. What I can do is speed up decisions, and fire people so rooted in the old ways of doing things that they cannot adapt to new systems of management. This is not quite democratic but it is what the situation demands.'

'To whom are you accountable?'

'To the Adjara council of ministers and to the supreme praesidium of Adjara and to the president of the republic. I was nominated by the local parliament and ratified by President Gamsakhurdia.'

'What happens if the people of Batumi are unhappy with your performance? What can they do about it?'

'The local parliament can let President Gamsakhurdia know that they are not satisfied with me, and he can make changes. It has happened elsewhere.'

I asked him what had happened to land reform and privatisation. He replied that the postponed session of the Supreme Soviet was to have introduced these measures, and despite the political tension he was confident they would.

'When?'

'Soon.'

'Months? Years?'

'In a month.'

My next meeting was with the Union of Adjari Writers. Ghia was alarmed to find the Union building locked; this had never happened before. We hung about for half an hour, but nobody turned up. Some phone calls established that the president of the Union had been summoned to a meeting with the president of Adjara. Perhaps some other time . . .

We whiled away an hour at a beach café, then returned to the hotel. The BBC reported that the National Guard had moved out of town to the Sea of Tbilisi. Supporters of both camps were gathering in the city, accusing each other of betraying Georgia. Gamsakhurdia was broadcasting appeals to his people to come to the Parliament building to defend him.

The afternoon had thickened with the mood. The weather had turned heavy and sultry. I wandered down to the docks, where half a dozen cargo ships were moored. Yellow plastic benches facing the quay acknowledged the universal fascination for watching ships come and go. A smart blue-and-white pleasure boat, the *Iveria*, was docked but was going nowhere. Near an outdoor café, clocks reliably told the wrong time.

Batumi's main department store was miserably stocked. Everything looked improvised. Plyboard shelves tottered on metal racks; glass-topped formica cabinets displayed a clutter of bric-à-brac. You could buy dolls, religious paintings, paintbrushes, candlesticks, anything other than necessities. Visiting the store was like turning up at a jumble sale just as it was closing. My attempt to buy black shoelaces failed; the only shoelaces for sale were green and maroon. In contrast, the covered market nearby was well stocked. Chickens were in ample supply, and women picked them up and sniffed their rear ends, checking for personal freshness before choosing one for their pot. Shoehorned into basements were the private shops, with their racks of clothing in synthetic materials gaudily decorated with glitter and velveteen strips. The most popular items were American cigarettes and Turkish bubble gum. A month's salary would buy a small bottle of French cologne.

Behind the cathedral, built in a crudely neo-Romanesque style as a Catholic place of worship but since converted into an Orthodox church, the railway station doubled as a social centre. On the platform a private shop stood next to a shooting range. Exhausted shoppers rested on benches behind hillocks of suitcases, stoves, bags of fruit and bread, bundles of pillows, toy bikes, and crates of lemonade.

I walked back to the shore along Marx Street. It was unevenly paved, and piles of rubble and cement flowed from building sites and blocked the pavement. Pretty villas were crumbling, their make-up cracked, their flesh peeling. Opposite a small park a pompous town house with excessive ornament showed that decades ago somebody had at least cared about the building. Nobody has cared about it since. Half the carved wooden doors were missing, and from the door a cascade of rubble had poured into the street. In the park the pool had been drained long before, and the grass was overgrown and untended. After dinner I strolled along the edges of the shore park. There was no light, but a few people sat on the benches, smoking and talking softly. The seafront on this balmy evening could have been a delightful spot, but the cafés and ice-cream parlours had long been closed.

The latest bulletins from the BBC spoke of increasing tension in the capital, with demonstrators along Rustaveli divided by only a thin line of police. Rumours multiplied: Kitovani was advancing on the city, Gamsakhurdia had hired mercenaries to attack the Opposition. Nobody knew what was true, what was fantasy, and what was mischievous rumour.

Violence erupted overnight in Tbilisi. Government troops had fired on Opposition demonstrators and throughout the night there had been fighting on Rustaveli. People had been killed. When Ghia arrived at the hotel he was plainly worried. Last night, he told us, people had been bussed from Batumi to Tbilisi to support the beleaguered president, who seemed to be exacerbating rather than calming the situation.

Svetlana was uncharacteristically downcast, but did her best to continue with our 'programme'. Ghia drove us down the coast into the Khelvachauri region just north of the Turkish border. The suburban roads were lined with boxy villas, as well as grander houses with classical pretensions and ornamental iron balconies. Tall eucalyptus trees shaded the road, and stretching up into the hills were tangerine groves and vineyards, usually glimpsed behind a band of scruffy workshops and factories of stained concrete. Watermelons were being sold at the roadside. Inland, along the valley of the meandering Djorokhi river, the hills rose sharply once we left the coastal strip, and shallow-roofed villas, reached up steep winding lanes, perched on hillsides among vineyards and tea plantations, cypress groves and copses. Svetlana would turn to me to admire the gorgeousness of the scenery, but she and Ghia were completely engrossed in discussing the political situation.

We had an appointment with the prefect of Khelvachauri, so we soon headed back towards the coast. Halfway there the car broke down. It had been been banging and shuddering since the day before; now it gave a terminal thump and would budge no more. Fortunately we were close to some houses, and Ghia prevailed on somebody to drive us back to the prefect's offices.

Tamaz Asanidze was the younger and less smarmy brother of the prefect of Batumi. He had been an engineer specialising in the technology of tea production. Four of his officials joined us around the conference table, where I found myself facing the only picture on the wall, a photograph of Zviad Gamsakhurdia.

Asanidze told me that the prefect system was still not fully in place. Municipal councils still exist alongside the new structures, but it was clear from his account – as it had not been from his brother's – that the prefect had the upper hand. When I asked Asanidze how he had become prefect, he said plainly that he had been appointed by Gamsakhurdia. Prefects were in effect the president's representatives and local executive officers. Gamsakhurdia had the power to replace prefects whose performance was unsatisfactory, and this had happened to his predecessor, who had lasted only two months.

Asanidze insisted that he was not a stooge of the president. 'When

I was appointed some people here wondered why, because I had not always agreed with Gamsakhurdia. The president replied that he appointed me because he knew I had the support of the local people.'

When I asked him what was left for the municipal council to do, given his powers, he replied, 'The budget and some other matters must be agreed by the council.' So there was no doubt where the power lay – all initiatives, or lack of them, came from the prefect's office.

I asked him whether the paralysis which afflicted Tbilisi was also affecting Adjara. Not really, he said. The university was closed but schools, restaurants and many factories were open. Yet Tengiz Asanidze had told me that in Batumi factories were closed for lack of raw materials.

'So if everything is going so well, how come the shops are empty?'

'Because everything we produce is exported, especially to Turkey. Our tea, for example, is bartered for food from Russia.'

He asked me about British salaries and prices, and I did my best to explain our cost of living. This is a pointless exercise, since such comparisons don't take into account the variations of earning power and the colossal subsidies which underwrite public services in the former Soviet Union.

'So what does it cost in England if four people go to a restaurant and order a meal and twenty bottles of wine?'

I gasped at the very thought. But Georgians think big.

'About $140 for the food.'

He sniffed triumphantly. 'For that, we can go to a restaurant twenty times!' He wanted to demonstrate to me that in practical terms the earning power of Georgians and western Europeans was much the same. How wrong he was.

I changed the subject.

'Why is the government in Tbilisi firing on unarmed demonstrators?'

'You must not confuse two things. There are those in the Opposition who want changes, and there are people who want power at any cost. So we have a kind of anarchy. Some Opposition supporters are bitter because they have lost their positions of influence. The armed forces don't like this state of affairs, so they are shooting. People must understand that after the elections, a change of presidency is impossible by force. In the future elections must encourage people to think deeply about such matters. But change must come about by processes of law, or by collecting signatures in a petition. Unfortunately some people want power by any methods, and ignore the well-being of the people. But I'm optimistic that the fighting will stop.'

He then apologised to me but, like his brother the day before, he was obliged to leave for Tbilisi. He passed me to his colleagues, who would take me to lunch and then give me a tour of Khelvachauri. Ghia slipped away to rescue his stricken car, and Svetlana and I were driven to the restaurant by Avtandil Bolkvadze, the courteous, white-haired chairman of the council of Makhindjauri, a town of 15,000 inhabitants just north of Batumi.

The restaurant was in Makhindjauri itself, a pleasant resort town with many rest houses. A Japanese architect had designed the restaurant in 1917, I was told, and it was a striking building, with a wrap-around verandah and tall wooden arcades prettily carved and latticed. While the staff prepared a table for us, we sat for an hour on benches under the trees in the slightly shabby park nearby, sipping lemonade and Turkish coffee.

In addition to Svetlana and Bolkvadze, our party consisted of Yasha Yadznavadze, the deputy prefect of Khelvachauri; Nodar, the head of a collective farm or commercial company (I never gathered which); and Omar Khalvashi, another senior manager in a regional enterprise. Omar, who was ragged continuously by Yasha because of his dark complexion, looked considerably older than his fifty-two years. His voice had been roasted by years of smoking. He asked me whether men or women were more honoured in British families, a question which itself hinted at the cultural differences between semi-Asiatic Georgians and western Europeans. He also asked why, if we had high unemployment in Britain, we allowed foreign workers to come to our country. I did my best to answer both questions, although Svetlana ticked him off for asking them in the first place.

Eventually we were summoned upstairs to a wood-panelled private room, where a long table had been spread with food and bottles of white wine, pink champagne, and vodka. I stuck to the white Ereti, which is not a distinguished wine. Omar joked that only weak men drink wine, and drank vodka throughout. Avtandil Bolkvadze rose to his feet – he was our host – and asked that Yasha be recognised as *tamada*. Yasha, with his booming voice and ebullient manner, was happy to oblige.

More food arrived: the bubbling stew of liver, offal, onions and parsley known as *djigari*, and fried chicken and potatoes. The toasts began. Violence, said Omar, should not lessen our love for our country. Americans sometimes assassinated their presidents, but that didn't affect our esteem for the United States. He hoped that justice would prevail in Georgia: 'In a civilised country it is not necessary to defend justice with guns.'

Yasha, as *tamada*, told me he thought that Omar had spoken for too long. 'There is no democracy at the table. I will have to find a way to punish the previous speaker.'

'You're not going to punish me,' replied Omar, 'because as a younger man you are required to respect your elders.'

'Traditionally,' Yasha explained to me, 'there are ninety-nine toasts at any Georgian meal, and these are regulated by the laws of the table. But the constitution of Georgia has introduced some amendments.' Everybody laughed. The waitress entered and scattered boxes of Winston cigarettes around the table.

Yasha then proposed a toast to the enemies of Georgia and explained why. 'The reindeer is afraid of the wolf, and when the hunter kills the reindeer, its meat is especially delicious. Today there are hardly any wolves, so the reindeer is not frightened and doesn't run fast. Instead it grazes and grows fat, so the meat is less delicious. This teaches us that we need to compete, and that the presence of an enemy gives us the alarm. So we always ask God to give us clever enemies.'

Avtandil tried to clarify this abstruse point for me, and so did Omar, who quoted a poet who wrote that a good man always has enemies. Yasha added that in Georgia even enemies are given hospitality and safe passage. To lighten the mood, he proposed a toast to smiles, to gaiety. Smiles are everything, added Avtandil; they are our future. During this endless succession of toasts, I noticed the frequent use of the word *magram* – 'but' – as though every phrase had to be qualified and refined or, even better, given a paradoxical turn.

'Georgia is full of love,' Yasha continued, 'and love has its own purpose. There are different kinds of love, and now we are dealing with love of country, love of region. But there are other kinds of love, including the great love we have here, friendship.' In Georgia hyperbole is a way of raising the stakes, of adding another room to the house of brotherhood.

Avtandil echoed Yasha's sentiments, wishing me good health and long life, which would be derived from (or possibly contingent upon) the kind feelings I had towards Georgia. In other words he was making a deal: speak well of us and we'll shower you with blessings. Better, we'll shower you with our blessings, so you'll feel obliged to speak well of us.

Omar elaborated. 'Whatever the gender of our guests, friendship goes from generation to generation. Let your visit be a spark, and our children will be the fire' – which sounded like an invitation to go off for a romp with their womenfolk.

The four men launched into a song which sounded more like a long recitative, Yasha ornamenting it with quavering and sobs. More toasts: to our parents, to the dead. Omar talked about his octogenarian mother, a cue for the men to fall into a mournful song to 'mother' that began, confusingly, '*Dedi . . .*' (to compound the confusion, the Georgian for father is *mama*).

My hosts showed no signs of tiring. Toasting is not primarily an excuse for drinking but a means of reinforcing the self-esteem of the participants and of including the guest within the community. All compliments must be returned and, if possible, improved upon. In the feast's operatic format, there is little dialogue or recitative, and the toasts are like a string of arias, each more elaborate, effusive and emotional than those they follow. Now the four men began to toast each other, declaring that while they might sometimes have their disagreements, they loved each other like brothers. Omar compared friendship to crystal, which is delicate and needs to be cared for.

Nodar was praised as a shy but very generous man. A bashful smile lit Nodar's face in the intervals between slowly emptying his glass and lighting yet another cigarette. A slight man, with hair carefully combed forward over his bald patch, he looked like an elderly boy, and was indulgently treated by his friends, whereas Omar and Yasha slyly tried to upstage each other.

Avtandil told me he had never been a Party member, so he had been constantly discriminated against. When he had tried to found a small tourist agency, the local Party secretary closed it down. So he founded another business, and once again bureaucrats put obstacles in his way. Now he is establishing an industrial enterprise: 'My people believe in me and love me, so I can do my best for the people.'

By six-fifteen I was beginning to wonder what had happened to the promised tour of the region. Given my hosts' consumption of alcohol, I decided it was better not to ask. By now Nodar had gained sufficient confidence to express a few thoughts of his own. Wine, he announced softly, makes fools of kings as well as peasants. Drinking wine together enables you to get to know somebody, but of course hatred could flare up too. At this point he ran out of steam, looked up, thanked us all.

We'd now been at the restaurant for five hours. There were eight empty wine bottles on the table. Svetlana was drinking no alcohol, and Omar was drinking vodka only. I had drunk no more than one bottle, which meant that the other three men had got through seven bottles between them. Apart from some doziness on Nodar's part, there was no sign of drunkenness.

Avtandil drove us back to the hotel, where I took Svetlana aside. I told her that I thought I should return to Tbilisi as soon as possible. Tomorrow was a Sunday and we had no appointments scheduled; for Monday Ghia had arranged meetings that might well not take place. I feared that as Svetlana had made such efforts to bring me to Batumi she would be upset now I wanted to dash back to Tbilisi. Instead, she seemed relieved.

8 Vienna in the Caucasus

Svetlana had good news when we met for breakfast. While out walking she had met an acquaintance, Nugzar Karsidze, a specialist in German affairs at the foreign ministry. He was returning to Tbilisi that morning and would give us a lift. He joined us for coffee after walking over from the Hotel Medea, where he had been staying. When Svetlana told him that we had had no hot water for two days, he laughed. This morning he'd had no water at all.

The recent events in the capital had left him stupefied: 'We have eighty nationalities living in Tbilisi, and there is no conflict between any of them. The only conflict we have is Georgians against Georgians. It's terrible.'

By nine we were on the road, following the coast northwards and then climbing into the lovely mountains, dotted with gardens and villas and undulating tea plantations which hugged the ground. After the coastal resort of Kobuleti, we turned inland to begin the 250-mile drive east to the capital. As we passed through Lanshkhuti, Nugzar pointed out that despite its population of no more than 8000, its football team was the finest in the Soviet Union. These sporting wizards flourished in a town that seemed little more than a long broad main road patrolled by flocks of geese and free-range sows.

At Kvitiri we stopped at a large weekend market. Regular traders occupied cubby-hole stalls, and other people were selling goods off the bonnets of their cars. Nugzar inspected a pair of cheap-looking trousers. 'This man probably bought them for five dollars in Turkey, and has doubled the price. Come with me. There's a stall selling cooking oil over there, and I need some. It costs five times as much as it's supposed to in the shops, but it's impossible to find any in the shops.'

'Where does it all come from?' I asked naively.

'Most of it is probably filched from stores, and sold and resold until it ends up here. As you can see, there are thousands of people involved in this kind of speculation. And not only here. In fact it's far worse in Moscow. What we need is proper privatisation, not this kind of profiteering. If it doesn't come soon, the whole country will go down the drain. Let's say that about 70 per cent of the people in Georgia have regular jobs at modest salaries. I'm talking about teachers and civil servants and factory workers. Or take me, I have a responsible position in a ministry, and I earn a few hundred a month. Like most other people, I don't have the time or the inclination or the opportunity for trading and speculation. We have to live within our means with ever higher prices.'

'Privatisation will mean even higher prices.'

'Yes, but I believe it will benefit not only me, but my children and their generation. It must come.'

We skirted round Kutaisi, along boulevards lined with hideous grimy apartment blocks, and emerged into a more hilly district of large villas, some of which had not only the usual ornate verandahs and canopies but heavy Tuscan-style arcades, a touch of Houston *nouveau riche* extravagance in suburban Kutaisi. Nugzar's jeep needed petrol, but after a few inquiries he learnt that there was none available on this stretch of the road. At the bus depot we were told the same thing. The depot would sell him some petrol, but the attendant who dealt with such matters wouldn't be back until the evening. An elderly man recommended us to a garage a kilometre away, which he'd just heard had some fresh supplies. We went there and found an encouraging queue. The petrol was the inferior 76 grade rather than the 93 the jeep required, but Nugzar was past caring. Drivers were filling not only their cars, but 20-litre cans for emergencies.

We ascended the gentle Surami Pass through wooded hills and traversed the mile-long tunnel said to mark the boundary between western and eastern Georgia. At Agara an immense traffic jam loomed up ahead. Before wedging ourselves into the queue, Nugzar asked a passerby what was going on. 'Shooting,' he replied. Nugzar swerved left on to a dirt road which crossed a field and might bring us back to the main road ahead of the jam. A soldier told us that some members of the National Guard had decided that, with trouble in Tbilisi, they had to prevent yet more people pouring into the capital. Hence the roadblock.

'So the talk about shooting was not true,' said Svetlana, completing her sentence just in time for us to hear a crack of rifle fire. Nugzar manoeuvred the jeep on to the main road ahead of the roadblocks, and from then on he put his foot down and drove Georgian-style until we reached the capital.

The street next to the Hotel Tbilisi was blocked, as usual, but the front windows of the buses were shattered and we had to squeeze past them to reach the hotel entrance, crunching slivers of glass under foot. Almost all the plate-glass windows of the hotel were punctured by bullet holes or boarded up. I was assigned a room considerably less shabby than the one I had occupied before leaving for Batumi. It had been recently redecorated and nothing had yet had a chance to fall apart. Svetlana was aghast at the outward condition of the hotel, but I was glad to be back and assured her I would be all right.

Walking out on to Rustaveli, I was accosted by an elderly man in a shabby suit. He was unshaven, toothy, and wore spectacles. I had met him before, but had been in a rush and had not responded to his overtures. He was, he told me, the head of a languages department at the university, and spoke six languages. He certainly spoke good English. As he was a professor who needed to write all day, could I please give him a ballpoint pen? I explained that I was down to two pens myself, which was true, and could not risk running out of writing materials. This cut no ice with the professor. He kept poking me in the chest and saying that if I had two pens, surely I could part with one. I promised to give him my spare towards the end of my trip, but right now there was nothing doing. He had to write a good deal, he told me. So do I, I replied. I was beginning to doubt his story. Was it really credible that the head of a university department needed to beg for pens when his students didn't?

'You have two. Please give me one.'
'No. I'm sorry. But no.'
'Then please, do you have any English coins?'

A tank was positioned in front of the Parliament. Makeshift memorials made of stones and pebbles demarcated spaces within which flowers were strewn and candles flickered, presumably marking where people had been shot on Friday night. Yet if each cairn marked a corpse, casualties were higher than had been reported. One of these memorials was considerably larger than the rest and enclosed a simple wooden chair. Apparently, a government supporter had been killed by a stray bullet while seated here. I made my way up to the courtyard, which looked even more like an armed camp than before. Riot shields were stacked near the doors.

In the press office a handful of reporters were watching *Rain Man* on the video channel and waiting for a possible press conference. To assist Russian viewers, the television editors employ neither dubbing nor subtitles, but simply swamp all dialogue with a Russian translation, using the same voice for all parts.

A hefty Canadian cameraman told me he had witnessed the violence, though he had arrived about fifteen minutes after the shooting began, and claimed to have been the only foreign cameraman on Rustaveli. Even now nobody was sure about the sequence of events. On Friday evening the Opposition had gathered on Rustaveli for a rally. At about 1.15 on Saturday morning there had been a noise like a thud, which might simply have been a car door slamming, emanating from the Opposition side of the barricades. Soldiers positioned on the Parliament steps and behind the buses took this as a cue and opened fire on the demonstrators. However, since the hospital reported only seven gunshot wounds, André suspected that the soldiers were not using live ammunition or were firing into the air. The seated man killed in front of the Parliament was well inside the barricades, so he was almost certainly the victim of a stray bullet or a sniper. The government had claimed that Opposition snipers had been stationed on the rooftops, but André found this hard to believe. Once the shooting began,

Opposition supporters dispersed into side streets and nearby buildings, including the Hotel Tbilisi. The government supporters, according to André, behaved like a lynch mob, rushing about with batons and iron bars, beating up people and smashing parked cars. His own sources concluded that seventy-eight people had been injured and only one killed, but that toll did not include minor injuries which might not have required hospital treatment.

'I've just got back from three weeks in Yugoslavia, and let me tell you that the violence on Friday night was uglier than anything I saw there. People were just grabbed on the street and accused of being Opposition supporters. Many of the government supporters were blind drunk and were beating people at random.' When I asked him whether Opposition supporters had attacked government loyalists, he insisted that *all* the violence he witnessed was inflicted by Gamsakhurdia's supporters, though he had seen some stone-throwing by the Opposition. 'There was one moment when I saw about a hundred men with iron bars and other weapons rushing towards me. I ducked round a corner and into a doorway. There was another man with me and he clutched me, exposing me like a human shield. I could smell something peculiar and I realised he was shitting himself in terror. We were lucky. We weren't spotted, as the mob saw some Opposition supporters taunting them from further up the street and chased them instead.'

André said the shooting had died down by four in the morning, but resumed at seven, this time with real bullets. That some of the shooting was planned and coordinated he had no doubt, as the initial round of fire had been preceded by the use of water hoses from the fire engines and also by tear gas. He had been briefly arrested as a 'provocateur', but his bulk and his cameras and his forceful personality saved him from more serious harm. Whether all this happened exactly as he recounted, it was impossible to judge, and there were other journalists who took his version of events, especially his central role in any story he was telling, with a pinch of salt.

Robert Seely of *The Times* arrived. He too had been staying at the Hotel Tbilisi but had moved out.

'Why? The hotel's so convenient.'

'Maybe. But when on Saturday morning my room came under fire from the street, I thought it was time to go elsewhere.'

I was the only foreigner left at the Hotel Tbilisi. Indeed, as the only resident who was not an armed militiaman, I received some strange looks in the corridors.

Erekle came to the hotel the next day and gave me his account of what had occurred on Friday. After the National Guard withdrew to the reservoir known as the Sea of Tbilisi there had been a spate of rumours, government-initiated, that Kitovani's men were planning to attack targets including a children's home. The Opposition construed this as an attempt to justify in advance a government attack on the National Guard, and there had indeed been fighting between the two forces. When the Opposition learnt that Kitovani's forces were being surrounded by government troops, a large but peaceful rally gathered along Rustaveli. Many of the demonstrators had gone home later in the evening, but during the night they began receiving reports of violence. Erekle confirmed André's account: government forces had turned hoses on the crowd, fired tear-gas canisters, and then troops believed to be OMON riot police had fired from the Parliament. Opposition demonstrators either fled or dispersed into small groups. Radio broadcasts claimed that the Parliament was being attacked by armed Opposition supporters, and loyalists were urged to come to the building to defend it. There seemed no evidence to support the government's claims, including later assertions that many injuries had been caused by Opposition snipers on the rooftops. Since almost all the buildings in the vicinity were controlled by the government, the story was inherently implausible.

Erekle thought Gamsakhurdia was genuinely startled by the violence. On Saturday he had made a conciliatory speech. Without apportioning blame for the disturbances, he appealed for calm and peace and announced a new session of the Supreme Soviet. Two hours of television time would be allotted to Opposition speakers. Erekle's optimism was short-lived, when during the day government propaganda resumed, denouncing Opposition leaders as criminals. Gamsakhurdia's appeal for reconciliation began to seem little more than a public relations exercise. None the less the televising of the parliamentary sessions – on the day after they took place – was giving the Opposition access to the media for the first time in months.

Gamsakhurdia had persuaded the Parliament to ratify the state of emergency, thus neutralising claims that it had been declared without constitutional authority. There had been no debate today, Monday, but the session would resume tomorrow. Erekle believed that Gamsakhurdia planned to use the Supreme Soviet to ratify his decisions. The president was insisting, in defiance of the facts, that Friday's violence had been a 'putsch'. If, as seemed probable, the Supreme Soviet deputies agreed with this analysis, it would give Gamsakhurdia the authority to label Opposition deputies as supporters of the putsch and, consequently, to arrest them. These fears were not to materialise. Nevertheless, the anti-Opposition hysteria whipped up by the government was proving effective. Nodar Natadze had not attended the parliamentary debates as there were fears that he would be arrested at the Parliament. If such fears were exaggerated, they were certainly not groundless, given the consignment of so many other Opposition leaders to Gamsakhurdia's jails. Many deputies had only reached the Parliament and left it again, under the protection of the Georgian Union of Veterans of the Afghan War.

Kitovani and Sigua remained out at the Sea of Tbilisi. Government militia were positioned to hamper any move Kitovani might be contemplating. The non-military Opposition was now gathering in the small park in front of the university. Its strategy, according to Erekle, was to continue its strikes and rallies, but even he was doubtful about how effective they were likely to be.

We walked over to the university, where the crowd was being addressed from the steps by Irena Sarashvili, the wife of the arrested leader of the National Democratic Party, Georgi Chanturia. She was sharing the platform with another leading dissident, Luisa Shakiashvili. Irena Sarashvili looked desperately tired: her body was taut with tension and her dark liquid eyes gazed wearily from her oval face. She later explained that after she and her husband had been arrested in September, they had been charged with attempting to organise an illegal meeting and with causing disorder in the streets. Ironically, this was the very same law under which Chanturia had been jailed for two years during the regimes of Brezhnev and Andropov. The state prosecutor had described her husband and other prisoners as 'criminals', which struck her as a peculiar statement for a prosecutor to make before a trial had even begun.

I asked her how many political prisoners there were in Georgia. She found it hard to estimate, since the placing of new charges and the dropping of old ones kept altering the status of prisoners. Moreover, some arrests seemed personal or vindictive rather than unequivocally political. None the less she thought that the figure of eighty would be close to the mark. Among these were Georgi Khaindrava and Djaba Ioseliani.

Ioseliani was a superb example of the Georgian composite – he was a playwright, theatre historian and expert on Georgian folklore. He was also the leader of a militia group known as the Mkhedrioni, the Horsemen. More notoriously, he had begun his career in jail after a robbery in Leningrad. He was pardoned and released in 1965. In Georgia a shady past is not seen as a disqualification for an illustrious career. Kitovani's past was unsavoury too. Ioseliani shared Gamsakhurdia's nationalist fervour but he had found Gamsakhurdia's recantation at the behest of the KGB hard to swallow.

After the massacre of April 1989 he founded Mkhedrioni as an armed group which intervened in South Ossetia as a kind of peacekeeping force. It also tried to rescue Georgians who felt threatened by Ossetian guerrillas. This didn't go down well with Gamsakhurdia, whose policies in the region were aimed at stirring up the conflict rather than resolving it. Ioseliani was also involved in a group known as the Georgian National Congress, in which Gamsakhurdia had participated too. The Congress favoured civil disobedience, but Gamsakhurdia argued that dissidents should participate in the electoral process in order to carry out nationalist policies from within the governing structure. Such a view was considered collaborationist by the Congress, but in retrospect Gamsakhurdia had the more realistic strategy. He and his supporters split off to form the Round Table coalition, and after the coalition's electoral successes Gamsakhurdia argued that the Congress was superfluous and should be disbanded. Late in 1990 he ordered Ioseliani and the Mkhedrioni, now 5000 strong, to disarm, but they refused. Ultimatums followed, to no avail. On 19 February 1991, with the aid of Soviet troops, Gamsakhurdia arrested Ioseliani and his followers and charged him with the capital offence of 'organising an armed band with the aim of attacking state or public institutions'.

Gamsakhurdia denied that Ioseliani was a political prisoner, yet he was repeatedly refused access to the lawyer of his choice. Ioseliani responded by going on hunger strike for forty days, a risky strategy for a man in his sixties. He was forcibly fed and the strike ended only after an appeal by Patriarch Ilya II. The trial was repeatedly delayed, but Gamsakhurdia, with his usual rush to judgment, declared that his former comrade was nothing but a criminal.

Ioseliani was clearly a potential rival to Gamsakhurdia, but the case of Georgi Khaindrava was very different. A cameraman who was not a member of any Georgian political party, he was arrested in September on charges of impeding the freedom of television broadcasting, which was laughable, given the constraints placed on the media. The Opposition suspected that he was arrested because he was performing his job too diligently, especially after he filmed another occasion when OMON troops fired on demonstrators.

Irena Sarashvili was continuing her efforts to obtain her husband's release. She had begun a hunger strike on the Parliament steps on 22 September, and been beaten up so badly that she had spent a few days in hospital. The government had represented her arrival at the Parliament with forty other members of the National Democratic Party as an 'attack' on the government. Tomorrow, she told me, the Opposition would march to the Parliament to demand a full analysis of what had taken place on Friday night. 'In my view, what happened that night was worse even than April 1989. Then demonstrators were attacked and butchered by Soviet troops. Last Friday Georgians were shooting and beating their fellow Georgians. We know that violence was initiated by the government, despite all their denials. I'm not saying that some Opposition supporters didn't give beatings too, but we did not initiate the attacks.'

'How do you know that you won't receive similar treatment when you march to Parliament tomorrow?'

She smiled. 'We must hope.'

'I don't think it is likely,' added Erekle. 'Like the Communists, Gamsakhurdia prefers to attack when it is dark. As long as it is daylight, the demonstrators should be safe.'

David Kakabadze was born in 1889 and studied science in St Petersburg before returning to Georgia to pursue an artistic career. Like Lado Gudiashvili, he was dispatched to Paris by the republican government in 1919 to continue his studies as a painter. He stayed there till 1928, exhibiting his work with Picasso, Braque and Picabia. After his return to Tbilisi he taught at the Academy of Arts throughout the 1930s but was dismissed in 1948 after his work was denounced as 'cosmopolitanist and abstractionist'.

While teaching at the Academy he met a seventeen-year-old girl named Eteri Andronikashvili, whom he married. In 1952 he died; she lives on, looking after his studio on Leonidze Street near the university district and showing it to interested visitors. Levan, who seemed to know everybody, arranged for me to visit the studio and gallery. The actual studio is a splendid room filled not only with paintings but with drinking horns, daggers, sheaths, ceramics, early Georgian jewellery and metalwork, and beautifully engraved Persian jugs.

Kakabadze came from a peasant family in the Imereti region, and his early landscapes depict its countryside as a kind of patchwork, a style he returned to when playing safe during the Stalin years. The most arresting of his early paintings is a swaggering and confident self-portrait with pomegranates, painted in 1913. In France he produced numerous charcoal sketches of outdoor scenes and a series of watercolours from Brittany in 1921, mostly of boats, painted on wet paper so as to create a fuzz of water, a fading of the sky. These mirage-like images are poised in the centre of the paper, with the edges left blank. At the same time he was adopting cubist techniques, and the accomplished if rather glum results show the influence of Braque, especially in their colouring. There was another change of style in 1924, when he painted brightly coloured abstracts enclosed like embryos within blobs. His collages of the same year employ glass and mirror and metal as well as paint, and also adopt embryonic forms. In 1927 he was painting other abstracts in a kind of blend of Miró and Klee, as though expanding amoebae were being surveyed under a microscope. On his return to Georgia he resumed a more conservative style, such as the Svaneti landscapes of 1939. The dreadful contrast between the inventive, dazzling work of the 1920s and the later run-of-the-mill landscapes speaks volumes about the repressions of the Stalinist years.

After leaving the studio, Erekle and Levan took me to Lagidze's on Rustaveli. Here the *khachapuri* are the variety popular in Adjara. The dough contains a central hollow into which melted cheese and a soft-boiled egg are dropped. With a fork the cheese and egg are beaten together and then prodded into the soft pastry before being eaten. We ate two each and afterwards I could barely make it up the stairs, as though I were pregnant with a pile of billiard balls. As we emerged from Lagidze's we saw a Mercedes come streaking down Rustaveli, no doubt carrying an Important Person to the Parliament.

'I thought it must be the president's car, but it wasn't,' said Levan. 'Did I tell you about Gamsakhurdia's cars? When he became president, the story goes, he asked Moscow to send him a large car. The authorities in Moscow said to him, "I'm sorry, but now Georgia is independent you will have to get your own car, or we can sell you a large Zil." Gamsakhurdia was very angry, so he bought two large Mercedes from Germany. The problem was how to pay for them. Then one day a big Georgian company was unable to pay its workers' wages. When the workers asked why, they were given some bogus explanation and told it wouldn't be possible to pay them for some time. Of course what had really happened was that Gamsakhurdia took the money to pay for his German cars. There were questions about it, but Gamsakhurdia always got very angry and said it wasn't true, that the cars were a gift from Chancellor Kohl.' (After Gamsakhurdia's downfall, a government official declared that the Mercedes had been paid for out of a hard-currency account of monies intended for medical supplies.)

Levan lit up a cigarette. 'Do you know why it is that Georgia produces the best tobacco in the Soviet Union but makes the worst cigarettes? Well, it goes like this. A typical cigarette factory boss would be given a plan to produce 10,000 cartons. He orders good Georgian tobacco. But he also orders the same quantity of grass from another source. He blends the two, delivers his quota, and sells off the remaining 10,000 and pockets the profit. Now the mayor or whoever appointed him knows he's going to do this, so he demands a rake-off. Whoever appointed the mayor knows that he's going to be receiving kickbacks from his appointees, so he gets a rake-off from the mayor. And so it goes all the way to the top. Simple.'

Levan and Erekle left me at the hotel, and I continued to the Parliament, where the crowd was being urged to take up battle stations. Marksmen were assuming positions behind the sandbagged arcades of the Parliament building. Buses were being shifted to form a double line of barricades. Facing the avenue were about two hundred policemen and militia. Soldiers were donning helmets. Since the avenue was completely empty, apart from a few pedestrians, I wondered what the fuss was about.

So I walked to the other end of Rustaveli, from which the assault was clearly expected. A line of buses blocked the avenue. Just beyond this new barricade I saw Irena Sarashvili and Luisa Shakiashvili leading a procession of about two hundred Opposition demonstrators. Here at last was the unarmed demonstration she had been planning. Here was the dreadful threat to law and order which had prompted the mobilisation of troops half a mile away.

The demonstrators were not allowed to proceed down Rustaveli, so Irena Sarashvili sat down in the street and the other marchers followed suit. As a protest it was hardly impressive, and I was struck again by the poor organisation of the Opposition. Both Erekle and Levan were acquainted with Opposition leaders, yet they had had no idea that this march was even taking place. Irena, looking pale but determined, addressed her supporters through a megaphone. I went to talk to a demonstrator on the front line, a member of the Free Democrats. He told me that the demonstration was intended to show the people that the Opposition was presenting its case peacefully. He explained the small turn-out by saying that some groups discouraged their supporters from participating because in a city filled with roaming gunmen the dangers were considerable.

Robert Seely of *The Times* was in an excitable mood, predicting broken heads before the day was done.

'I doubt it,' I said. 'The howling mob is half a mile away at the Parliament.'

'Yes, but all they have to do is move the barricades and they'll come streaming down.'

I wandered back to the Parliament. The barricades were still up, but there was less tension than when the rabble was being roused. Women still stood on the steps waiting for the barbarians to come storming down Rustaveli. The whole situation was preposterous, and I was astonished at the gullibility of the government supporters, for this was not the first time they had been urged to defend the president against putschists who had failed to materialise. They were lied to over and over again, but every time believed what they were told. As I made my way past the police lines I noticed that they wore no identification.

I returned again to the Opposition sitdown. It was growing dark, so Irena Sarashvili rose to her feet and announced the demonstration was over and they would return to the university. The Free Democrat told me this was simply prudent, because any violent reaction from government hoodlums would occur under cover of darkness. As the demonstrators walked back, they chanted 'Ceaucescu!' and 'Satana!', both of which seemed slight over-statements of the case against Gamsakhurdia, but it raised the spirits of the marchers after hours spent sitting on the chilly tarmac.

'There's a joke making the rounds,' said my acquaintance, 'that the Kurds gather outside the palace of Saddam Hussein and chant, "Zviad, Zviad!'"

Helga, a reporter with a German news network, had overheard me speaking in German to Georgi the medical student, and had asked me to join her for dinner one evening so that we could exchange views. I tried to book a table in a private restaurant. One restaurant wasn't sure whether it would open at all, and another would stay open only until six. I went to her hotel.

The Metekhi Palace Hotel dominates a hillside opposite the Narikala fortress and Mount Mtatsminda. It's built in a smart ziggurat design, and not only is there a neon sign over the roof but none of the letters is missing. Outside the main entrance the hotel's Volvo limousines were parked, still bearing Viennese licence plates. Everything whispered 'joint venture' and 'hard currency'. The lobby exemplified classic international hotel design, complete with atrium, internal glass lifts, splashy fountains, hanging plants, uniformed doormen and receptionists, shopping arcades, and a 'business centre'. The hotel even had a Viennese coffee shop with authentic-looking cakes and tarts priced at three to four dollars each. The bar was well stocked and evidently Gamsakhurdia's prohibition order did not apply to those paying for their booze in dollars. Men in suits were wandering about the lobby, just as they would be doing in Zürich or London or Chicago. Who were these people, and why did I never see them elsewhere in Tbilisi?

The Metekhi Palace is a handsome hotel, but Georgia it ain't. It's a foreign enclave for those who have no wish to deal with the awkwardnesses of Soviet existence. The enclave even has its own currency, which bears no relation to the currency employed beyond its doors. The Tbilisi and Iveria hotels had the gall to charge $33 for a three-minute phone call to Europe, but here the same call cost $45. This Vienna-in-the-Caucasus catered only to businessmen, trade delegations, and journalists, all of whom paid with other people's money.

Helga asked me to wait for a few minutes while she completed a radio report. I left her to it but a minute later she was at my side.

Before she filed her story she wanted to know how the sitdown demonstration had ended and what had been discussed at the Supreme Soviet that day. I was happy to tell her what I knew, and then she dashed back to complete her story.

This made me feel a lot better. I had been struggling to weave together an impartial account of the political situation and it had not been easy. Government and Opposition did not speak the same language, and the fragmentation among the Opposition could lead to different versions of the same events. All sources were biased. Now here I was, an itinerant Englishman, having my brains hurriedly picked by the correspondent for some major German-language networks. Some of the information I conveyed to Helga was first-hand and reasonably reliable; the rest was probably fourth-hand. My information was probably accurate, but who could be sure?

Helga had had a good day. After waiting three hours for the privilege, she and her crew had been granted an interview with Gamsakhurdia, who had been in a genial mood. On the subject of arrests and trials he had been emollient, saying he didn't believe in punishment, but he still viewed his political opponents as criminals and traitors. When Helga mentioned the name of Sigua, the president had just laughed: Sigua was not worth bothering about.

What interested me was whether Gamsakhurdia believed his own rhetoric. 'Is he cynical and manipulative, an intellectual turned crude populist, or does he really believe all this rubbish about criminals and drug addicts?'

'I don't think he does. It's just a political ploy. But he told me he does believe strongly in good and evil, and I am sure he means it. He really thinks he is on the side of the angels, and by implication his opponents are bad, even wicked.'

As I left the hotel I could see an orange glow in the distance; it was clearly a fire. I dashed back to the lobby and phoned Helga, suggesting it might be worth her while to take a look. She was down seconds later, tried unsuccessfully to locate her cameraman, and phoned for a taxi. Taxis were usually easy to find, as drivers summoned to the Metekhi Palace could hope to be paid in dollars, but not tonight. One of the doormen roared up in his car and offered us a lift to the scene. His motive was self-interest: his flat was not far from where the fire seemed to be. Behind us a roadblock had been set up, but we were within the cordon and soon reached Avalabari Metro station. A nine-bay building opposite was ablaze, but there was no reason to assume it was a politically inspired conflagration. Helga returned to her hotel, while I stayed to watch the fun.

The fire engines were out in force, and two extension ladders were close to the roof, from which smoke and flames were shooting out. A fireman wearing no protective clothing at all climbed one of the ladders, while others entered the building through a first-floor window. The fire was gradually brought under some kind of control. A young man tapped me on the shoulder and shouted, 'Guy! Guy!' This was not a case of mistaken identity, but the name of the Soviet traffic police, and the blazing building was one of their offices. No wonder the crowd was enjoying the fire: thousands of parking tickets had been reduced to ashes.

9 We Have Everything

'This doesn't look right,' I said to Erekle. 'Let's try the other side of the reservoir.'

We were looking for the National Guard camp. Kitovani's men were still based at the Sea of Tbilisi, and I thought he might appreciate a visit. Eventually the taxi driver found what we were looking for: a series of small blocks within a compound by the shore where trade unions had once organised residential courses. Heavily armed soldiers sat by the main gate checking the credentials of visitors. Mr Gabashvili's signature worked its usual magic, and we were allowed in. As we walked through the encampment, I kept an eye out for weaponry, but all I could see were a few armoured vehicles, two pieces of heavy artillery, and half a dozen lorries. Not a single tank. It was hard to estimate how many soldiers were living there, but it couldn't have been more than a few hundred. If this was the rebel National Guard, it wasn't very impressive.

The dormitories were in use and blankets had been slung across the windows to provide makeshift curtains. Some soldiers were enjoying the morning sunshine, either sitting on benches or strolling about. There was nothing for them to do except chat and sip cans of German lager. Inside the buildings there were left-over photographs of fraternal trade union activities. I could see the faces of glum diners, a pool table, a grim cloakroom attendant, recording the joyless good cheer of enforced camaraderie. As we approached a building near the reservoir, I spotted Tengiz Kitovani standing on a balcony. He agreed to talk, but he was not his usual bouncy self. His father had died the day before, and he was in sombre mood. He was wearing not the fatigues sported by most of his men, but a kind of Breton fisherman's jersey with thin black and white stripes, and in his belt he carried a dagger. He seemed distracted, weary.

I asked him how he saw his role now that he and his men were outside the city.

'The president has admitted that my forces are the real National Guard, and without our existence he would suppress the Opposition.'

'How long will you stay here?'

'Till the democratic movement triumphs.'

'Is that likely?'

'Yes.'

'But Gamsakhurdia has the political advantage at the moment.'

'Yes, but nobody knows the strength of both sides, and at the moment the people aren't being told the truth.'

'What should the strategy of the Opposition be?'

'The Opposition will make gains as the economic crisis worsens and leads to a political crisis which will bring an end to Gamsakhurdia's rule. The president recently declared that only he can guarantee that the Georgian people will have water and bread and other essential supplies. If he were to die tomorrow, he's saying, Georgia would be ruined. This is demagoguery.'

'How much support does the Opposition have outside the capital?'

'About eighty per cent.'

'I have to tell you that nobody I have spoken to on either side shares that view.'

He hedged. 'That's because many people have a stake in the system. Their jobs depend on it.' This didn't make much sense, but perhaps he meant that people were afraid to express their real views for fear of losing their jobs.

'Have your forces shrunk since you came out here?'

'No, they have grown.'

'People have volunteered to join you?'

'Yes.'

'How many troops do you have at your command?'

'Let me put it this way. We were attacked by 2500 of Gamsakhurdia's troops and held them off. That should give you some idea of our strength.'

'Why is the president letting you sit here unmolested?'

'Because he saw the consequences of the last time he attacked us.'

'Last Friday peaceful Opposition demonstrators came under vicious attack on Rustaveli. There was nothing you could do to come to their aid. How can you prevent a repetition of those scenes in the future?'

'We didn't want to interfere last Friday because if we used force against the government, we would lose our moral authority and the respect of the people. We would be regarded as putschists.'

'Are there any circumstances in which you would use force?'

'Only in the case of repressions, arrests.'

'Do you consider those likely?'

'Yes.'

Kitovani was clearly not his usual expansive self, so I ended the interview. It was becoming increasingly clear that his National Guard was an irrelevance, a judgment proved, two months later, to be completely wrong. But standing by the Sea of Tbilisi it seemed to me that Kitovani, by withdrawing from the city, had cut himself off both physically and psychologically, and that both he and Gamsakhurdia knew it. He and Sigua were stranded, for if either left the compound he would be arrested.

We hitched a ride back into Tbilisi. At the Parliament I learnt of a prime ministerial press conference to be held that afternoon. Outside the building women were collecting signatures for a petition which asked for the 'putsch' to be suppressed, and demanding that if Parliament wouldn't act on behalf of the Georgian people it should be dissolved and replaced by presidential rule.

'You mean the people are asking for a dictatorship?' I asked one of the organisers.

'In the Parliament there are many deputies who are not in favour of Georgia. It was a mistake. It is better that Parliament should go.'

'You want to give up your freedom?'

'We have no freedom now.'

It was enough to make one weep, but of course this petition was being organised from the top. The cynicism of the government was beyond belief. The previous evening the sixty-three Communist deputies had been expelled from Parliament – less an ideological move than an attempt by government supporters to prevent a coalition of Communist and Opposition deputies. Even this expulsion was not enough for Gamsakhurdia's supporters.

Nobody at the Parliament had the faintest idea where the press conference was being held. I wandered about the halls for a while, and was pleasantly surprised to see Nodar Natadze trotting down the stairs unmolested. After two days of absence because of fears for his safety, he had gauged, correctly, that he would be all right. Eventually I found the right room. I was half an hour late, but so was everybody else.

The prime minister, Besso Gugushvili, walked in. He was a dapper man in a grey suit and wearing large spectacles, with a trimmed bushy moustache above neat features, and a general air of self-satisfaction. He invited our questions. Robert Parsons began by suggesting that despite Gamsakhurdia's appeal for reconciliation on Saturday, there had been few signs of it subsequently from either side. Gugushvili explained that there were external forces that opposed reconciliation. There was a third force – mystery, mystery – which supported the Opposition. The next few minutes of his reply were totally incomprehensible. He concluded by saying that certain matters could be settled swiftly, but there were forces that were receiving their orders from elsewhere (subtext: the Kremlin).

Robert Parsons wanted to know whether the prime minister had any evidence for these allegations. Gugushvili smiled, and asked us whether there was any evidence that the KGB had been active in Britain? ('Yes,' I muttered.) Parsons pressed him: what precisely was the prime minister alleging? Gugushvili said he was talking about the supply of weapons, ideological support and so forth, but he didn't want to be too specific now. And there had been telephone messages.

'Oh,' said Parsons, 'do you have any recordings?'

'A prime minister is not asked such questions, but I can assure you such talks are being held with the Opposition. If I give you our evidence, then our sources will be blocked. I recommend that you read some books about espionage.'

I asked a question: 'Since the president has repeatedly stated that Opposition leaders are criminals and traitors, would the prime minister let us know which elements of the Opposition the government regards as legitimate?'

'Any person who doesn't break the law is beyond suspicion. The government does not regard opposing opinions as criminal, only certain actions by Opposition figures.'

Parsons picked up the baton. 'Most Opposition deputies were present at the Television Centre, the seizing of which was an illegal act. Does that mean that the government won't speak to those deputies?'

Gugushvili was magnanimous. 'The Television Centre was occupied by rebel elements of the Opposition. We shall have to forgive some actions, actions that would not be so easily forgiven in the West. Our country is young, our governmental structures are weak, democracy is still being weaned, and the population is still getting used to democracy and responsibility. The third force has a fertile soil here.' His reply rambled on. He was a historian, he said, and knew the history of the West well, and he knew that under similar circumstances in Britain martial law would have been declared by now. Had we heard of Lord Haw-Haw? Yes, we had. Well, Lord Haw-Haw was hanged.

Parsons was looking completely exasperated, but the prime minister wasn't done with his historical lecture. He referred to race riots in London, and how our police use tear gas and rubber bullets and armoured cars. He waffled on about Ireland, and how our experience there should help us to understand the situation in Georgia. He regretted that the Western press didn't accept the existence of the third force. 'That's because you've forgotten that the bear is still alive.' (Code for the Soviet Union.) 'But the bear can still reach Berlin or Paris.' He had now been declaiming for fifteen minutes. I tried to interrupt, unsuccessfully. Parsons had better luck. 'Since the Supreme Soviet ruled that the events of last Friday were a putsch, why don't you arrest its leaders?'

'It has also been decided that those persons, if they stop their activities, won't be prosecuted.' But since 'activities' were broadly defined, this still left the government options open.

By now Parsons had had enough, and walked out in a huff, followed by the AFP correspondent, followed by me. The AFP man said he was so fed up with having his time wasted that he was returning to Moscow the next day. Certainly Gugushvili, who was in the habit of treating the press to lengthy lectures, had treated us with faintly disguised contempt. I couldn't tell whether he was being deliberately obfuscatory or was just too conceited and ignorant to behave otherwise.

I had been invited to a small private concert organised by the singer Nunu Gabunia. I was late because of the press conference, and arrived to find her flat full of people. Her mother was stirring pots in the kitchen, and her daughter was keeping an eye on her own two small children. In the living room four young women, all musicians, were chatting. Nunu ushered us immediately to the table, laid with numerous dishes of stuffed red peppers, ratatouille, sturgeon, layered *sulguni* cheese, caviar, a delicious bean salad in a walnut dressing (*mtsvane lobio niguzit*), and other hors d'oeuvres. My arrival unleashed a series of hot dishes from the kitchen: fried *khinkali, chakapuli*, a lamb stew with herbs and greens in its own juices; *chakokhbili*, an equally delicious but drier stew with herbs, diced tomatoes, garlic and onions; the *tkemali*, sour plum sauce to accompany the meats; and an exquisite sauce made from crushed walnuts and garlic, blended with salt and pepper and saffron. All the food was delicious, quite the best tasting dishes I had come across in Georgia.

After lunch the musicians moved to the piano. On the left stood Maya, a shy young contralto, and on the right Piso, whose name means 'cat' in Georgian. Between them was the principal singer, Nukri, a dark woman in severe black clothes. The trio was accompanied by Nino, known more familiarly as Nutsiko, a piano teacher at the conservatory. Maya and Nukri were chemists, and

Piso worked as an interpreter with a theatre company – or did before the theatres were closed down.

Many of the songs were love songs, mournful and typically Georgian. Sometimes I would catch Nunu looking at the trio intently, her lips slightly pursed, and this usually meant that she had composed the song. Very fine her compositions were too. I loved the intimacy of this music; these weren't operatic compositions, they were songs for the night club, ballads with long reflective stretches. They usually began delicately, with Nukri launching into the song softly while the other singers provided a subtle harmonic substructure. The songs rose to climaxes of extraordinary intensity, then subsided again, and it was these variations in mood and dynamics that made this informal recital so gripping. Nukri gave the music everything she had, throwing her head back and closing her eyes with concentration, and Piso too sang with her eyes shut most of the time. Their teamwork was so immaculate that they could keep them closed and stay in time and in tune through songs which were rhythmically and harmonically complex. How sensuously the liquid richness of the Georgian language was savaged by those harsh throaty *kh* sounds and the knots of consonants.

As well as the love songs, they treated me to folk and gypsy songs, which I enjoyed less. Here Nutsiko came into her own, her hands flying up into the air as she set a tremendous pace and rhythm. Chewing gum incessantly, she played at hair-raising speeds with the utmost nonchalance. Nukri too was in her stride, and surged into the climaxes with her head thrown far back, her neck tendons taut as cable. During one of the gypsy songs the two granddaughters came quietly into the room and clung to the singers' arms for a while before subsiding into sofas, listening attentively and chewing the bubble gum I had given them. A light as yellow as the glow in a Vuillard domestic painting fell over the scene, and I found myself entranced by the tableau of the rapt musicians. In the warm old-fashioned flat we seemed far away from rhetoric and riflefire, and I was making the most of this temporary retreat from the more volatile reality outdoors.

When the performers paused to refresh themselves, Nunu moved to the keyboard to accompany her granddaughters, aged six and four, who took it in turns to sing Neapolitan songs. They stood up straight, hands by their sides, and sang with the utmost seriousness and aplomb. They were performing for their guest, not a duty to be taken lightly. So these carefree songs were sung as solemnly as dirges. When Nunu slipped a cassette into her VCR of a television programme that had featured her singing, I realised that this kind and unassuming woman had the voice of a Tebaldi.

The tape came to an end, and politics intruded again. The broadcasting of the previous day's parliamentary session had begun and, though we were trying to direct our attention to other matters, it was impossible not to watch. Nodar Natadze gave a tremendously feisty performance. With his blockish bald head and his toothbrush moustache he resembled a compact Japanese netsuke figure, but he blasted his way through his speech, disposing curtly of hecklers. He denied vehemently that the Opposition was launching a putsch, and attacked the government for firing on its own citizens, whatever the provocation. Throughout the speeches, the speaker of the Supreme Soviet, Akaki Asatiani, was doing his best to remain impartial, but it must have been difficult with Zviad Gamsakhurdia seated next to him and whispering in his ear.

At nine I thought I should release my hosts. As I was saying goodbye to Nunu's white-haired mother, who had cooked most of the food, I told her how fortunate she was to live in a home always filled with music.

'I only wish,' she said, 'that you could be as happy as I am.'

'This region,' said Soso, as we drove southwest out of Tbilisi, 'used to be forbidden to tourists. You can see the radar installations on the hilltops, and there are many tank bases in the area.'

'Why here?'

'You may well ask. We're five hundred kilometres from the Turkish border, so obviously the tanks were here to keep an eye on us, not on potential invaders.'

We were passing through a region that looked exceptionally fertile, where a benign climate allows fruit and vegetables to be grown almost year-round. Most of the farmers are Azerbaijanis. According to Soso, they have lived here since the time of Shah Abbas and have always been loyal allies of the Georgians. They are not the only 'outsiders' in the region; many other villages here are Armenian.

Plastered against the walls of the large army base in the drab village of Koda, signs warned off intruders in Georgian, Russian, and Azerbaijani. Just beyond the village, shepherds on horseback were driving flocks of sheep down from the hills. Donkey carts trundled along the lanes. On a hillside the huge Ageti statue reared up, one of those monumental war memorials of which the Georgians are so proud. This one depicts a statuesque Georgian mother handing her husband's sword to her two small sons, who hold it in their hands, symbolising the next generation of Georgian warriors ready to defend their nation. From the monument there was a depressing view on to a plain filled with smoking factories, overlooked by hills where the radar installations were flapping their sails. These factories used to produce concrete and tinned food, but not all were still operating: the shortage of sugar has forced jam production into temporary retirement. None the less, the air looked badly polluted.

We stopped at a roadside stall run by Azerbaijani women wrapped in a primitive version of the layered look, usually with two head shawls and leggings, all in colourful but faded flower prints, none of which matched. When a purchase was made there was a flurry of cloth, as hands groped up skirts for that gap in the leggings into which bills were stuffed for safe-keeping. I inspected buckets of apples and pomegranates, and we bought corn on the cob which was being steamed in large tubs by the roadside. They were rubbed vigorously in salt before being handed over. They were tough. I tasted the local medlars for the first time. Shaped and coloured like a small but smooth-skinned orange, the pulp has the colour of halvah or grained wood and the texture of a not-quite-ripe pear. In taste it was lightly sweet and fibrous.

We continued to Bolnisi, a small town which had a large German population until World War II, when the remaining Germans were deported. One of the businesses they had established was wine-making, and the winery still exists. The technical director showed me round, and for a change the buildings were well maintained, although many of the tanks and filters looked venerable. Until recently the winery exported almost all its production – mostly fortified wines – to Russia, where it was bottled. Now it is free to sell its wines where and to whom it wishes, but the absence of a bottling line has made them difficult to market. The managers long for privatisation, and claim that Western investors are queueing to develop the winery, but I suspected these were the attentions of scavengers.

As we were leaving, a lorry loaded with grapes was pulling into the entrance from the main road, and passersby and children were helping themselves liberally to bunches as they walked by. We drove to the outskirts where Soso wanted to show me a quarry which produces basalt and some of the lively yellow tufa one sees on public buildings in Tbilisi. The manager, Temuri Gabidzashvili, told me he already exported stone to Russia, but, like everybody else, he was looking for other opportunities on the export market. To beef up his portfolio he also had a sideline in bottling mineral water. Tufa is usually expensive, but he could offer Western purchasers a good deal – a year's free supply in exchange for modern equipment. Soso added that if I could bring the attention of Western investors to this splendid opportunity, of course I would earn myself a piece of the action. I was gradually realising that this little outing, announced as a tour of the Georgian countryside, had a little business activity spliced in, for Soso too had a commercial interest in Temuri's enterprises. Like every other businessman I had encountered here, Temuri was bitterly critical of Gamsakhurdia, describing the regime as neo-Bolshevik.

Temuri hopped in the car and guided us as we continued south towards the Armenian border. The road narrowed and twisted through a valley lined in places with rugged cliffs. At Dmanisi we passed very close to the dig which just a few days earlier had yielded a jawbone said to be 1.6 million years old, about the same age as the African bones believed to be the earliest example of *Homo erectus*.

Here in the hills of southern Georgia the map of pre-history had just been redrawn.

We pulled off the road into what looked like a farmstead in a dell surrounded by fields and orchards and hayricks. A donkey grazed contentedly. A shed with a corrugated iron roof turned out to be a restaurant. The surroundings did not look promising, but the food proved excellent. The usual hors d'oeuvres were supplemented by two kinds of sturgeon. The main dishes included glazed pork, squares of pork fat and rind ('very delicious', according to Svetlana), the salty brisket dish *khashlama*, excellent pressed beef (*basturma*), cornbread both fried and baked, juicy shashlik, and slices of baked potatoes. Two other men arrived halfway through this feast, experts on agriculture and forestry who just happened to be business associates of Soso's. They did not come empty-handed, and contributed chicken, green peppers, delicious cheese, and brandy.

Soso explained that this corner of Georgia was packed with natural resources, with first-rate fruit and walnuts and hazelnuts and mineral springs. He and his friends had plans. They were keeping an eye out for an American firm to help them build a hotel and to revive the former German cheese factory. To achieve this, they were planning to inseminate the local cows with specially imported American sperm. I had to tell them that there was little I could do personally to help.

'We have another project,' continued Soso. 'The sweetbriar jelly from this region is a unique product, so we will market it if we can obtain the technology to produce it on a commercial basis. In exchange we will supply the product free of charge for two years.'

'It is a great opportunity,' someone else urged me.

I asked these eager entrepreneurs whether in the hoped-for rush towards privatisation and foreign investment there was a danger that Georgian resources and industries would end up in foreign control. They thought not. It was only a temporary phase, while Georgian businessmen exchanged goods for the technical assistance they needed to stand on their own feet.

We rose from lunch at four. As in Batumi, there had been talk before lunch of visiting local monuments, but after a couple of bottles of wine my hosts' enthusiasm for sightseeing rapidly diminished. On this occasion I was determined to see more than the insides of cars and restaurants. The important excavations at Dmanisi were inaccessible because of the damp weather, but instead they would show me the Sioni church near Bolnisi.

What's striking about Sioni is the beautiful green tufa from which the broad west façade of the church is built. The lowest sections date from the fifth century, but the later additions, though easy to pick out next to stonework over a thousand years older, were sensitively made. From the porch, steps lead down into the lofty aisled church with its high arcades and brick vaults. Without candlelight and electricity the church would be impenetrably gloomy, for the only natural lighting comes from the door and from deep-set lancets in the aisles and a single lancet high in the rounded apse. The carved capitals are damaged and the remaining frescoes in the apse are faded. What has survived is the lintel over the north door (now replaced with a copy), carved with the oldest inscriptions in the Georgian language found within Georgia itself, which dates the construction of the church: 478–93. I trudged back through the sopping churchyard to the waiting car, wet feet a small price to pay for the chance to see this remarkably impressive church.

Mr Gabashvili, receiving me on my weekly visit to his office, looked up. 'Mr Brook,' he said, very mournfully, 'after all this time here, what are your impressions?'

I had to be careful. My papers were still on his desk. 'They are varied.'

My reply was of no interest to Gabashvili, who was using the pretence of dialogue as an overture to a speech. After careful study, he wanted me to know, he had concluded that the Western media had no understanding of the Caucasus and no desire ever to arrive at any such understanding. That is what the distortions of the Western press suggested to him. He attempted the famous lines by Kipling on the failure of East and West to meet, and I gave him a helping hand with the scansion. He regaled me with lists of the terrible errors respected reporters had perpetrated and was at a loss to understand why they had failed to check their facts. Had he really wanted to know, I could have told him: trying to get information out of the Georgian government, other than tiresomely self-serving press releases, was exceedingly difficult.

'Democracy,' he admonished me, 'is not something that survives by itself. It has to be worked at every day.'

'Very true.'

'Why, even Mrs Thatcher was criticised because on occasion she acted in ways that some people felt were repressive.'

'Indeed.'

'In Ireland you have these problems.' I sat back and let Gabashvili roll on. I was his prisoner until he chose to hand my new accreditation to a typist, so I might as well relax and enjoy the experience. Once I had the piece of paper in my hand, I had little to lose.

'If I may say so, Mr Gabashvili, it might be easier for the press to report with complete accuracy if the government would make information accessible to us. Some press conferences, supposedly held for our benefit, have, frankly, been a waste of everybody's time.'

I waited for a rebuke but it did not come.

'I agree with you,' the minister unexpectedly replied. 'Sometimes it is hard for you to have the correct information. This is because of subversion, because of former Communists who want to obstruct the workings of the government.'

I had momentarily thought we were close to understanding each other, but no. I let the point go, as I needed to hurry off to an appointment for which I was already late. As I crossed the Parliament courtyard I saw Zviad Gamsakhurdia slipping out of the main building, flanked on either side by bodyguards. He gave a quick glance at the scene from beneath his hooded lids, then kept his head down and hunched his shoulders as he strode towards the doorway opposite. As he entered it he sneezed, which I found oddly endearing. I tried to follow him in, but the guards did not think this a good idea.

*

Relations with the supercilious waiter were now rock bottom. I had rewarded a Russian waiter who was always pleasant, if not efficient, with cigarettes, but saw no reason to lavish gifts on this one. On this occasion he ignored me for fifteen minutes. When the restaurant administrator ambled past I gave him a despairing look, which he interpreted correctly. He whispered something in the waiter's ear. The waiter came over and flung crockery and cutlery in no recognisable pattern on my table, which I construed as a hostile act. Ten minutes later he had still not taken my order, so I went to the desk to complain, the first time I had taken this drastic measure. The manager walked me back to my table, and at the same moment the waiter arrived with dishes I had not ordered.

The administrator said I would be getting shashlik tonight and was that all right? I said that it was, but added, 'I do the ordering here, not the waiter.' He nodded, and asked me whether I wanted Borjomi or lemonade. I chose mineral water, whereupon the waiter returned with lemonade. To his astonishment I refused to accept it, and he eventually gave me what I had asked for. I worried that my outburst might be seen by the other diners, all Georgian, as the tantrum of a spoilt Westerner. It wasn't. Everyone knew the waiter wouldn't have dared treat Georgians as he was treating me, and some men at the next table came over and offered me a consoling slug of vodka, but I pointed to the bottle of wine in my bag, and they laughed. I drank the wine openly throughout the meal. Nobody objected.

The next day I was out of the waiter's clutches, as Erekle's family invited me to lunch. We were joined by Rusiko Beridze, clothed as usual in black. She told me about her family background, how her father had been arrested in 1937 and how her mother had accompanied him to prison, where she became pregnant with Rusiko. Her mother had left the prison to give birth, but her father was never heard from again, and it had to be assumed that he was executed. I learnt that when Merab Kostava had been sentenced to ten years in Siberia, he and Rusiko were divorced. They remarried in the KGB offices where he was being held, and during the ceremony he cheekily toasted the free Georgia for which he longed.

She remarried him because as his wife she would have the right to visit him in prison; otherwise he might not have received a single visitor for the entire decade. She travelled vast distances, often unaccompanied, to reach Kostava in the depths of Siberia. She also had the right to occupy his flat, which would otherwise have been confiscated by the KGB. As if his own death were not grievous enough, she had to endure the suicide of their son, although there were doubts as to whether he had indeed killed himself, but she had no way of knowing the truth. When Demo toasted Rusiko as the paragon of Georgian womanhood, it was impossible not to agree.

She also denied that Merab Kostava had been a close friend of Gamsakhurdia. There had been times when they were friends, she said, but there was also much conflict between the two nationalist leaders. 'Zviad always had to be the dictator of his small circle, and now he is president, he has to be dictator of a larger circle, Georgia.'

They asked me what I thought about Shevardnadze, and like most Westerners, I expressed a high opinion of the man. Georgians, who were ruled by him as the tough Party boss of the republic, are more cynical, though they admit that he is extremely clever.

'He became foreign minister and knew nothing, no foreign languages,' said Erekle. 'Within a month you would have thought he was truly familiar with France, with America, with Italy. He is very clever. But he no longer represents Georgia, and we hope, but do not expect, that he will help us.'

Zeinab emerged from the kitchen with my favourite Georgian dessert: the wonderful *nigozis muraba*, walnuts in syrup. These are made from whole walnuts picked while still green, and marinated repeatedly in slaked lime and water before eventually being boiled, still in the shell, with sugar. This process darkens the nut to the colour of a black olive and provides a thick sweet syrup, spiced with cloves, cardamom and vanilla. Teeth sink luxuriously through the syrup and encounter only a slight resistance with the shell; the reward is the dense succulence of the nut within, now moistened to the texture of a marron glacé.

I mentioned that this was the first time in weeks that I had eaten anything sweet. Rusiko leant across the table. 'That is because we have no sugar. We have no oil, no petrol, no fish, nothing. But we have Gamsakhurdia, so we have everything.' The irony was delicate but savage. Even a bite into a walnut had its political interpretation. In Georgia politics penetrated everything; it had become a national obsession, especially among those who believed that Gamsakhurdia was an unmitigated disaster for their country. Nationalism was a vehicle that had taken Georgia to independence, but to carry the republic beyond fine words and passionate sentiments, a different philosophy was called for. Gamsakhurdia had no ideas other than his own sense of mission and its dreadful underside, his hatred and fear of those who disagreed with him. There was not only anger among those who saw through the president's windy rhetoric; there was shame, and that was much more telling.

Of course the volatile Georgians exaggerated their plight. Nobody was starving, yet, and Gamsakhurdia, for all his faults, was not another Stalin, as some of his most hysterical opponents liked to claim. The feasting may not have been as extravagant as in the past, but food and drink, although expensive, were cheaper than elsewhere in the Soviet Union. Nevertheless, Gamsakhurdia's rigidity and intellectual bankruptcy had brought Georgia to a standstill. Disdainful of Russia and incapable of developing trading relationships with the rest of the world, he was isolating a country which had, in the past, combined nationalist fervour with cultural catholicity. It had dispatched its finest young painters to Paris in the 1920s, it produced and performed Shakespeare brilliantly at its best theatres, its intellectuals (including Gamsakhurdia) were well informed about literature and culture in Europe, its scientists and researchers avidly sought contacts with their counterparts in Britain and America. Gamsakhurdia the politician was turning his back on all that. The economy was in decline and cultural life, once the pride of Georgia, was frozen. His only policy was to bicker. The fears of those who believed Georgia was rapidly being turned into a new Albania were not unfounded.

PART TWO

10 Normal Situation

'Problem. Problem'. That was all they would tell me. Aeroflot officials are notoriously uncommunicative. I was at Moscow airport at 5 a.m. to catch the 7 a.m. flight to Yerevan, but the check-in desk was refusing to take my luggage. A young man shepherding a small Japanese group muttered for my benefit, 'Aeroflot, very wonderful airline.'

Whenever I asked for information, the officials registered my request but ignored it. I spotted two Americans checking in for a flight to Dagestan, and I asked one of them, who spoke excellent Russian, to take up my cause.

'You want information? Have you been to the Soviet Union before?'

I nodded.

'Well, then. Apparently your flight has been delayed, and it'll be delayed for as long as they want it to be delayed. You won't get any more information than that.'

I resigned myself to a long wait. All available seating was occupied by sleeping bodies left over from the previous evening's non-flights. I tried to make myself comfortable on top of a large sack of rice belonging to a dozing Vietnamese. A few minutes later there was an encouraging development – I was summoned back to the desk and told to check in my luggage.

Free now to go up to the departure lounge and cafeteria, I joined the Americans, who were embassy officials on a spree. I asked at the counter for tea or coffee. There was none, I was told curtly, although Aeroflot officials at the next table were steaming their noses over glasses of hot tea.

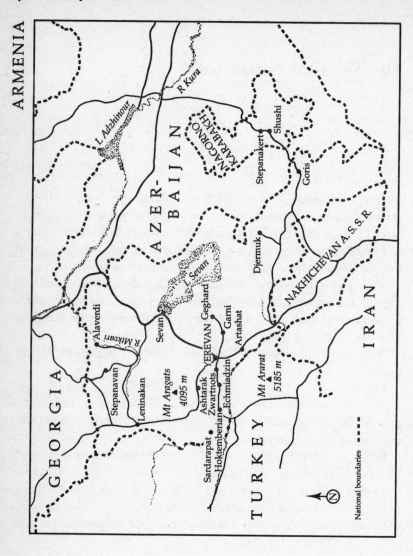

YEREVAN

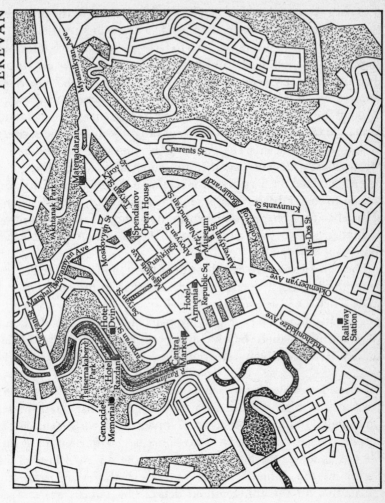

'That's Aeroflot for you,' sighed the American. 'All the problems of the Soviet Union wrapped up inside a single organisation.'

The young man had never been to Georgia but was well informed about the situation there. All Russians, he told me, were convinced that all Georgians were racketeers. There was a sizeable Georgian community in Moscow, and not long ago a rumour had swept through the city that all Georgians were to be granted refugee status in the United States. It had taken considerable diplomatic severity to inform supplicants that nothing of the kind was on offer. Meanwhile Armenians, another rumour had it, were to be given parcels of land in Pasadena. Whereupon many Armenians had rushed to the embassy to apply for their hand-out, and the young official had been charged with explaining to them that homesteading had ended a century ago and was not about to be revived in suburban southern California.

The Americans were called for their flight, and I returned to the departure lounge. I queued outside an office in the hall. I didn't know what the office was for, but all queues in Russia are worth joining. Inside I found a mighty woman behind a desk, and when I asked for information she actually picked up a phone and made an inquiry. There was no information, she eventually told me. I should wait.

I waited, positioning myself as far as possible from the screens blasting out rock videos. I sat among Angolans, Vietnamese, Ghanaians, Indians, Poles and Germans with an inexhaustible supply of lager and brandy. Two hours later I queued up again. There was news: the flight would take off at 8 p.m. I headed off glumly to the Intourist office to ask whether there was any explanation for this thirteen-hour delay. The woman was sympathetic but couldn't enlighten me. The plane from Yerevan had failed to arrive, so the flight was delayed. I settled down with a long Dickens novel. At 5.15 the Intourist official rushed up. A plane had unexpectedly arrived and would be leaving for Armenia at 6.30; we had to hurry. Minutes later I was out on the tarmac next to the plane. A row was developing between the waiting passengers and the stewardesses standing in the door of the plane, who were forbidding us to board. A few exceptions were made in the case of small children vulnerable to the freezing temperatures on a November evening in Moscow, but the white-bearded Indian bishop standing next to me was left to shiver.

The baggage had been loaded, but unfortunately there was no fuel, and it was unclear whether fuel would be forthcoming. Hence the reluctance to allow passengers to board. While I was grumbling to the bishop about the confusion, the increasingly drunk German Red Cross workers behind me remarked that thirteen hours was a modest delay by Moscow-Yerevan standards: the previous year they had waited forty-eight hours for their flight.

A young Armenian standing nearby explained: 'This plane belongs to the Armenian branch of Aeroflot. It was bought after Armenia became independent. So now the Aeroflot authorities say, "You want to be independent? Fine. Be independent. You must also find your independent fuel."'

A fuel truck eventually arrived and at 7.15, thoroughly chilled, we were allowed to board. I was naively surprised to find at least a hundred army officers and other dignitaries and their wives already comfortably seated. Passengers continued to trickle on for about an hour and a half, followed by the police, who threw some of them off again. At nine, the top cop, with much-studded epaulettes riding his shoulderblades, began shouting at us and whacking the seats with his truncheon. Apparently, some people had boarded who were not entitled to do so, and they had to get off. There was a slow trickle of passengers towards the door. At ten we took off. Passengers continued to stroll about the plane as we roared, soared and banked over Moscow. In-flight movies took the form of two American films shown in black and white, but we were allowed to see only half of each. There were no headsets, so we were all compelled to listen to the relentless voiceover, a single Russian monotone obscuring all the dialogue.

Moonlight threw a gleaming silvery sheen over the snowy slopes and crevasses of the Caucasus, which I glimpsed through a cloudless sky. We landed at 12.15 Moscow time, but Armenia, although at the same longitude as Georgia which pitches its clocks one hour ahead of

Moscow, adds on one more hour as an energy conservation measure. My guide Arman and his driver were still waiting, assuring me that they were well used to such delays. Indeed, just two months earlier Arman had been stranded in Moscow for a week and had taken the train instead, a dangerous 100-hour journey which he couldn't recommend.

Even in the middle of the night, as we drove in to Yerevan from Zwartnots Airport, there were shashlik stands, the skewered meat turning over a spattering yellow blaze. Arman had booked me in at the Hotel Dvin, the only one in town with hot water. The room was fine, equipped with a television and refrigerator, but there was no heat and no hot water. Had Erekle been here he would have smiled and murmured, 'Normal situation.'

The Georgians, perhaps out of excessive pride, had thought it peculiar that I also proposed to visit their neighbours to the south, the Armenians. I hadn't been in Armenia for long before I found similar attitudes among the Armenians. Each culture seemed to regard the other as uncouth, and the Armenians certainly distrusted the Georgians. Outwardly the two societies have much in common, quite apart from a shared frontier. Both are ancient Christian cultures, with long literary and artistic traditions.

Georgians were rarely encountered outside the Soviet Union. Despite their identification with European culture and their passion for Shakespeare, they travelled little; their cosmopolitanism was most obviously manifested at the level of the mafiosi quickstep, for they were the acknowledged masters of the Soviet black market. The Armenians, like the Jews, were a nation with a vast diaspora, with ancient communities flung about the world, from California to Iran to France. Relatively isolated by the ranges of the Caucasus, Armenia was geographically more remote than Georgia. There was no Black Sea from which to sail to the Mediterranean; there were no palm trees swaying along an Armenian shoreline – the terrain was harsh and extreme. So was the climate: Yerevan, 1000 metres up, enjoyed North African summers and Baltic winters. Georgia was the master of its territory, but Armenia's hold on its lands had always been precarious. The turn of the century had been marked, horrifically, by the genocide perpetrated by the Turks, but now the threat was coming from the east, from Azerbaijan, and the conflict was focused on the disputed status of Nagorno-Karabakh.

The only manifestation of that conflict in Yerevan in November 1991 was the blockade. Oil and gas were failing to reach Armenia, lack of heating was ubiquitous, power cuts routine. That first morning I kept warm by taking a long introductory walk and returned to the hotel at lunchtime so that Arman could present me to Kevork Zakoyan. In Tbilisi Svetlana had operated independently, despite her association with the official Friendship Society. In Armenia it was the Friendship Society itself which had invited me, and Mr Zakoyan was its acting director. Arman was charged with looking after me and keeping me happy. He was adept at welcomes, outgoing and talkative, well armed with assurances and encouragements. He was a forty-year-old globe trotter who had spent years in Africa and India, and had clearly been sufficiently trusted to be given foreign assignments and rewarded with a country house. He advertised his wealth, such as it was, by wearing a sumptuous leather jacket; meanwhile he and his family lived in a single room in a tall modern block near the city centre.

Kevork Zakoyan was a more formal figure. Except on days when he was tired and tetchy, he looked younger than his forty-five years. Arman, with his Nixonian jowls, was developing a touch of sleek plumpness, but Zakoyan was slender and vigorous, with only his lightly lined face to indicate his true age. Remarkably, for an official charged with furthering good relations with foreign countries, he spoke no European languages, but like Arman he had travelled widely.

After introductions were completed, we walked upstairs to the restaurant, only to find it closed. The manager had no explanation to offer, so we walked over to the Hotel Razdan, located in a nearby cul-de-sac on the edge of the Razdan gorge. There was no sign to identify this elegant fourteen-storey tower as a hotel. Like other establishments of its kind in Russian cities, it was a hotel for the use of the government and its guests. In 1979, as a member of a small delegation sent to Moscow, I was lodged in a similarly anonymous and equally comfortable hotel, the Krasnopresnenskaya. The Dvin was dreary, ill-lit and rather grubby. The Razdan was modern and well maintained, not as luxurious as the Metekhi Palace in Tbilisi, but bright and comfortable.

The lunch was good. Any hardships being experienced by Armenians as a whole were not in evidence here. There were plates of tomatoes, parsley, cheese, greens in a yogurt dressing, sausage and tongue, olives, cabbage, and plenty of brown bread. The main course was a slab of minced meat with fried noodles, washed down with a bottle of soft, attractive Areni red wine. As we ate, Mr Zakoyan eagerly explained how the Friendship Society was being revitalised now it was independent of Moscow. There were some influential Armenians who felt the Society was superfluous, but he had persuaded the government to keep it alive. Because it is not government directed, the Society can further government aims while absolving the authorities of responsibility for its projects and actions. The Society, for example, supports the government's wish for closer ties with Armenia's age-old enemy, Turkey, and can work with the government rather than at its behest.

As we were finishing our lunch, Yura, the hotel cook, joined us at our table. Arman told me the gravel-voiced cook was one of the finest in Armenia, so I should ask him about the country's gastronomic traditions. Lamb, he told me, used to be the most popular meat, but had been displaced by pork, beef and chicken. Fish is less plentiful than it used to be, although a few days later I would be served a delicious fish from Lake Sevan called *sig*; a large trout, it was introduced in 1968 and has flourished despite the pollution that afflicts Armenia's largest lake. Garlic and peppers, Yura told me, were essential ingredients in Armenian cookery, but high prices were restricting their use; garlic now cost sixty roubles per kilo. Flour and sugar are in short supply, so cakes and sweets and stewed fruits are becoming rare. Good quality meat products such as sausages and hams have virtually disappeared from the markets, and he admitted that the cold sausage he had served us was mediocre. Milk and yogurt do occasionally turn up at the markets, but you must queue for ages to get your hands on any.

He had a question for me about English cooking. Was it true that a popular British dish consisted of cutlets composed of chicken tongues? I said that I had never encountered it in England, though I couldn't answer for the Scots. Still, it sounded unlikely, if only as an economic proposition. Our learned exchanges continued, and as he rose to return to his kitchen Yura invited me to eat at the Razdan whenever I wished. Arman said that this was an offer I should grasp, as the food was much better here than at the Dvin.

After lunch Arman's driver took us to the square in front of the Spendiarov opera house, a rather ugly building from the 1930s of which the Armenians are very proud. In the small park across from the opera house the weekend art market was still active. Laid out on tables and benches along the paths are examples of artwork supposedly with a commercial appeal. For the most part the paintings were soupy garish landscapes and glossy nudes, but a handful of abstracts made concessions to more sophisticated tastes. The handicrafts were marginally better: frames of dried flower arrangements, ceramics, jewellery, accomplished wood carvings and large, well-worn carpets. A sign by one table welcomed barter. As in Tbilisi, art books were very expensive.

As we strolled through the park, Arman expressed considerable dissatisfaction with the changes that had taken place in Armenia. Land has been returned to the farmers and peasantry, but this has not resulted in cheaper food. Bribery and corruption persisted. Many people, in his view, had entered politics with the clear intention of lining their pockets.

'But at least under the new system,' I said, 'you can throw the rascals out after a few years if you don't like them. Under the old system you had people lining their pockets until the day they died.'

Arman wasn't convinced. He told me how parliamentary deputies were beholden to local rather than national interests. I had to tell Arman that it was no different in other democracies. He also complained that there were members of parliament who had never once spoken and who often fell asleep during debates. I said that there were members of the British House of Commons who hadn't opened their mouths in years, except to order food and drink, and who used the chamber as a place for sleeping off over-indulgence. Indeed, many debates were so tedious that it would take heroic self-discipline to avoid falling asleep on the benches.

'But it is not so forgivable here because conditions are more extreme. We have serious problems. And now everybody wants to look back and blame the Communists for everything. Yes, there were many bad things under the Communists, but not everything was bad. There were Party members who served the people well. We must have reform, but those in favour of reform should adopt what was good in the old system rather than condemn every aspect of it out of hand.'

I was back at the Dvin by five-thirty, and at eight wandered across to the Razdan for dinner. The manager was none too pleased to see me at such a late hour, so I asked for Yura. The cook came rushing out of the kitchen and sat down opposite me. We beamed benignly at each other, while I tried to communicate that I had come in the hope of getting some dinner. Yura returned to the kitchens, and a short while later a waiter appeared with kebabs, thick ropes of spicy minced meat wrapped in the delicious and chewy handkerchief bread known as *lavash*. My meal over, I returned to my chilly room, threw a blanket over my shoulders, and watched American basketball on television.

Two of the German Red Cross workers, also lodged at the Hotel Dvin, were enjoying a vodka breakfast the next morning, swigging from a bottle while hauling their luggage to the van that would take them north to Stepanavan, where their team was building 500 houses and a kindergarten to replace those destroyed in the 1988 earthquake. I had a vodka-free breakfast with Arman in the Dvin restaurant, which had reopened. The manager explained that he had closed up the day before because most of his staff had been off sick. Lack of hot water was also complicating matters in the kitchens. Arman and I sat hunched in our coats as we spooned in a kind of porridge. Our breath condensed in the air as we talked.

Arman reported that tension between Armenia and Azerbaijan was rising again, since an Azeri helicopter had been shot down a few days earlier over Nagorno-Karabakh with considerable loss of life. The original Armenian explanation for the crash had been fog, but the Azeris claimed a rocket had brought down the helicopter. Since the twenty-one dead included not only Azeri officials but representatives of the Russian Federation who were trying to broker a solution, the incident was being taken very seriously. In Baku there was mounting pressure to put Azerbaijan on a war footing with its neighbour. There were rumours that Azeri troops were gathering along the border.

Like South Ossetia, Nagorno-Karabakh was an enclave within the boundaries of another republic. It differed from South Ossetia in two important respects: the Armenian population of Karabakh was proportionately far higher than the Ossetian population of South Ossetia; and whereas South Ossetia shared a border with North Ossetia, Karabakh was entirely surrounded by Azeri territory and separated from Armenia by a strip of land about ten kilometres wide. This made contact between Armenia and Karabakh difficult, since the only access was now by air, and the hazards of air travel in that part of the world were all too evident.

The historical claim of Armenia to Karabakh was strong. In 1923 95 per cent of the population had been Armenian. Since then the proportion had declined to about 85 per cent, but the mountainous province was filled with about 4000 Armenian monuments which were centuries old. After World War I the Armenians, exhausted and depleted by genocide and war, agreed to let Azerbaijan enjoy provisional control of the enclave. From then on Azerbaijan, soon to become a Soviet republic, kept up the pressure to have Karabakh included within its borders. There had been periods when Moslem shepherds had grazed their flocks on the hills of Karabakh, so Azerbaijan had some historical claim to the region, though less powerful than that of the Armenians. When the briefly independent Armenia was about to submit to the Soviet embrace, a compromise was worked out, in which the Azeri leader agreed to allow Karabakh and the region of Nakhichevan, tucked between Armenia and Turkey, to be regarded as part of Armenia. But subsequent treaties disregarded this offer, and in October 1921 Nakhichevan – after yet another massacre of Armenians instigated by the Turks – was put under Azeri control as a sop to Turkish sensitivities, while the problem of Karabakh was simply ignored. Stalin came up with a solution, proposing that Karabakh should become an autonomous region within the republic of Azerbaijan. And so it remained, an island of Christian Armenians within a sea of often hostile Moslem Azeris.

Karabakh Armenians complained bitterly of their suffering under Azeri administration. Their so-called autonomy was meaningless, as they were entirely at the mercy of the Azeris. Economic life was stifled, the teaching of Armenian history forbidden, churches closed, television programmes from Yerevan jammed, and the population was subject to random violence from the Azeris who moved into the region in an attempt to dilute its Armenian identity. Compared to the rest of Azerbaijan, the region was seriously undeveloped. In the 1960s the Karabakh Armenians took the bold step of petitioning the central authorities in Moscow as well as the government of Armenia for amelioration of their position. Nothing was done. Mikhail Gorbachev's rise to power seemed at first to offer them some hope, but the new Soviet leader regarded these disputes between nationalities as a headache and a distraction. He had no inclination to start tampering with borders. The pursuit of *perestroika* did, however, encourage the 200,000 people of Karabakh to take matters into their own hands, and in February 1988 the regional soviet passed a resolution calling for reunification with Armenia. Fears of Armenian expansionism were countered by observations that the large Armenian communities within Georgia were not calling for secession or reunification; it was only the Azeri denial of basic rights to the Karabakh Armenians which had provoked the problem.

In Moscow the Politburo was unmoved and refused to contemplate any change in the status of the region. By this time Armenian intellectuals in Yerevan were taking up the cause and responded to the Politburo's intransigence with a series of demonstrations. Any chance of a peaceful resolution of the dispute became negligible when, on 27 February, Armenians living in the Azerbaijani town of

Sumgait, not far from Baku, were brutally attacked by Azeris, who outnumbered them by ten to one. The pretext was a radio report that two Azeris had been killed in clashes in Karabakh. It turned into an old-fashioned massacre, although it was acknowledged that many Azeris had come to the rescue of their Armenian neighbours, often at considerable risk to themselves. Nobody knows how many died in Sumgait; the official figure of twenty-six Armenians and six Azeris was widely regarded as a gross underestimate. Many are convinced that the KGB had a hand in instigating the slaughter, and the pogrom sent shivers down the spines of a people who must have hoped that massacres and genocide were a thing of the past. The large Armenian community in Baku was rightfully alarmed, and within six months 100,000 Armenians, half their population in Baku, had arrived as refugees in Armenia.

The demonstrations continued and strikes were organised by the newly formed Karabakh Committee. In June 1988 the Supreme Soviet of Armenia, by accepting the resolution passed in February by the assembly in Karabakh, forged closer ties between the autonomous region and Armenia. Karabakh experienced a cultural revival; television links were renewed and Armenian books were on sale for the first time in years. On 12 July Karabakh formally seceded from Azerbaijan and changed its name to Artsakh, a name routinely used by many Armenians today. Of course none of this was acceptable to the authorities in Moscow, who declared such moves illegal. Soviet interior ministry troops (OMON) were dispatched to the region, sparking confrontations with Armenian demonstrators. Azeri hostility towards Armenians still living in Azerbaijan continued, especially after a man implicated in the Sumgait massacre was sentenced to death in November 1988. By the end of the year about half the Armenian population of Azerbaijan had fled. The movement of refugees was matched by about the same number of Azeris from Armenia. Many Armenian refugees settled in the north of the country where their plight was compounded by the appalling earthquake in December 1988.

Early in 1989 the Soviet authorities instituted direct rule over Karabakh, but the administration reverted to Azerbaijan in

November. There was ample evidence that Azeri and Soviet troops were taking part in joint operations against Armenian villages in or close to Karabakh, claiming that they were merely disarming those in illegal possession of arms. By now Karabakh and Azerbaijan were virtually at war, and the Armenian death toll would rise into the hundreds, and by late 1991, to a thousand and more. As in South Ossetia, both sides would regale anyone who cared to listen with atrocity stories featuring their opponents. In January 1990 there were more killings of Armenian civilians in Baku itself, and those who had not fled after the Sumgait pogrom now wasted no time. Some 360,000 Armenians had fled from Azerbaijan, and all but 100,000 had settled in Armenia.

While the persecution and deportation of Karabakh Armenians continued, the Azeri authorities veered from a conciliatory line to a tough stand and back again. President Ayaz Mutalibov said he was prepared to negotiate with the Armenians, but added that the secession of Karabakh was unacceptable. Although the Armenians had complained about the partiality of Soviet troops in the conflict, the dissolution of the Soviet Union in the autumn of 1991 made the situation worse; their refusal to intervene encouraged armed bands on both sides, and the fighting worsened.

Now with the shooting down of the helicopter, even those doing their best to mediate were joining the lists of victims. The situation seemed increasingly intractable. Moreover, whereas the fighting in South Ossetia impinged little on daily life in the rest of Georgia, the conflict in Karabakh had a direct impact on the Armenian economy. The Azeris had long been maintaining a blockade against Armenia. Previously, 85 per cent of the republic's oil and gas and other supplies had been transported via Azerbaijan. No longer. Sometimes the Azeris would lift the blockade briefly, and a few goods would get through, but this had not happened for months. The only other access to Armenia, apart from air freight which was inordinately costly, was through Georgia, and that route too was proving erratic. Armenians believed that Georgian officials and bandits (if the two could be distinguished in their minds) were stealing goods destined for Armenia, although Georgians I subsequently spoke to indignantly denied the accusations. The uncertainties of the Georgian route could be debated, but no one could doubt the reality of the Azeri blockade. We could feel the consequences: the cold rooms, the power cuts, the closed factories and schools.

11 My House is Your House

There were plans afoot to move me to the Razdan. I told Arman that I could manage at the Dvin, but he replied, 'After two days, okay, but after ten days, maybe not okay.' They were hatched at the offices of the Friendship Society in an elaborate old building on Abovian Street, where Mr Zakoyan was waiting for us. There was a long discussion about what was to be done with me, and after letters had been typed to establish whatever credentials were required of potential guests at the Razdan, we took them to offices elsewhere for authorisation. We drove along broad streets lined with buildings faced in buff and dirty pink tufa, a stone in which Armenia, like Georgia, is rich. Here the façades had been given an Armenian stamp by constructing lofty rounded arches which rested on capitals as thick as an elephant's foot. Other buildings, especially along Bagramyan, showed the influence of heavy-handed Soviet neo-classicism.

There was no lack of traffic congestion despite the fuel shortage and the fact that petrol cost three times as much as in Georgia. I once asked Arman which trolleybus I should take to reach the centre from my hotel, and he told me that he had no idea as he never used public transportation. Inefficiencies and breakdowns plagued the tram and bus services, and those who could afford to travel by car had no hesitation in doing so, even if it did entail lengthy waits in queues for petrol.

Autumn was fading into winter, and there was a constant cold haze over the city. The unclouded sky resembled a dusty and washed-out baby blue blanket. Sometimes the sun filtered through to penetrate the general chill, though not with sufficient force to persuade office workers to remove their coats as they sat behind their desks. A lucky few could warm their feet at small electric coil heaters which provided puffs of warmth within a two-foot radius.

While government officials were considering my status, Arman took me sightseeing. We drove east out of Yerevan, past the suburban high-rises now swollen by refugees from Azerbaijan. A few years ago the population of the city stood at just over a million; now it had gained a further 500,000 inhabitants. The price of land and housing, always in short supply in this mountainous little republic, had skyrocketed.

A cobbled road climbed steeply out of the city into a treeless landscape of rolling hills and moorland. The village houses, as in Georgia, were quite spacious, though the verandahs were more cramped, reflecting the less benign climate of Armenia. They were built from tufa blocks, often of different colours including black and orange, so that tortoiseshell cats would have been perfectly concealed against their sides. Many houses were unfinished, as the blockades had disrupted the supply of building materials. Everywhere there were signs of improvisation, and the results resembled an orderly scrap heap. Old stone walls had been patched with stretches of concrete and wire netting; roofs were of corrugated iron or wood, or both. The larger houses were set within gardens filled with peach, apricot and apple trees, among vegetable plots where cucumbers and tomatoes flourished. The commercial greenhouses dotted along the hillsides had closed for lack of fuel, reducing further the supply of tomatoes, peppers, herbs and flowers.

As we gained height, the snowy peak of Ararat emerged through the haze, its great fuzzy-edged cone filling the horizon. I recognised it from photographs, but checked for confirmation with Arman. It struck me as odd that he hadn't pointed out this most celebrated feature of the Armenian landscape. Perhaps his remark, 'It is now in Turkey', contained the explanation.

About twenty-five kilometres from the capital we came to Garni, a small but perfectly proportioned first-century classical temple perched on the edge of Asia, on a spur above tall cliffs. A long way below the River Azat skitters through the valley. In the fourth century, just after Armenia adopted Christianity, the site was adopted as the summer residence of the kings. The temple was destroyed by an earthquake in 1679 and only reconstructed in the 1970s. This reconstruction was painstaking but clumsy. It clearly wasn't possible to match the texture of the new stone with the more weathered stone of the ten-foot plinth. Moreover, the new sections are battleship-grey in colour, whereas the original masonry and carvings are honeyed. Most of the twenty-four columns are new, but they support original sections of the capitals and lion-headed friezes. A few paces away are the remains of third-century baths, the floors covered in mosaics depicting fish and sea gods and lettered with Greek inscriptions. Despite the exposure of the site to the elements and to the predations of man, I found none of the graffiti which disfigure so many Georgian monuments.

From Garni we continued up the winding Azat gorge to Geghard. This monastery complex, which once supported a school and a famous scriptorium, cowers beneath awesome black cliffs jaggedly crenellated by erosion. The complex is fortified, and surrounded by cliff faces and, closer in, by high stone walls. Within the cliffs are caves where local people and their livestock took refuge in times of war, reaching them with ropes they pulled up after them. Everywhere you look there are *khachkars*, the wonderful carved ornamental crosses of stone which are such a powerful feature of the Armenian landscape. They perform numerous functions. Some are inlaid in church walls; others are tombstones, or commemorate historical events or generous donations to a church, or mark crossroads. It's said that no ornamental design is ever copied from one *khachkar* to another; with thousands of these crosses surviving, the range of arabesque and other sinewy stylised ornament is astonishing. There's a distinct resemblance to the Celtic crosses found in Irish churchyards, but the carving of the *khachkars* is often more intricate.

Some kind of church has existed here since the fourth century, but the present church, hunched and clenched against the cliffside, dates from 1215 and the subsidiary chapels carved into the rock were created a few decades later. The portals and much of the exterior arcading are carved with birds and bulls and inlaid with *khachkars* and inscriptions. The interior is stern and dark, since black basalt is not exactly a luminous building material. The church is divided into chambers, with a substantial stone portal leading from the arcaded nave (which some call a narthex) into the choir. The squarish choir is lit by deep-set lancets within the cupola, whereas light crawls down on to the nave from a lantern over the crossing. The drum beneath this lantern is sculptural in form, with extraordinary chunky tiered carving which mounts from the tops of the arcades to the lantern, thick with brackets and pendants and sharply angled projections. Set into the walls are more *khachkars* and inscriptions, hard to make out in the gloom, except where the tendrils of stone catch the inconsistent light.

Doors lead from the nave into the churches gouged from the cliffs. The floors are simply the solid rock of the caves. One chapel is dominated by an extraordinary relief carving of two lions, linked by a knotted chain like a leash; beneath the knot a stately eagle rests its claws on a lamb. It's believed that this carving represents the coat of arms of the princely Proshian family, who owned the monastery in the thirteenth century. The cupola which illuminates the chapel is extravagantly carved with geometrical patterns. Further west, and reached through a separate entrance from the main church, another cupolaed chamber is designed in an entirely different fashion, with four arches on each side of the squarish space intersecting in each corner. The Russian writer Andrei Bitov has captured the experience of standing here and looking upward: 'The arcs of the walls extended into the dusk, and the columns rushed upward to become the dome, from whose summit the round blue eye of the sky gazed at me. All this was inside the cliff, all of one integral stone.'

On leaving the dark dank rock churches, I walked around to the back of the church, where steep worn steps climb the cliffside past more *khachkars* to a series of tiny hollowed-out chapels. From a terrace a tunnel leads into yet another domed church with a central skylight. Strangely angular string courses dip and swerve above the rounded arches. The heavy capitals are decorated with abstract stencilled patterns gouged out of the stone, and an inscription identifies the architect: Galdzag.

The cowering church, its enclosed terraces, and its secluded back-against-the-wall chapels spoke volumes about living conditions in mediaeval Armenia, when terror must have been the only constant in one's daily life. Even the climate was hostile; it had been cool in Yerevan, but here there were ice patches along the ground.

We returned to the car and headed back down the valley. A small stone public lavatory was inscribed with the insulting English slogan: Turkish Ambassy [*sic*]. As we bumped along the badly patched road, I was surprised to see shards of glass strewn across the tarmac every few hundred yards. It seemed odd that accidents should occur with such regularity. Then I spotted a bus ahead. The rear window was shattered and the remaining chunks of glass were being prised out by children who tipped the jagged fragments on to the road as the bus sped on. It must have been enormous fun for the children, and hazardous for drivers behind.

Armenian buses would be turned down by Rent-a-Wreck. Like most encountered in the former Soviet Union, they are manufactured by the Hungarian firm of Ikarus. Nowadays the Hungarians, increasingly Western-oriented, demand hard currency for their wares, including spare bus parts, and Armenia, like the other republics, has very little currency at its disposal. If spare parts are unobtainable, the buses must be taken out of service, which is one reason why public transport in Armenia is in such poor shape.

That afternoon I moved into the Hotel Razdan. My room was smaller than the one I had just vacated, but better furnished and blessed with hot water. The television picked up two cable channels, one of which specialised in congressional reports from Washington alternating with recipes for quails in French; the other was CNN. I soon discovered that the hotel was part of an enclave of privilege. At the top of the cul-de-sac stood another unmarked building of smart modern design which I took for well-built flats. No sign of sagging balconies, stained concrete, or haphazard patchwork of corrugated iron. It was a hospital, and its exemplary condition signalled that it was still reserved for the use of government officials and their families. Arman told me that one of the surgeons was a mate of his, a useful connection should illness strike his family. Just beyond the hotel entrance the lane was blocked by a metal gate guarded by police twenty-four hours a day. Beyond the sliding gate I could see landscaped grounds and the green roofs of spacious villas. When I asked Arman about this compound, he said he had no idea. When I pressed him, he put the question to one of our drivers, who came up with the unsurprising answer that these were the summer houses of government officials. Democracy may have come to Armenia, but privilege remains entrenched.

The door opened. We stepped from the unlit hallway, where I had been warned to duck to avoid cracking my head against an invisible concrete beam, into the aromatic heat of the flat, scented with roasting meats and pungent spices, loud with the yap of television. Roupig was standing in the threshold, hands clasped in front of his chest, face beaming with the pleasures of welcome, the opportunities for hospitality. Introduced to me, a complete stranger, probably not even expected that evening, he leant down from his great height, grasped my hand and murmured, smiling, 'My house is your house.' For the rest of the evening he behaved as though that were true.

I had been appropriated for the evening by Rita Balayan, who was also staying at the Razdan. Somehow she had discovered that I was a fellow guest and had invited me along to Roupig's. Rita, born in Beirut, had left with her husband and children during the civil war in 1975, and settled near Washington. She devoted her inexhaustible energies to bringing Armenian causes to the attention of those with power and influence in Washington.

She was travelling with an entourage. Her son Raffi, with his large dark eyes and shadowy beard, looked more Armenian than his mother, but his appearance was the consequence of fatigue as well as genetic inheritance. After ten days in Armenia with a mother who seemed to require no sleep, he was exhausted. Rita strode; her retinue stumbled in her wake. For another member of the entourage, Charles Garoian, visiting Armenia was a spiritual homecoming. His parents had escaped from the massacres in western Armenia, migrating via Paris to Fresno, California, where Charles was born. Until the age of six, he told me, he spoke only Armenian. As he grew up, he was unable to resist the Americanisation which the United States then demanded of its immigrants, but the reality of Armenia dwelt in the stories and memories of his parents, which they patiently relayed to him.

Now in his late forties, Charles was in Armenia for the first time, and he was glowing. He had disinterred the language of his childhood and was communicating with only slight hesitation with the Armenians around us. More importantly, he was discovering that all the things his desolated parents had spoken of with such sadness and longing were indeed rooted in reality, and he was learning that the mental map he had carried with him was not fictive at all. The culture his parents had striven to preserve, with only partial success, beneath the skies of California, was not a nostalgic recollection but a continuum.

There was more than filial piety to Charles's visit. A specialist in visual education, he was here to study the Children's Art Museum founded by Henrik Igitian in Yerevan. It was the first museum of its kind in the world, established in association with a number of aesthetic education centres in Armenia which offered classes to both adults and children. Charles was in awe of Igitian, to whom he gave much of the credit for the revival of Armenian culture after decades of Soviet suppression, and would be collaborating with Igitian on a book about his visionary undertakings.

Rita took me round the room. The tall, elderly, dark-suited man with a self-consciously dignified demeanour was Dr Karlen Dallakian, a distinguished literary historian and critic, who ran an institute at the Academy of Sciences studying the history and culture of the Armenian diaspora. This linked him with Roupig, whose job involved maintaining contact between Armenia and its long-dispersed communities abroad. The diffident man with the broad shy smile was Levon Malkhasian, the president of the Armenian Jazz Club and a disciple of Oscar Peterson, whose records, he told me, he avidly collected. The old man in the armchair was Roupig's father, who doggedly watched television while waves of conviviality splashed around him.

The small, tense, red-faced man standing in a corner was Henrik Igitian himself. He looked very cross, and his grizzled beard was as peppery as his mood. My attempts to communicate with him were met with a brusqueness I interpreted as shyness. Later, after dinner, he handed me a business card – Senator Henrik Igitian, Honoured Art Critic – which I took as a conciliatory gesture. Charles had no doubt that Igitian was a national hero. Not only had he founded the Children's Art Museum and amassed, by hook or by crook, some 150,000 works from around the world, but he had established Armenia's Modern Art Museum in 1972. Whenever I walked past the modern concrete building which houses the museum on Mashtots Avenue, it was closed. Igitian, concerned that during Armenia's economic crisis it was no longer possible to control the interior climate of the building, had closed it and removed its contents to avoid any further neglect or damage to the collection. He was also a deputy to the Supreme Soviet in Moscow – hence his title – although a month later the job would cease to exist. Charles assured me that Igitian was renowned for his eloquence, his gift of oratory, his integrity, his power to communicate with people in all walks of life.

When it was time for the nine o'clock news, everybody gathered in a hushed circle to see if there were any fresh developments, especially in Karabakh. They watched and I sweltered. I had dressed in preparation for inadequately heated rooms, but Roupig's flat was as thickly warm as a greenhouse. Large brick flues, heated from stoves in the hallway, pummelled warmth into the living room and dining room – ugly intrusions into the bourgeois domesticity of the heavily furnished salons, but extremely effective.

A later section of the news featured an interview with Rita, who watched the transmission with some satisfaction. It wasn't really an interview. A man with a microphone asked a single question and Rita responded, almost without taking breath, for five minutes or more. When she finally stopped, her eloquence, in praise of the gallery of art and music which constituted modern Armenia thanks to Igitian and others, won her a burst of applause from her friends. The news over, Roupig, hands fluttering nervously, ushered us into the dining room, where we squeezed around a large table. A huge platter some three feet long, like a ship ploughing down the table, bore an explosion of vegetables and peppers and herbs, baroque swags of dripping, bulging growth. Glass vases were stuffed with carnations, with more blooms arranged in rings around the bases of the vases. Dishes were filled with hors d'oeuvres, many of them sprinkled with chopped walnuts. Such profligacy in a land of shortages was astounding, yet it was an expression of hospitality and generosity rather than ostentation. Who knew how many weeks or months the family had saved to welcome its guests in style?

Roupig, wincing with nervousness yet expansive in gesture and speech, proposed a toast to Professor Dallakian, whom he hailed as a great teacher, scholar, philosopher, diplomat and father figure to a generation. Rita had earlier described him to me as her mentor. Dallakian took the honeyed praise with graceful nods, oozing a satisfaction far more senatorial than Igitian's feistiness. Rita translated Roupig's toast for my benefit, and then asked me to follow his example. I replied that I would gladly do so in principle, but it was rather difficult, since I'd only just met the professor and knew nothing about him.

'This is the Armenian custom,' insisted Rita. 'I want you to toast this distinguished man.'

'Yes, with pleasure, but it's not going to be easy for me to make much sense –'

'Just do it.'

'Armenian coercion,' whispered Charles from across the table. There was no escape. I said I would propose instead a more general toast, which would of course include the Dallakians, and I thanked all my hosts for their hospitality. Rita nodded, said I had spoken well. She would have made it very clear, she intimated, had I not met her standards.

After the main course, a kind of rissole with rice, Levon moved to the piano, and many of the guests shifted on to the sofas around the sides of the room. Armenia's foremost jazz pianist boogied away, grinning hugely as we applauded. Meanwhile Roupig and his mother were scurrying into the dining room with dishes brimming with diamond-shaped pastries filled with chopped nuts, fresh and dried fruit, figs in syrup, walnuts and raisins. New to me was an acorn-shaped fruit called *pshat*, identified as the fruit of the oleaster. It tasted like a mouthful of talcum powder.

Henrik Igitian proposed a toast to love. Referring no doubt to Armenia, he said that we love a child all the more when it is sick. So even if a bomb were to devastate his land he would still love it deeply, and he wanted especially to toast Rita who had an ocean of love for Armenia.

'*Genartzet!*' And we raised our glasses.

Rita turned to me. Did I know what this Armenian word meant? Not exactly, but its context suggested it was a version of 'Cheers'.

She looked at me sternly. Toasts, she explained, reflected national character. The gloomy British wished for cheer, the liver-fatigued French desired *santé*, Arabs hoped for the cups of their chieftains, and Armenians, like the Jews, longed for life. '*Genartzet!*'

Levon, back at the piano, temporarily jettisoned his riffs and rags for a traditional Armenian song. Rita jumped to her feet, not to propose a toast but to dance, stretching out her arms and twisting them with almost Indian sensuousness, and shuffling either sideways or back and forth, according to whim. Charles, revelling in his recovered Armenian identity, was dancing alongside her, but after a couple of minutes of enthusiastic onlooking, I saw, to my dismay, that Rita's slinking form was edging in my direction. I tried to look away, but too late. She grabbed my wrist. Nobody argues with Rita, and my attempts to do so were dismissed with scorn. 'I'll teach you.' And she moved her feet about in a pattern as complex as a transistor circuit. I did my best – 'Just feel the rhythm,' she exhorted – but after a while she graciously allowed me to drift away and slither to a halt.

Charles came and sat beside me. He too had soon flagged. Days, even weeks, of hard work and hard play had worn him down. He recalled one feast at Lake Sevan that had continued for fourteen hours. Yet despite their hosts' insistence on fêting the Balayan party in the grandest fashion, he couldn't help feeling that all the boisterousness was in part an escape from the intractability of their position. Soviet domination had been exchanged for economic constraints and conflict with Azerbaijan. The Armenians he had met were impatient and frustrated by the government's inability, for perfectly understandable reasons, to make much progress restructuring the economy.

'Armenians are tired.'

The fresh graves I saw near the monument to the genocide the next morning were emblems of that weariness. Some of those who had died on Armenia's borders with Azerbaijan were buried here, and one newly turned grave was ringed, like the festive vases on Roupig's table, with carnations. The monument was erected in 1956 in the face of Soviet disapproval. Compliant with Soviet sensitivities to displays of nationalist pride, it carries no inscriptions but relies for its power on symbolic effect. A tall tapering obelisk rises sleekly, like the nose of Concorde. But it is not symmetrical, for a portion is splintered away from the rising needle; truncated, the splinter has slightly less bulk than the principal obelisk. This lesser portion symbolises Turkish Armenia, where the genocide took place, and the taller portion represents modern Armenia. Alongside the spire is a stupa-like basalt structure, curved and leaning in over a broad central wall. There are gaps between the twelve segments, each of which represents one of the former Armenian provinces. Within the well, which is open to the sky, a vigorous flame blazes day and night, despite the shortages of fuel, and bouquets are strewn around it. Every 24 April Armenians, led by political figures and the Catholicos, gather here to commemorate the massacres.

Armenia's history stretches so far back that its earliest days are obscure, but megalithic structures prove its antiquity. Some of the earliest examples of metalworking were excavated on Armenian soil. In the ninth century BC the tribes who lived here were united under the Urartu kingdom, which flourished for two centuries. Thereafter a series of invasions destabilised the country until, in the fifth

Lenin's head used to grace the frieze
on Georgia's Institute of Marxism-Leninism.
No longer.

Tengiz Kitovani bides his time at the Sea of Tbilisi.

Levan and Erekle

Local boy who made good:
the statue of Stalin in Gori.

The churches at Ananuri on
the Georgian Military Highway.

Keeping putschists and criminals at bay: barricades near the Parliament.

Yeranos and his family in Leninakan.
Passing a third winter in a wooden cabin.

Municipal buildings in Leninakan.

Ashot, Aram, Armine and Vladimir making their English guest welcome.

These sheep have only minutes to live:
the animal sacrifices at the church of St Gayane in Echmiadzin.

Christmas Day in Tbilisi, as Opposition gunmen advance
along Rustaveli Avenue.

Zviad Gamsakhurdia keeps up with the latest news in January 1992.

After the civil war:
the Georgian Parliament
and its gutted neighbours.

The shell of the Hotel Tbilisi.

Eduard Shevardnadze prepares
to chair Georgia's state council.

The church at Shushi, freshly
emptied of Azeri missile cases
in May 1992.

Latchin burns as Armenian troops establish
a corridor to Nagorno-Karabakh.

A donkey grazes close to the bridge near Latchin
where dozens died in the battles of May 1992.

century, it became a province of Persia. Alexander the Great, in vanquishing the Persians in the fourth century, brought Greek civilisation to Armenia, with lasting influence, as I had seen at Garni. In the first century BC King Tigran II reunited Armenia and expanded its territories in a spectacular way. His empire reached the shores of the Caspian to the east and the Mediterranean to the west. It was a short-lived grandeur, and in 66BC Tigran's forces were defeated by Pompey, and Armenia reverted to the buffered, battered existence that was to become the norm. To the west Armenia was constantly threatened by Turks, to the south by Kurds and Persians, and to the east by Mongols and other nomadic tribes.

None the less the Armenian kings maintained strong links with the Mediterranean, which assisted two crucial events in the nation's history: its adoption of Christianity as the state religion in roughly 301, and the invention in 404 of the Armenian alphabet by Mesrop Mashtots. As an outpost of Byzantium, it remained in the forefront of European intellectual and cultural life, despite periods of Arab, and thus Moslem, conquest. In 885 King Ashot Bagratuni inaugurated a dynasty which brought a renaissance of Armenian culture. In the tenth century the splendid city of Ani, now in Turkey, was established, filled with palaces and churches which succumbed, almost inevitably, to waves of Turkish depredations. In 1064 the city was destroyed, initiating the first Armenian diaspora.

There were few bright moments during the centuries that followed. The Mongol invasion of 1236 was followed a century later by Tamburlaine's even more devastating onslaught. Gradually the country, or what was left of it, split, with a substantial colony in Cilicia exercising more and more autonomy. Cilicia's independence was threatened just as often as the motherland, and by 1375 its period of sovereign authority was over. In 1554 the Turks razed Yerevan, and fifty years later it suffered the same fate at Persian hands. By the early seventeenth century the Persians were back in Armenia, which had become a pawn in the power struggle between Shah Abbas and the Ottoman empire, a conflict which ended with the virtual partition of the country in 1639. Eastern Armenia fell into Russian hands in 1828.

There are varying assessments of tsarist rule over Armenia in the nineteenth century. Russia imposed a fundamentally despotic régime, but it was more tolerant and progressive than the Persian and Ottoman régimes which preceded it. The historian Christopher Walker points out that Russian Armenia was an agricultural province which prospered under tsarist administration, while Armenian intellectuals abandoned provincial life in Yerevan for the more alluring commercial prospects of Baku or Tbilisi. In Baku it was they who developed the oil industry on which Azerbaijan's prosperity would be based. Yerevan in the early nineteenth century was scarcely a pearl of the east: it was an unsanitary little town of 12,000 inhabitants, but gradually its Russian masters improved conditions and established municipal facilities such as schools and hospitals. Yet, as in Georgia, there were determined attempts by the Russian authorities to stamp on Armenian culture and education, and dissatisfaction with Russification spawned social democratic and revolutionary resistance which, for obvious reasons, was usually clandestine. The Russians' most foolish move was to try to secularise the Armenian church, a policy guaranteed to win the lasting enmity of the entire population.

The sense that the Armenian heartland lay in Ottoman Turkey rather than in the province of Yerevan fuelled nationalist fervour. Conditions within Armenian Turkey, as eastern Armenians under Russian rule were well aware, were deteriorating. Ottoman laws prohibiting Christian subjects from bearing arms laid the Armenians open to attack and persecution, and their commercial prowess, especially in Constantinople, made them vulnerable to official extortion and punitive taxation. Their commercial and intellectual prominence, instead of winning respect and honour, had the opposite effect: they were easily set up as scapegoats by their imperial masters, who in some obscure way feared them.

The ensuing genocide remains inexplicable. From the 1890s onwards, any self-assertion by the Armenians of Turkey was ruthlessly suppressed. Pillage and massacres were usually attributed, especially in rural eastern Turkey, to wild tribesmen, especially Kurds, or to self-defence by the Turkish population. This was mostly nonsense, and the massacres in which hundreds and sometimes thousands of Armenian civilians died were clearly organised, and in some cases carried out, by the Turkish authorities. Sometimes, it is true, Armenians responded violently, even with assassinations, but such response was then used as a pretext for organised pogroms on the most horrific scale. Terrified civilians taking refuge in their churches were murdered by troops not bothered by the niceties of sanctuary. Well-documented tales of atrocities are legion.

By 1896 it was clear to many urban Armenians that they had no future in Turkey, and they emigrated in their thousands. In the early years of this century there was a lull of sorts – if you can call only occasional massacres a lull – but by the time World War I broke out the situation had deteriorated again. This time it was the impoverished rural Armenians in the heartland who were most vulnerable in the face of rising Turkish nationalism, expressed in the almost racist rhetoric of the Young Turks, who distrusted the Christians in their midst. The war brought Turkey and Russia into direct conflict, and early defeats in Ottoman attempts to invade Transcaucasia did not endear the Armenians near the border to their Turkish masters.

In 1915 Young Turk theoreticians decreed that it was time to move decisively against the Armenians, who were not responding to hopes that they might assimilate into Moslem Turkey. The only alternative, in the view of the extremists formulating Turkish policy, was to exterminate these awkward vestiges of a different civilisation. The interior minister Talaat Pasha issued explicit instructions for the genocide to begin 'and no regard must be paid to either age or sex, or to any scruples of conscience' (though some Turkish historians dismiss this document as a forgery). The war provided a perfect cover. The Armenians might cry for help, but the world had other matters on its collective mind.

The sequence of events is sketched in Christopher Walker's account: 'In the last 10 days of February Armenian government officials and employees were dismissed; and in the army Armenian soldiers were taken out of any combat positions and enrolled in labour battalions . . . At about the same time the civilian population was ruthlessly searched for arms. Armenians had been permitted to bear arms for self-protection in the years following the revolution of 1908, when the Young Turks realised that it was impossible to disarm the Kurds. Now these same arms were held to be evidence of plans for treason and insurrection . . . The total number of arms fixed in each case was arbitrary and quite in excess of any reasonable estimate of the number of arms held by Armenians. The arms searches became a pretext for brutal persecution . . . That the killings were deliberate none but dedicated Turkists deny . . . The pattern was this. Initially all the able-bodied Armenian men of a certain town or village would be ordered . . . to present themselves at the *konak* (government building) . . . Once at the *konak*, they would be jailed for a day or two. No reason was given. Then they would be led out of jail and marched out of town. At the first lonely halting place, they would be shot, or bayoneted to death. Some days later the old men, and the women and children, were summoned in the same way . . . They were forced to walk, endlessly, along pre-arranged routes, until they died from thirst, hunger, exposure, or exhaustion.'

These forced marches were described as 'deportations', ordered by the authorities in what they described, to those who cared to inquire, as 'self-defence'. Thousands of Armenians, inadequately clothed and shod, perished on the marches through wintry eastern Turkey or in the brutal concentration camps to which the survivors were consigned. The Turkish killing machine seems to have been every bit as efficient as the Nazi *Einsatzgruppen* twenty-five years later. At the beginning of 1915 there were believed to be 17,000 Armenians in Trebizond; six months later the Italian consul had difficulty locating one hundred.

Nobody knows exactly how many Armenians were butchered in 1915 and 1916. Even allowing for the flight of 250,000, and the conversion to Islam of approximately the same number, a conservative estimate would place the casualties at over one million. When, later in 1916, Russian troops successfully occupied parts of Turkish Armenia, including Trebizond and Lake Van, hardly any

(

Armenians were left there to celebrate. The two million or so living within Russian borders were more determined than ever to gain their independence, and various bodies were set up, some composed only of Armenians, others attempting to find common cause among all the peoples of Transcaucasia. The Turks were not inclined to ease the process along: the treaty of Brest-Litovsk, which ended Russia's participation in the war, called for the return to Turkey of Kars and Batumi and other districts after fifty years of Russian rule. When the peoples of Caucasia resisted, the Turks punched their way into Armenia, causing more havoc and prompting the mass flight of inhabitants who knew that to be overrun by Turkish troops was equivalent to a death sentence. The Turks swarmed into the fertile Ararat valley and it seemed only a matter of time before they captured the rest of Armenia. At the battle of Sardarapat in May 1918, Armenian defenders had their last chance, and took it. The Turks were driven back and Armenia was saved from probable extinction.

The country was now confronted by a dilemma which persists today: it was debatable whether Armenia, small and defenceless, could survive on its own. It was fine for nationalists to make speeches about independence, but the tiny territory was in constant danger of being squeezed between Russia and Turkey. Many Armenians favoured a Transcaucasian federation, but the debate came to a swift end. Georgia declared its independence just one week after the battle of Sardarapat, leaving the Armenians with no option but to follow suit. Armenia was free, but it was impoverished, underpopulated, and insecure.

Independence did not mean an end to the killings for Armenians living outside the tiny territory. Those brave or foolish or desperate enough to return to their former homes in Turkey faced further massacres, though not on the barbarous scale of the genocide. In September 1918 Turkish forces entered Baku and set up the government of Azerbaijan. In the process at least 20,000 Armenians living in the city perished, and the appalling winter wiped out thousands more, including refugees unable to cope with hunger and the unusually severe conditions. Nor was there much joy for

Armenia as a result of the Versailles peace conference in January 1919. Promises given by the Allies proved almost worthless, as Armenia's independence and security were not guaranteed by the participants. With the Turks still armed and pursuing their ambitions in the southern Caucasus, there could be no peace of mind. Another year passed before, in January 1920, the republic of Armenia was recognised by the Allies.

And in the autumn the fighting started again, as Turkish troops poured across the border, causing civilian casualties estimated at 30,000. The Turks captured Kars, a dreadful setback, and were closing in on present-day Leninakan, and again the Armenians faced the threat of extinction. On 17 November 1920, they sued for peace. The terms proposed by the Turks were predictably humiliating, and the shrunken Armenia envisaged by Turkey would, of course, continue to be vulnerable. Squeezed between Scylla and Charybdis, the Armenians jumped in the other direction: they agreed to cede power to a Bolshevik-dominated coalition. Three years of struggle had brought them back to square one and on 29 November they were back under Russian control.

The Bolsheviks treated Armenia no more gently than they had treated Georgia. Nationalisation was total, and the Armenian army was decimated, with many of its officers arrested or deported. Opposition was crushed, and many independent-minded Armenians were executed. On the other hand, however brutal the Soviet domination, the tiny republic did at least exist and, insofar as one could make predictions in Transcaucasia, was likely to continue to exist, which is more than one could say for an independent Armenia in the face of unrelenting Turkish threats.

The history of Soviet Armenia was predictable: repression and enforced collectivisation on the one hand; industrialisation and reconstruction on the other. Yet viewed across the decades, the Armenians were not too roughly treated by their new masters. They were allowed to retain their identity, not, of course, in full-fledged nationalist form, but their religion, their language and their cultural traditions were not suppressed. Most importantly, Armenia enjoyed a measure of security for the first time in decades, if not centuries.

They learnt to live with the absurdity of Azeri rule over Nakhichevan, where the Armenian population has shrunk from 50 per cent in 1923 to 2 per cent. The Azeris had also destroyed many ancient monuments of Armenian origin. Nagorno-Karabakh was another matter, and protest about the status quo reached a crescendo in the 1980s, with wretched consequences. Azeri vindictiveness, both against the hapless residents of the enclave and against Armenia as a whole, brought misery and discomfort to the Armenian people.

When the earthquake unglued thousands of ill-constructed dwellings and brought them tumbling to the ground, burying the contents, human as well as material, the Armenians would have felt justified in regarding themselves as peculiarly marked out for suffering. No wonder, as Charles had observed, they are tired.

12 Bibles and Bread

Just as Mother Georgia stands, an almost sacred image, high on a hillside overlooking Tbilisi, so Mother Armenia looks down on Yerevan. Not long ago this prime site was occupied by another family member, Uncle Joe Stalin. Lower down the hill, but still on a prominent slope, stands the Matenadaran, a stern building of grey stone, completed in 1957 in the monumental round-arched style. The Georgians have consigned the written relics of their history to an academic institute; the Armenians chose a more public display of their collections. Of the 26,000 Armenian manuscripts still in existence, just over half are here. The Matenadaran is not just an archive, but a unique storehouse of the Armenian cultural heritage.

Among the stylised statues in front of the library is one of Mesrop Mashtots, who formulated the Armenian alphabet and translated the bible into the vernacular. The alphabet was an ingenious invention, consisting of thirty-six letters which also functioned as numerals. The letters could be arranged in four rows of nine, with each row a different level of a decimal system: single figures, tens, hundreds, thousands. Two more letters were added in the tenth century. The dispersal of the Armenians led to the development of regional dialects, many of which still flourish. Armenians from Tbilisi, from Istanbul, from Karabakh, all speak differently, but mass communications have begun to iron out the differences. Armenian lacks the crackling melodiousness of Georgian. Its relative harshess seems in tune with the landscape. As Osip Mandelstam memorably noted in his *Journey to Armenia*, 'The Armenian language cannot be worn out; its boots are made of stone.'

Fragments of manuscripts from the fifth century still survive. Even at this early period Armenian academies were copiously translating works from Greek, Syriac and other ancient languages into the vernacular, and the works of Plato, Aristotle and Euclid were all available in Armenian. Many of these translations acquired enormous importance when, as frequently happened, the originals were lost, but not all the early manuscripts are translations. In the seventh century, a thinker called Shirakatsi wrote a treatise arguing that the earth was not flat. He was right, of course, but not right enough, since he concluded that the earth was, in fact, egg-shaped, suspended in the air between opposing forces.

If scientific progress was a bit uneven, there were more success stories in the field of medicine. There had been hospitals in Armenia from the third century. Autopsies were permitted for three centuries before they became accepted procedure in Europe. Not surprisingly, anatomical studies were far advanced. Folk medicine, using the plethora of herbs and spices commonly found in this mountainous country, was based on ancient recipes, tried and tested over time. Many were old wives' remedies of doubtful medical value, but some of the books of prescriptions and diagnoses dating from the twelfth century are still studied today. A treatise of 1482 with the unpromising title of *Useless for the Ignorant* by Armidovlat is by any standards a work of awesome scholarship, listing names and synonyms of 3500 flora, fauna and minerals, and including the names of drugs in five languages, Arabic and Persian among them.

Plutarch wrote about Armenian theatre before the birth of Christ, and musical traditions are equally ancient. A system of musical notation originated in the eighth century: the notation, known as *khaz*, usually appears in red ink above the text. After Western notation was introduced in the seventeenth century, the principles of *khaz* were abandoned and forgotten. The musicologist Komitas claimed to have cracked the code in 1915, but his work was lost during the genocide; scholars have resumed the quest but so far without success.

Armenian scribes routinely attached lengthy colophons to their manuscripts and these have proved invaluable sources of information.

One touching example records how a leading scribe of the fifteenth century found, at the age of eighty-six, that his eyesight was beginning to fail, so his work had to be continued by a more youthful monk. Other manuscripts, like the Armenians themselves, have survived against all the odds. The colossal Chronicles of Moosh were written in the early thirteenth century and preserved in the monastery of that name until 1915. As Turkish forces were approaching Moosh, two women volunteered to take the precious manuscript to Armenia. Since it weighed twenty-eight kilos, they divided it between them. One woman reached Armenia safely, the other perished at Erzerum, where her half of the manuscript remained until it could be brought to Armenia and reunited with its other half.

The art of the miniature was known as early as the sixth century and reached great heights in the twelfth century, when Cilician scribes produced many exquisite designs. They obtained their colours from a variety of sources: red from cochineal worms, pink from plants, blue from lapis lazuli, and green from copper. They used garlic juice to adhere gold leaf to paper and it also functioned as a preservative. The oldest miniatures are found in the Gospel of Echmiadzin, a tenth-century manuscript which incorporated older illustrations and also preserved a magnificent ivory book cover with relief panels from the sixth century.

As for printed books, the earliest volume in the Armenian language came off the press in 1512 in Venice, where the famous Mechitarite monastery kept the culture alive. Only in 1772 was an Armenian book printed on Armenian soil. Present-day Armenia was a backwater, while the diaspora communities flourished, and I was not greatly surprised to encounter an Armenian magazine published in 1794 in Madras.

It was cold in the Matenadaran, and colder still in the halls of the Museum of Children's Art in central Yerevan. Young artists provided 150,000 works for the collection, but not all of these are housed here; many are distributed among other museums in Armenia and in other former Soviet republics. Not surprisingly,

Armenia's economic plight was making it increasingly difficult to acquire new works.

On the evidence of the exhibits, Armenian children enjoy a highly developed sense of colour, vigorously deployed for expressive purposes. Paint is not the only medium employed; there are 'tapestries' of string and wool, varieties of batik, skilful embroideries and dolls. In the basement are some of the contributions made by children from 110 countries. Distinct themes were repeated in works from certain countries, and I wondered whether thematic, even ideological content, had been determined by the choice of the Armenian curators or by the submissions of the countries concerned. It seemed no accident that paintings from Nicaragua, Palestine, Vietnam and Syria included scenes of war, and that one from Nicaragua incorporated the banner of the liberationist FSLN. All the contributions from North Korea showed scrubbed, smiling, well-behaved children, an instance not only of dreary propaganda but of the misplaced assumption that children's art must necessarily depict children. Works from Austria and eastern Europe were drenched in folkloric elements and traditional costumes, which seemed evidence of a teacher's guiding hand. But there were also some wonderfully idiosyncratic paintings, highly detailed, emanating from Mongolia and Bolivia.

Arman suggested that I might like to continue my cultural tour by looking at some video films of architecturally rich regions of Armenia. It sounded a peculiar idea – inviting me to his country and then showing me films of it – but I agreed to his proposal. The studio was frigid, but the staff were helpful, plying me with that rare commodity, coffee, and pushing the single-bar fire alongside my chair.

The first video showed amateur dramatics in a provincial town, the activities of a fabric cooperative and the showrooms of factories producing buttons and baby clothes. An interview with the boss of a cooperative was conducted with a single hand-held microphone, which the boss was unable to operate. Perhaps my stretches and yawns suggested that none of this was of riveting interest to me, so we tried a different tape. This showed a couple in Roman togas in a horse-drawn chariot, from which they descended to sprinkle bystanders with water. I asked Arman whether this was some revived pagan tradition. He hadn't the faintest idea. The tape continued with folk dancing, a religious procession, a display of tightrope walking, and a stylised street ballet in which two lines of folk in mediaeval costume solemnly filed past each other and then declaimed poetry. Nobody knew what this was about either. We fast-forwarded. A third tape panned over Lake Sevan and showed the region's *khachkars* – endless shots roaming slowly up and down the carved stones; and continued with a visit to the spa of Djermuk – endless shots of the resort hotel and of sodden cliffs. After a twenty-minute inspection of the hotel and every stream that flowed through Djermuk, Arman asked me whether I wanted to watch any more videos. I answered decisively. Perhaps, then, I would like to return tomorrow to watch an entirely new selection? I had to indicate politely that I found the whole exercise a waste of time.

Arman had another appointment lined up for me, in response to my interest in modern architecture. Our driver took us to Government Building No 3 to talk to a ministry official who, by happy chance, turned out to be the brother of Henrik Igitian. On entering Igitian's office, we found him laid out on a row of chairs. He staggered to his feet but the poor man was clearly ill with severe stomach pains. Colleagues came in with food and cups of tea to revive him, and he managed to totter back to his desk. But the expression on his face made it clear that a cosy discussion was out of the question. Arman left me with Igitian while he went to find an official in better health. Igitian and I blinked at each other. Arman returned beaming: he'd found an acquiescent deputy minister. We strolled into his anteroom, which was overpoweringly heated with electric bar heaters and the roaring air-conditioning unit, which must have been eating up more energy than any central heating system.

The deputy minister, seated in an empty office, seemed wary and reserved. He explained that new projects were planned, in response to requests by local councils, by architectural committees at the ministry. Simultaneously, a separate committee produces plans from which district councils can make their choices. This was all rather academic, since very little new construction was now in progress. Shortages continued to be severe, even in the earthquake zone. Lack of petrol was hampering the efficient operation of machinery such as cranes. There was ample evidence, he continued, of Azeri sabotage against goods destined for Armenia; materials contributed by other republics as aid for the earthquake zone had been pilfered, stolen, or destroyed as they passed through both Azerbaijan and Georgia.

I was curious to know whether it would be possible for an individual entrepreneur or company to buy land and build flats which could then be offered for sale? The minister replied that there had been talk of such things, but no decision had yet been made. And how about the privatisation of flats? This decision too had not been made, but it was imminent. After privatisation, who would maintain the common parts of apartment buildings, who would deal with malfunctioning lifts, who would replace broken windows and fix the roof?

'We have put these same questions to the committee discussing privatisation, and we haven't had an answer yet.'

'What can you do to improve the quality of design, which during the Soviet period was fairly wretched?'

'We hope to have more competition which will lead to cheaper construction.'

'You mean competition between various architectural firms for new projects?'

'Well, this is the aim, but we're not yet at that stage. At present we can only order plans from the best architects we have.'

It was not an illuminating exchange. To recognise the failings of the old system was easier than to devise the policies that would replace it.

I was struck again by the absence of character in these ministerial offices. Not a picture, not an ornament, just a few rolled-up plans gathering dust on top of an empty cupboard, and a bank of phones. Arman explained that this was a survival of Communist times, when most officials occupied sinecures and were paid to do nothing. There was no incentive to work hard, because you got paid anyway and promotions depended on connections more than performance. The office was not an important place.

'Things haven't changed much either,' he added.

The news from Azerbaijan was not very encouraging, despite Gorbachev's invitation to the presidents of the two disputatious republics to go to Moscow to discuss their differences. News reached me via the World Service or from CNN. The former was more reliable, since transmission on the two cable channels was intermittent and the screen sometimes remained blank for days. Arman, after his initial enthusiasm for discussing the Azerbaijani situation, had gone strangely silent, replying, whenever I asked him about latest developments, that everything was calm.

Nor were the other Westerners at the Razdan better informed through their official contacts in Yerevan. I often breakfasted with a telephone engineer, who, in harness with European colleagues, was installing new long-distance circuits. In addition to facilitating contact between Armenians and the rest of the world, the new system would prove profitable for the government. After nine months of work, Joe was now looking forward to his Christmas leave before returning to Yerevan for the last time.

'You been here all along?' he asked me one morning.

'No, I was at the Dvin for two nights. I moved here because there was heat.'

'There is?'

'There was the day I moved in. Naturally there isn't any now. Still, it's a nice hotel and the staff are friendly.'

'It's definitely the best place in town. But you have to keep on the right side of the manager. A couple of months ago he told me that an important American delegation was coming here, so would I mind going to the Dvin for two nights. That was going to be a damn nuisance. I've got my office here, lots of equipment. So I said no. They begged, they pleaded. We came to a deal when they offered me a couple of cases of brandy. So I moved to the Dvin. Ten days later I was still there. I insisted on having my old room back as agreed, but they said no, they were sorry. So I threatened to cut off the new phone circuits I'd installed. They just shrugged. So I went ahead and for forty-eight hours there was no phone link between Armenia and the West. It still made no difference. It took me eighteen days to get back here. Now I'm trying to persuade the manager to let me keep my room while I'm back home for Christmas. I just want to be able to leave my stuff here, rather than drag everything halfway across the world and back on Aeroflot. The manager's very suspicious. The concept of paying for a room in advance and not using it is alien to him. So he's thinking about it.'

Up early one morning, I walked into the town centre. A power cut meant that the only light available within the shops came from open front doors which admitted chill as well as light, or from an ineffectual candle on the counter. Racks were laden with coats priced at between 2000 and 10,000 roubles, and beneath the glass counters were the usual array of candies and gums, watches and video cassettes, combs and cosmetics, all at prices that made most browsers shake their heads in disbelief. Other shops, state-owned, were closed, because they no longer had any goods to sell. Others were open, but also had no goods to sell. Butchers sold no meat but jars of jam and packets of Georgian tea were stacked on the shelves. Greengrocers had better stocks, but the quality was abysmal.

Along the central thoroughfare of Mashtots Avenue, I came across the basement Dessert Bar, which served coffee but no desserts. There were six lanes of traffic, none of which paid much attention to the rules of the road. A trolleybus came charging through the red lights, hoping that clanging noises alone would ensure its safe passage; in the next lane a Volga flashed its lights at a car old-fashioned enough to halt at the red light. I made it across the avenue by sticking with the crowd and advancing *en masse*. Across from the Dessert Bar I found an art gallery, which offered mediocre contemporary paintings and older objects such as carpets. Next door the principal Armenian wine shop in Yerevan sold glassware but no wine.

All along Mashtots stood the street hawkers. Although there was little wine or vodka or coffee to be found in any shop, these commodities were available at dozens of stands throughout the city, where their ubiquity could only be explained by corruption. The official price of a half-litre of vodka was about 10 roubles. Should a shop receive a consignment of vodka, the managers know that they can obtain a much higher price by selling the whole batch to middlemen for, say, 15 roubles per bottle – instant profit. Order another Mercedes. The goods then filter down through more middlemen until they reach the street stands priced at about 40 roubles. That was still a bargain compared to Turkish sunflower oil at 180 roubles and a 750-gram bag of coffee at 150. The mayor of Yerevan had declared that the only goods which could be sold in this way were those not derived from state enterprises. Those who took the trouble to import products from other republics, such as Georgian wine, could charge what they wished in accordance with the laws of the free market. Nevertheless it was evident that profiteering was rampant, and little was being done about it.

I turned up Bagramyan Avenue, walking past the shallow-roofed mansions with their rounded Armenian arcades imposed on a form which is essentially neoclassical, with repetitious side bays and central pediments. The massive Central Committee building, set in a park of clipped hedges and empty pools, pays swift homage to Armenia in the rounded arch that pierces the central pediment, but in other respects the building is solidly and Sovietly neoclassical, providing the model to which the other lesser buildings along the avenue unsuccessfully aspire. Behind these ministries villas rise in tiers up the wooded hill.

At the top of Bagramyan a handsome if unadventurous modern tufa building is perched on a hill. Arman had told me that this was where the Communist Party had held meetings and assemblies, but this was only a half-truth. It was in fact the former Department of Political Education. The steady rows of identical windows seemed emblematic of rigidity of thought. Now it was used in part (Arman said nothing about this) by the American University of Armenia, which had been established with government support in September

1991. It offered courses in computing, business studies, earthquake engineering and industrial engineering. Fees were very high, though for some the financial pain was alleviated by stipends and scholarships. There had been considerable criticism from those who argued that the money spent on the AUA would have been better used to develop the country's existing universities, but AUA supporters point out that these are based on antiquated Soviet models and there is a need for a less restrictive approach to higher education. Since the enrolment is about ninety students, its impact will be slight.

Arman collected me from the hotel for a mystery tour. I would be given some notice of excursions and a vague indication of where we might be headed, but the vagueness, no doubt, was deliberate, and much depended on such variables as supplies of petrol, the weather and Arman's whims. Today we were driving north towards Ashtarak, a town of about 20,000 inhabitants built on a series of hills. As we drove I could see the clear snowy peak, rising smoothly up from the valley floor, of Mount Aragats, not to be confused with its even mightier colleague Ararat to the south. An ancient town located at a strategically important crossroads, Ashtarak is best known for its apricots. For me it was a relief to be out of Yerevan, with its smoky skies and pall of grime. Here the sky was blue and the air limpid.

Arman had arranged for us to visit the winery at Ashtarak. Awaiting us as the Volga pulled into the forecourt was a small welcoming party: Ashot, a district architect, and various officials who led me to the director's quarters. We were also joined by Yura, a courteous watchful elderly man, a judge and a great authority on the region.

The lugubrious fellow slumped behind the desk was the director. He roused himself sufficiently to shake my hand, then returned to his post and lit another cigarette. He looked more like a warning against the perils of drink than an advertisement for the pleasures to be derived from it. He had the head of a raddled Placido Domingo, but this promising start was unsustained as the eye moved down his length. He was neither welcoming nor informative, and left all the talking to Misha, a cocky little man who was head of production for the wine marketing coordination committee in Yerevan. (It was always impossible to work out the precise bureaucratic status of anyone I was introduced to.) If I understood Misha correctly, the winery was founded in the late 1930s by the Armenian-born politician Anastas Mikoyan, and the present director was, surprise surprise, a relative of the great man.

Ashtarak specialises in fortified wines. Its version of 'sherry' does develop the same yeasty layer found in Jerez and known as *flor*, and production methods, including a simplified solera system, are modelled on those used in Spain. Misha even speculated that the production of sherry-style wines may have originated in Armenia rather than Andalusia.

In the cellars I was shown a handful of old casks and butts, and hundreds of metal tanks. The battery of filtration equipment piled up in a corner was among the most antiquated I had ever laid eyes upon. The smug Misha and I had a slight misunderstanding when he denied that the wines went through a fermentation process. It turned out that by fermentation he meant distillation, which seemed an odd confusion, even allowing for lapses in the translation. Misha also denied that Armenia had suffered greatly from Gorbachev's loathed anti-alcoholism campaign, which encouraged the grubbing up of vineyards. According to Misha, Armenia had resisted strongly, because of its ancient winemaking traditions, but from other sources I heard that a considerable proportion of the vineyards had been uprooted.

Were these wines exported? Yes, to Germany, Japan, and the United States. But exports had declined because of the shortage of bottles. In Georgia the winery directors had been excited by the thought of privatisation and foreign investment in their flagging, under-financed enterprises. Not Misha. If the Ashtarak winery were sold off, he told me, he feared that its new owners would simply want to bottle the production and sell it as fast as possible. Thus the patient traditions of sherry production would be lost. (Actually, most of them were jettisoned long ago, since most Ashtarak wines are aged for only two years.) In his view the wine industry should remain a state monopoly.

I asked him who makes this kind of decision now: the winery director, officials in Yerevan, or a ministry? They were made at government level, and this, he intimated, is the way it should be, since if every winery were free to devise and implement its own marketing strategies, there would be a free-for-all. By keeping such matters under government control, wine could be traded for badly needed foodstuffs. None of this differed greatly from the old Communist line on agricultural production. Misha, of course, had a vested interest in the present system, as his role might become superfluous if wineries became autonomous. Sensing that his answers didn't glitter with innovation, Misha threw me a sop: 'But maybe in the future, we can choose another path.'

A tasting had been organised in the small restaurant adjoining the winery. There were only two wines to taste, so we would do so over lunch. I sampled a two-year-old sherry called Byurakan, which resembled a dry Amontillado, and a three-year-old which was sweeter and much more alcoholic. Misha and I preferred the Byurakan – at least we agreed on something – and once personal preferences had been established, our tumblers were filled with the sherry of our choice and the toasts began.

In a two-car convoy, the party drove to the village of Oshakan, where Mesrop Mashtots was buried in 440 at the wish of his noble friend Vagram Amatuni. The aisleless church of charcoal-grey tufa does not look especially ancient, but I was assured that its fabric dates from the fifth century. Down in the crypt the simple tomb is covered with a new slab of Italian marble. In the churchyard, deferentially set in the wings, is the canopied tomb of his benefactor Amatuni.

From here we drove up the valley of the Kasakh river, which has ploughed a gorge through the uplands. The great church of Sagmosavank was built in 1235 in a meadow on the edge of the canyon. A few yards from its walls the land falls away and plunges a few hundred feet down to the pulsing river, and beyond the gorge the slopes rise gently towards the snowy mountains. The asymmetrical church presents a varied profile, piercing the sky with its drum and cupola and two open belfries. Decoration is minimal, but *khachkars* are attached like large postage stamps to the thick stone walls. The main west portal, with its sensuous curves, surely echoes Persian designs.

The south door leads into a cupolaed chamber, the former book depository. The main ribs of the vault spring from capitals and intersect, binding the space together. Vestiges of carved angels flutter above the altar. The cupola of the narthex is inlaid with quatrefoil panels and with a lacy *khachkar*, cunningly positioned so that the sun falls directly on it just twice a year. As at Geghard, a large portal separates this narthex from the choir, which is narrow and gaunt. A tall drum above, lit by lancets, illuminates the choir, and on either side the slender vaulted passages, originally used as sacristies, lead to other lancets with views over the gorge.

On our way to visit another important church at Hovannavank, a distraction awaited us in the village square. Large ovals of *lavash* had been slapped down to dry in the bright if cool sunshine. The farmer who had baked the bread urged us to enter his farmyard; his wife bustled me into the bakery behind the house where the dough had just been cooked against the sides of a subterranean oven. Heat was too precious a commodity to be wasted, and a cauldron, nodding over the top of the oven, would provide the household with hot water for the rest of the day. Once the bread was dry it would be laid in sheets inside a wooden cupboard, where it would keep for months, requiring only the addition of water to revive it.

Stringed walnuts hung from the rafters. A pungent decadent whiff pierced the air, emanating from a freshly decapitated calf's head flung into a corner. Next to the upended barrel which served as an impromptu table were four hooves, recently torn from the slaughtered calf, and, next to the bread cupboard, the unfortunate animal's skin, freshly flayed. Stacked against the side of the dank passageway between the square and the farmyard were crates of apples. I asked why the peasants weren't selling them, and they replied that they were keeping them a while longer, hoping that the onset of winter would drive prices even higher. Everybody was invited to raid the *lavash* cupboard and delicious crumbly white cheese was brought out to accompany the fresh bread, followed by homemade yogurt which was tangy and very rich.

Our party was enjoying itself thoroughly. The appetite of these men who had just completed a substantial lunch was remarkable. But the farmer's wife was more agitated. As she chatted away, tears came into her eyes. One of her sons had been called up by the National Guard, and she dreaded the possibility of war. The visitors did their best to reassure the old woman, and helped themselves to more fruit and cheese. After thanking her profusely for her hospitality we walked over to the church. My wish to visit these old churches was regarded by Arman and the others as a mild eccentricity, a fit of antiquarianism that needed to be indulged to keep me happy. Only Ashot, himself an architect, seemed to share my interest.

A chapel here dates from the fifth century, but the main church, a sturdy hulk of black and reddish brown tufa, was built in 1217. The façade was covered with crude wooden scaffolding, and the interior was a wreck. Squinting through a gap in the west door, I saw that it was roofless; makeshift beams were propping up the rafters. The church's most attractive visible feature was the inscribed tympanum. Like the church of Sagmosavank, Hovannavank stands on the brim of the canyon. This precarious siting was of course defensive. It protected church and village from potential enemies from the east, and torches lit in the belfries alerted a whole string of villages to impending threats.

We drove back to Ashtarak, and stopped beneath the seventeenth-century bridge which spans the river. From this spot I could see three churches, two of them extremely old, perched high on crags. Alongside the bridge a nineteenth-century mill has recently been restored and is now being privately operated by a family who had been millers for generations. I shook hands with the miller and his assistants, their hair greyed by the flour that constantly dusted them. I wandered into the mill through a haze of flour dust and inspected the wheels, which were being fed with wheat through inverted pyramidal wooden buckets; the ground flour then sifted down into a trough, from which it was being packed into sacks. It was taking about one hour to fill a sack. The former bakery adjoining the mill, where clients used to have their flour turned into bread, was being restored.

During the afternoon our party had grown, then diminished, and was now reduced to the truly committed: Yura the judge; Haik, the financial director of the town council; Ashot the architect; Surik the driver; Arman and myself. We dusted the flour off our clothing, then drove back up the gorge for a mile or so to a newly built restaurant on the cliffside. Balconies leaned out over the gorge, and on the upper floor there was a series of private rooms, one of which had been prepared for us. Haik, a proud investor in the restaurant, was our host.

I gazed at the table before us with dismay. I had eaten amply at the winery on the assumption that I might be returned to my hotel after the dining room had closed. But now it was only five in the afternoon and the table was crammed with dishes. Haik, a hearty handsome man with a grand moustache and greying hair, was clearly determined that we were all to have a most wonderful time, so I resigned myself to an onslaught of bonhomie. A waitress brought in a dish of dumplings not unlike *khinkali* but smaller and without the indigestible topknot. These were eaten with yogurt flavoured with crushed garlic. She returned with a huge plate of grilled pork with tomatoes and green peppers, which my hosts peeled before eating. A platter of *kyufta* and noodles followed: this version was made from pulped meat seasoned with butter and brandy and then fried. The recipe was more promising than the results, which were rubbery and tasteless. On top of each slab of *kyufta* were generous pats of butter, but it was so cold in the room that the butter refused to melt.

The meal was washed down with lemonade and tinned Cuban grapefruit juice, a choice item on the black market. The toasts required vodka, and the incessant eloquence achieved the social purpose of binding each member of the group to every other. Surik, our eager and friendly driver, participated in the exchange of tributes just as much as the boisterous Haik. It was a splendid and joyful occasion, but I was bored to distraction. I had a raging headache, a limited capacity for neat vodka, and Surik insisted on replenishing my plate with kilos of meat and vegetables for which I had long ceased to have any appetite. My companions indulged themselves in long courteous monologues extolling each other, while I sat among them trying to look interested. Arman had long ago given up translating these ever more flowery tributes. The air was thickened by the fug generated by three dedicated smokers, and the fumes rasped at my throat, already sensitive from a slight cold. I recognised that my reaction, which I tried to conceal, was one of appalling ingratitude, as the feast was nominally in my honour.

At 8.15 we rose and descended to the car park, where my companions stood about for another fifteen minutes until Yura noticed that I was shivering with cold. There were three Mercedes parked outside the restaurant, one of them a recent model. I asked Arman who could afford to buy such cars. The owners, he replied, might be successful Armenian businessmen or those with rich relatives abroad, or officials who had worked abroad and been able to bring a foreign car back with them. Why, he himself had had the opportunity to pick up a Mercedes cheap in Africa, but had declined because of the problem of obtaining spare parts in Armenia. The other explanation, which he omitted to offer, is corruption. The old Communist system of fixed plans offered factory managers innumerable opportunities for profitable scams.

In the meantime we were struggling back to Yerevan in the Society's Volga. Surik, despite an impressive intake of vodka, negotiated the tricky and completely unlit road junctions without difficulty. Along the highway to Yerevan, he had to stop repeatedly, either to replace the bonnet, which had developed a tendency to spring loose, or to fiddle with some component which was acting up. There was something to be said for a Mercedes after all.

13 Mozart-Strasse, Leninakan

'I like this area very much,' said Arman, waving beyond the car windows towards the fields. The peak of Mount Aragats was poking up in the distance above a shroud of white cloud. Fields were being fenced as farmers took advantage of land reform to claim their acres and demarcate the boundaries.

The area Arman was fond of was the Talin district, just north of Yerevan, where he had begun his career as a schoolteacher in the villages. Many of the inhabitants had settled here after fleeing from Turkey in 1915, and he recalled frequent encounters with old folk who remembered life in western Armenia. The Soviet authorities, always keen to squash manifestations of nationalism, had forbidden the singing of patriotic Armenian songs, but Arman recalled private gatherings where the songs were sung and recorded in an attempt to preserve the vanishing Armenian heritage.

The town of Talin was mesmerisingly unattractive. Erected at random throughout the town were ugly tufa houses, blockishly conceived without ornamentation, the masonry crudely mortared. At the municipal buildings we called on the boss of the district: an agro-technician by training, Kevork Ghiraghosian was a more impressive figure than the prefects I had met in western Georgia. He was a slight man with a large nose which swelled as it descended; his eyes were alert and keen.

I asked him how he had ended up as local leader. There had been elections of deputies to the district council, he explained, and then the deputies had elected him to this post.

'And what were you doing before that?'

He smiled. 'This is my twelfth year in this job.'

So Ghiraghosian had been the district chief under the Communists too. Arman vouched for his competence, and I was inclined to believe him. He certainly had considerable experience of regional administration, which was more than could be said for many recently elected local leaders. Despite his background, Ghiraghosian had traded ideologies with few pangs. Two large collectivised farms had recently been privatised, a move rewarded with increased productivity. Moreover, privatisation provided revenue, since both land and livestock returned into private ownership would be taxable. With rising prices for fruit and vegetables, farmers were earning a good living. Agricultural productivity was compensating for the closure of some local factories because of fuel shortages. Ghiraghosian was confident about the district's long-term future because of its wealth of raw materials, including building stone and the volcanic glass known as perlite. Nor were there any serious shortages of foodstuffs. The rural population had ample supplies of wheat, flour and milk, which may have partly explained why city dwellers did not.

Although local councils still worked closely with ministries in Yerevan, there was more freedom of action than under the Soviet régime. Local leaders were at liberty to come up with new ideas and to develop their own foreign contacts. Ghiraghosian was in a stronger position than most, since he was also a member of Parliament. He told me he was optimistic about the future, even though he expected the blockade to continue.

'How will the Armenians survive another winter in these conditions?'

'We have made plans. We have bartered for coal and other provisions, and there is enough fuel stored away for a few months, as well as stores elsewhere that can be moved here if we need them.'

As we continued northwards, the ground became less fertile. We crossed a stony treeless plateau and passed through a range of gentle hills before descending into the Shirak valley. Surik, who normally drove steadily and well, had taken to driving in the middle of the road, a pointless strategy, since every time traffic approached from either direction, he had to slip back into the right lane. The only explanation seemed to be that he wanted other motorists to know that our official Volga was top dog on the highway. Driving was made no easier by the black curtains that blocked his, and my, view through the rear window. When I asked Arman about this widespread Soviet custom, he agreed that it was a stupid habit signifying a snobbish wish to appear official and exclusive. None the less, the curtains stayed.

After an hour we approached Leninakan through its heavily industrialised outskirts. The city (which in 1992 changed its name to Gumairy) had been badly damaged by the 1988 earthquake and it still showed. Most large apartment blocks on the outskirts had been abandoned. Even in buildings with no outward signs of structural damage, windows gaped blackly from deserted apartments. Closer to the centre, clusters of hurriedly built wooden cabins provided 'temporary' accommodation for hundreds, if not thousands, of displaced families. It was no coincidence that most of the buildings that had collapsed had been constructed during the last twenty years. Examining the ruins, building experts had established that construction methods were shoddy; for example, joints which should have been welded had not been. Short cuts had been taken, no doubt in the interests of enriching the industry bosses, yet nobody had been punished for tricks of the trade which had condemned to death thousands of people who might otherwise have survived.

It had been cold in Yerevan, but it was colder here. The trees were already bare of leaves. We searched for the former English-language school near the town centre, but found that its buildings were being used for temporary housing, even though the structure was thought to be unsafe. The school had moved into temporary cabins next to its former premises, but lack of heating was keeping it closed. In the main square the clocktower, as in other cities struck by disaster, still recorded the time of the catastrophe: 11.41 a.m. Traffic lights were not functioning (probably an electricity cut) so cars jostled for position as they turned the corners of the square. A street away wooden huts temporarily housed the municipal offices. Arman left me with Surik while he dashed in to see whether any official would be available to meet me. It was impossible to phone from Yerevan to Leninakan, said Arman, which is why my 'programme' had to be improvised at the last moment.

Andranik Kevorkian, the deputy mayor, viewed me as blotting paper. Yes, he might answer some of my questions, but he preferred to give me his views on whatever happened to interest him at that moment. Unlike Ghiraghosian, he was not a professional politician. A former historian, Kevorkian was closely allied, as he frequently reminded me, with another intellectual, President Levon Ter-Petrossian. About forty years old, with a round dark-complexioned face and thinning hair, he throbbed with nervous energy. His round eyes bulged from a large head which had a cocky lift to it; his fingers strummed the desk and when moved he would whack the table with his fist, not out of anger but simply to add emphasis.

Before the earthquake, he told me, there had been about 250,000 inhabitants. Of the 28,000 who were killed that day, about 18,000 died in Leninakan and many more were injured. The population had shrunk after many families, justifiably unnerved, moved to other parts of Armenia or to other republics. Eighty per cent of the city's structures had been damaged, and of those built in the last two decades the figure was as high as 95 per cent; 70 per cent of the sixty schools had been destroyed. Before the disaster the city had 2200 hospital beds. Now, despite the efforts of charities and governments, there were only 490. Industry too was wrecked; the situation was compounded by the blockade, and only 10 per cent of Leninakan's factories were functioning. Kevorkian had no unemployment figures, but others in the town estimated the figure at 100,000.

A new city was rising on the northwest outskirts, but it would not come close to replacing the lost housing capacity. The new city was designed to withstand earthquakes in the future, but the blockade was preventing some materials specified for the new buildings from getting through. Three years after the disaster foreign relief workers were still active in the region. Yet Kevorkian believed all this foreign aid had its negative aspects too. The reconstruction effort had, he argued, been hampered by the Communist system. The victims had demanded help, reasonably enough, but by so doing had acted as beggars, a condition exploited by Moscow to increase Armenian dependency on the Soviet Union. People now understood this, he said, but at the time it was less apparent. Nowadays the people of Leninakan would rather rebuild their city themselves than rely on charity.

Kevorkian criticised the West for accepting Gorbachev's analysis of the situation. 'The West was more anxious to protect Gorbachev, and did not give enough thought to the plight of the Armenians.' This seemed excessively harsh on the thousands of Westerners who gave money for the victims for the purest of humanitarian reasons, but I later understood what he was getting at. The earthquake and its aftermath had come at a bad time psychologically: just as Armenians were contemplating independence as a realistic possibility, they were thrust once again into a position of dependency.

Today, he continued, Armenia was at liberty to make its own contacts with the West, but in 1988 Moscow deliberately limited freedom of choice in such matters. Leninakan had wanted to establish itself as a free-trade zone, but Moscow had stamped on the scheme, fearing, no doubt rightly, that it would strengthen Armenian ties with the West. Joint ventures with Western businesses had also been forbidden by the Soviet authorities. Even now Moscow was encouraging Azerbaijan to hamper Armenia's continuing economic development. Moscow knew how resourceful Armenians are and how rapidly the republic could develop if left alone to do so. All Armenia wanted was the same opportunities for progress that other countries enjoyed.

Kevorkian was now in full bumptious flow, and had been speaking and thumping for about twenty minutes without pause. While Arman translated, Kevorkian stared haughtily out of the window, as though oblivious of my presence except as a dutiful recording instrument. He wanted me to know that his view of the situation was not an idiosyncratic one – on the contrary. He knew everybody in the republic, and was a friend of the president's, and his opinions were widely shared. Although he was doing everything possible to get my back up, I rather liked Kevorkian. Arman did not. He clearly felt happier around the old-style administrators, the men who had worked the system for years and had successfully adapted themselves to the changes taking place. Men like Kevorkian were wild cards, unpredictable, shooting off at the mouth, vain and grandiloquent. To me all this was refreshing. He was a devoted supporter of Levon Ter-Petrossian, but added, a trifle apologetically, 'The president can only do what is possible.'

As he paused to take breath, I rushed in with a question. 'What is not possible?'

'To become completely independent overnight. Ter-Petrossian wants our country to prepare for independence, but other parties are pressing for immediate independence. We are not yet ready for that. Right now Armenia would shrivel alongside the huge republics such as Russia and the Ukraine. I see the Union as a powerful electrical magnet. As the current diminishes, the particles, namely the republics, will gradually become detached without damage.'

I remarked that it sounded paradoxical to support the concept of the Union while denouncing central authority.

'We're a small country,' he replied. 'We have a small economy, so we have to take a gradual approach to removing ourselves from the Union. My ideal, of course, is complete independence, but this is a time for tactics rather than ideals. The West seems afraid of the disintegration of the Union, but at the same time won't recognise us as an independent nation. Why not?'

'Because your economy is totally dependent on that of the Soviet Union.'

Kevorkian nodded, as though I were confirming his argument, which, in a sense, I was. In the months that followed Armenia, conscious of its dependency, was to take a more internationalist view than its neighbour Georgia. It was eager from the start to join the Russian-led Commonwealth of Independent States, whereas Gamsakhurdia set his face against such a course.

Arman was anxious to find his friend Yeranos, who was deputy director of the best of the three English-language schools in Leninakan. After many inquiries we were directed to a hut among a group of temporary cabins reached along a muddy lane. Yeranos was not there but his eleven-year-old daughter was happy to show us the way to the new school. Following her directions, Surik drove north towards the new city, and stopped outside the Lord Byron School, funded by the British government and supplemented with dona-tions of materials from British firms. It had opened in June 1990. The school, one of only three so far rebuilt in the city, was Britain's principal contribution to the reconstruction of Leninakan.

The school amazed me. It was spacious and brightly furnished, carpeted too, and far more luxurious than any British school I had seen in years. We found Yeranos in the computer room, which was equipped with about fifteen monitors. He was a handsome man with the same Italianate good looks and lined features as the conductor Giulini. He spoke excellent English and had just returned from a short visit to the school at Hucknall in Nottinghamshire where Byron is buried.

The school, superbly equipped by British standards and astonishingly so by Soviet standards, was for obvious reasons the first choice of every parent. Built for 400 students, it now taught 1000 in two shifts. About one hundred of those children had lost one or both parents in the earthquake. Because demand is four times greater than the number of places available, the school operates a lottery system to decide which children shall be admitted. The classrooms were well equipped, the library was well stocked, posters of the British royal family smiled from the walls, reminders of privilege and class dispatched to a once egalitarian land. Solar panels provided heating, but selectively. In the large gym, children were playing basketball fully clothed, and there was talk of closing the school during the coldest months and holding classes through the summer instead. I marvelled at such amenities as the lavatory for disabled students, the drinking fountain, and the seating areas where students and teachers could relax. Most astonishing of all was the pristine physical condition of the school. In use for eighteen months, it still looked spotless. Not a wall had been cuffed, not a surface scratched, not a floor muddied. The Lord Byron School was being treated not as a facility but as a treasurable possession.

It was hard to say the same about many of the other new buildings in Leninakan. The other republics, notably the Russian Federation, had contributed new apartment blocks, but many of them already looked shabby and discoloured. Families had been rehoused on the basis of need. Those with young children, or whose losses during the earthquake had been most grievous, had been housed first. I tried to look impressed as the car jolted along rutted lanes beside the new blocks. 'It's very impressive, but I can't see any shops.'

'There are some,' said Yeranos.

'Shops?' intervened Arman. 'Who needs shops? There's nothing to put in them.'

The Austrians had contributed a 'village' of bungalows, mostly semi-detached, ranged along roads called Mozart-Strasse and Franz-Werfel-Strasse (Werfel having written about Armenia, and Mozart honoured as though he had set operas on Ararat). The village was neat and respectable, impeccably bourgeois in the best Austrian traditions. The Italians too had left their national stamp on Leninakan in the form of a hospital designed with just enough chic to make it attractive but not so much that it would appear ostentatious and flashy. Kindergartens had been constructed by the Danes, the Germans, the Swedes.

It was four o'clock and we were all hungry. Yeranos directed us to a private restaurant, the Ani, on the outskirts of town. The decor was thoroughly garish, and featured the heavy ruffled curtains of which British urban gentry are so enamoured. The light fittings were as heavy as was compatible with their remaining attached to the ceiling, and the doors were panelled with swirling coloured glass. Despite the austerity which afflicted the stricken town, there were plenty of revellers in the restaurant, even if all of them kept their coats on. We were served colossal pork chops and succulent mushrooms moistened with yogurt. Arman, Yeranos and Surik made short work of a couple of bottles of vodka, and I was provided with bone-dry Georgian wine which I thoroughly enjoyed. As Arman slipped away to settle the bill I reflected that the cost must have been about the same as Yeranos's monthly salary.

Yeranos told me about the moment when the earthquake had struck. 'I was on the third floor of the old English school, and when it began, I just stood there and waited for death. Then I ran down and found my two daughters – they were both safe – but they were running around crying, "Where is our brother? Where is our brother?" He had been buried under the rubble, and it took four hours before we got him out. Luckily he was all right, apart from some injuries to his leg. But nine children in our school died.'

'And your flat?'

'Ruined. We lived in a tent for seven months, right through the winter of 1989, and then we were given the wooden cabin where we still live. The earthquake also destroyed most of our possessions, but what made me particularly sad was that I lost almost all my books. I have collected books all my life, I have published poetry and translated books from English, and everything perished.'

A week later, in Yerevan, I watched a film made immediately after the earthquake. Coffins provided the dominant image – strapped to the roofs of cars, being carried by relatives along the streets, and stacked in their hundreds like firewood by the roadside. Shapeless sacks of bloodied sheets containing the remains of victims were being lowered into shallow coffins before the boxes were slid into graves. Side by side in one grave lay four coffins, one tiny, an entire family extinguished. Passing among the coffins were the survivors, grief-stricken and dazed, either weeping or standing about numbed by the transition from everyday routines to death and dislocation.

Today the physical damage is still visible, but the pain of the survivors is less tangible, until one encounters people willing to discuss their experiences. For survivors, life in the wooden huts had been grim. Many people, Yeranos's wife included, had become ill, and rheumatism was widespread. Yet he and his family were luckier than most, despite their cramped living conditions. Thanks to contacts in Europe he had been given a Swedish prefabricated house, which he has erected in Voskelask, the village where he was born. It would be habitable, he hoped, by the spring, and he wanted to show it to me.

Driving along a very rough road to Voskelask, we encountered, to Surik's surprise, a petrol tanker parked in a lay-by. He turned in. He removed one canister from the boot, and Arman removed another, so that he too could lay in an extra supply of the precious commodity.

Voskelask is a large village of about 5000 inhabitants, most of whom live in private houses. On a ridge overlooking the village we bumped along some exceedingly muddy lanes until we reached Yeranos's house. It was small, with two tight bedrooms and a modest living room, but he was thrilled with it, since it represented an independent life. It stood in its own garden, where he was already growing vegetables. After years of living in a shantytown, he looked forward to returning with his family to the place where his ancestors had lived and, in the case of his parents a year earlier, had died.

From the garden I looked down on to the undulating roofs of the village, smoke rising from chimneys and workshops but remaining trapped beneath a layer of low cloud. The light was fading fast, and dogs howled at the ending of the day. Beyond the village the Turkish frontier lay no more than a kilometre away.

We drove back towards Leninakan, passing a church, or the remains of a church, left untouched after the earthquake: the west front and the choir were standing, but the entire nave was a pile of rubble. We entered Yeranos's cabin through the tiny kitchen, and then descended a couple of steps into a windowless living room, which adjoined a small bedroom. The heater from his Swedish prefab had been installed here, and it was performing magnificently. Yeranos had managed to acquire some new furniture, but he could not replace the books and manuscripts pulverised in December 1988. I was ceremoniously introduced to Yeranos's wife and three children. Despite the cramped ship's-cabin conditions and his wife's poor health, there was no indication of poverty or distress. The rooms were neatly kept, the family's clothes impeccably clean. A bottle of vodka was placed on the table together with a box of chocolates, and I was embarrassed to see that Yeranos had bought a bottle of wine for me at the restaurant which he insisted on opening immediately. I drank small glasses more out of politeness than thirst.

'Sometimes I think it is an act of heroism just to live in Armenia,' reflected Yeranos, and I recalled that he had just returned from England, a land of abundance compared with Armenia. He was not the grumbling kind, and such an admission was an expression of the despair Armenians usually prefer to conceal from visitors. He reminisced feelingly about English pubs, simply because they were places where one could meet one's friends in an informal atmosphere without having to spend a fortune. In Leninakan hardly anybody could afford to frequent restaurants such as the Ani, and there was nowhere else to go. Soviet-style cafés, as I well knew, were specifically designed to depress the spirits.

When Arman decided it was time to begin the journey back to Yerevan, Yeranos's younger daughter presented me with a badge, two pretty handkerchiefs and a pen embroidered with the names of Leninakan and London. I was touched beyond measure, because I knew that even the smallest gifts involved considerable sacrifices. I wished, and not for the last time, that Arman had briefed me before setting out so that I could have offered more appropriate gifts in return than those I routinely carried with me.

I left with a heavy heart. I had urged Yeranos to contact me if he and his family came to London, and he smiled wanly. We both knew it was unlikely. The worthlessness of the rouble and the dire conditions within Armenia meant that prospects of foreign travel were receding all the time. The vast majority of Armenians, and Georgians too, were marooned. Eager to reach out to a world from which they had long been excluded, they realised to their dismay that their isolation was, if anything, greater than before.

14 French Love

Very little remains of old Yerevan, but wandering along Mashtots Avenue I saw, tucked into a courtyard, a charming eighteenth-century Persian mosque. Only some of the turquoise and yellow tiles which adorned the dome and the minaret are still in place, but there are plans to restore this lovely building, now used as the city museum.

Across the street from the mosque is the Central Market. Prices were considerably higher than they had been in Georgia two months earlier, reflecting the onset of winter, inflation and the greater physical isolation of Armenia. One tradesman was offering figs stuffed with chopped nuts and sugar. For this product, compounded of costly raw materials, the price was 200 roubles per kilo. Since the monthly dole for an unemployed Armenian worker was a mere 140 roubles (and even that ceased after three months), such prices were fantastical to most shoppers. The tradesman, seeing my interest in his confection, urged me to taste one, and it was indeed delicious. Did I think his sweetmeat would be popular in Britain? I said it undoubtedly would.

'Then invite me there, and we will do it!'

At the meat counters there was chaos. The problem was queue-jumping, actual or attempted. As there were two queues, both ill-defined, it was easy to see how misunderstandings could arise. As they inched towards the counters the queues were diverted by the presence of two upturned pigs' heads seeping blood and marrow on to the marble.

I wanted to know what was going on, and approached a watchful bearded man in glasses who, I guessed, might speak English. I was right. Aram was a sociologist and a writer of detective stories. Like others, he would wait an hour or more for whatever chunk of meat and bone the butchers chose to give him. No rack of lamb or boned-out leg of pork here. Rows were springing up between customers requesting particular cuts and butchers telling them to get stuffed. The fury was not only to do with meat, Aram admitted. The situation was deteriorating in Armenia, people were anxious and angry, and it was tempting to take that anger out on one another. Offering to continue our conversation in less strenuous surroundings, Aram gave me his phone number.

There was a marginally more relaxed atmosphere at the suburban meat market on the road to Echmiadzin. Metal counters identified with stencilled numbers lined three sides of a square. Farmers were queueing at a side gate to have carcases weighed before being offered for sale. Some were selling directly to retailers. They would accept a slightly lower price than they could obtain by selling directly to the customers, but would not need to spend half the day at the market. The same price of 30 roubles per kilo applied to pork, beef and lamb. As in Yerevan, people were attempting to jump the malformed queues, always with a plentiful supply of excuses. One farmer offered for sale a single item, a suckling pig proudly displayed on the bonnet of his Lada in the muddy car park. He was asking 300 roubles for it, but intimated that if I could see my way to 200 we could discuss it.

Leaving the Yerevan market, I walked back up the hill to meet Arman at the Paradjanov house. A well-known film director, Sergei Paradjanov had lived for most of his life in Kiev and in his birthplace Tbilisi. This handsome stone house near the sports stadium was planned as a museum and residence for the elderly director, but he died in July 1990, shortly before the house was completed. The rooms intended for his use were furnished as his home in Tbilisi had been furnished. It seemed appropriate that the portrait of Lenin had been consigned to the bathroom.

In his youth the director had enjoyed his first spell in jail (two years) for the offence of impersonating Karl Marx in a college play.

After his release, Paradjanov exchanged academic studies for film-making. His early films had surrealist overtones, but he also played safe with works of socialist realism. The first to awaken international interest was *Shadows of Our Forgotten Ancestors* in 1964, and there was even greater acclaim for *Sayat Nova*, directed five years later, the story of a famous Armenian monk of the eighteenth century. By now Paradjanov had become involved in human rights campaigns. In 1974 he was arrested again, this time on a bundle of charges which included trafficking in stolen goods, hard currency speculation, and homosexuality. Sentenced to five years in prison, he was released after four. In 1982 he was arrested yet again, but the French exerted so much pressure that he was spared a further sentence. In all he spent seventeen years behind bars.

Paradjanov was also a wonderfully inventive artist, specialising in collages made from jetsam. Some are sculptural, others take the form of tableaux. There are outlandishly dressed dolls and one of them, a bearded angel suspended from the ceiling, is a playful self-portrait. Everyday objects were contorted and manipulated until they resembled something quite different: an old portmanteau looks like an elephant viewed head on. There's a train in which the cab is adapted from a lantern, the sides are the piping of a dismantled clarinet, and the smokestacks are simple metal bowls. Many of these objects were contrived to while away the long hours in prison, and the materials at his disposal were limited. From aluminium bottle caps he carved small objects, using his nails to shape and define the outlines. Broken bottles, spectacle frames, combs or buttons or bulb filaments, were all put to new imaginative purposes. There's whimsy too. An icon is framed not in silver but in smashed ceramics. A series entitled 'Metamorphoses of Mona Lisa' takes reproductions of the famous painting and imposes other images or screens out parts of the work to create new versions. The addition of a simple luminous pearl earring, for example, transforms a Leonardo into a Vermeer.

I was lunching with Arman at the Razdan, and he gestured in the direction of a bearded man lunching alone a few paces away. It was

Paruyr Hayrikian, the leader of the Union for National Self-Determination. Hayrikian had spent nineteen years as a political prisoner during the Soviet period. Exiled in 1989, he had lived in the United States, where he received enthusiastic support from far-right politicians, presumably because of his stout anti-Communism. Hayrikian has long argued that progress towards independence has been too cautious. He and other politicians have also criticised the government for poor and inappropriate appointments to important posts, and have claimed that the policies for tackling the Karabakh dispute and relations with the Soviet authorities have been ineptly handled.

President Ter-Petrossian had always taken a more gentle, less ideological line. Like many leading Armenian politicians, his political baptism had begun with the Karabakh Committee. In May 1988 the Committee, previously concerned with the plight of Armenians within Azerbaijan, expanded its interests to include the development of democracy within what was still Soviet Armenia. At the same time Green issues became additional grounds for discontent with the status quo. In December 1988 many members, including Ter-Petrossian, were arrested and held without trial in Moscow for six months. A year later the Committee formed the Armenian National Movement, a loose association of some forty political and cultural groups. When the ANM triumphed in the parliamentary elections of August 1990, leading members of the Committee rose to high office: Ter-Petrossian became president of the Supreme Soviet, Vazgen Manukian became prime minister. One of their first tasks was to rein in the growing number of militias, armed with looted weapons, who were roaming the republic.

On 24 August 1990 the Armenian Declaration on Independence was adopted. The preposition is significant. This was not a declaration *of* independence, but a statement of intent with no deadlines attached. It set out the principles the government proposed to apply as the republic moved towards full independence. Many of the steps proposed have since been implemented, including economic reforms, freedom of the press and the widening of diplomatic contacts. Others, such as creating a new currency, are having to wait, which is leaving Hayrikian and his associates impatient.

A curious role in Armenia's political evolution has been played by the diaspora, which is organised into three political parties, two of which used to be deferential towards the Soviet régime. For the diaspora, independence was not an overriding concern. As the scholar and presidential adviser Gerard Libaridian has written: 'Armenia for us [in the diaspora] became a museum that attested to our past, that fuelled our need for cultural identity. Armenians in Armenia were the museum keepers. We asserted, almost with a sense of relief, that the Armenians of Armenia had no role to play in the making of history. We no longer recognised you when you acted as a living nation.'

Instead, the diaspora was obsessed with the genocide and Turkey's failure to acknowledge it. Diaspora Armenians, many of whose parents had fled during the massacres, yearned for the recovery of her 'lost' territories such as Nakhichevan and eastern Turkey. But they did not envisage this notional 'greater Armenia' as an independent nation, and assumed that the Soviet Union, wary of Turkish influence in the Islamic republics, might assist them in their territorial ambitions.

The most astute Armenian politicians were swift to point out that dependency on the Soviet Union, even with the well-intentioned Mikhail Gorbachev in the Kremlin, was misplaced. No outside force – whether the Soviet Union or the United States or the United Nations – was going to come to Armenia's aid. They pointed out that the superpowers had never lifted a finger in the past, most crucially after World War I when independence seemed within Armenia's grasp, and they never would in the future. For these politicians the primary issue was not territory but statehood. Only a truly independent Armenia could argue for the return of its former territories. Vazgen Manukian expressed this view cogently in a 1990 article: 'The unpredictable ups and downs of history may provide us with an opportunity to resolve the territorial issues we must face as an independent nation, a state, and not as an ethnic unit in the process of being assimilated in Russia. It does not mean, of course, that we must forget our territorial demands [but] territorial demands cannot constitute for us at this time a national or state policy.' To those who feared economic ruin if the umbilical cord to the Soviet Union were cut, he replied: 'When not on our own, we may at first fall faster into the abyss; but not being tied to the disintegrated economy of that large country, we can also pull out much faster.'

The ANM was offering an alternative to the politics of the victim, as represented by the diaspora parties. Armenians should abandon their colonial mentality of fear and accept that Russia would never be a protector; they should seek better relations with Turkey despite the unresolved problems over the acceptance of responsibility for the genocide; they should substitute for anxieties about pan-Turkism the struggle for democracy and independence. The ANM has won the argument, even though, as its leaders are the first to admit, true independence has not yet been attained.

Arman offered to introduce me to Hayrikian, and went over to his table, where he joined the politician for a few minutes. They seemed to be talking amiably enough, but on returning to our table, Arman merely handed me a torn-off corner of a paper napkin on which had been scrawled two telephone numbers, one in New York, the other in Paris. 'What's this?'

'These are the phone numbers of the party's representatives in the West.'

'I don't want to speak to them. I want to speak to him.'

'I know, but he says he is too busy over the next ten days.'

'And there's no one else in Yerevan from his party that can spare me fifteen minutes?'

'I asked, but he said no.'

'That's ridiculous.'

Arman nodded. 'I think he does not wish.'

The next morning there was encouraging news: the presidents of Armenia and Azerbaijan had agreed to meet before the end of the year. Other news was less welcome. The tourist exchange rate was being abolished, but the new rate of exchange had not yet been disclosed. As soon as Arman arrived at the hotel we went off to the nearest bank. The bank had no information.

We continued in the direction of Echmiadzin, the seat of the Catholicos of the Armenian Church. On the outskirts of the town we stopped at the Hripsime church. Built in 618, it is squat and compact, shaped like a Greek cross with a porch and belfry attached. A short polygonal tower rises from the centre. Ornament is limited to window-hoods and inscriptions around the porch. The tall broad interior is taut with power, and the crossing piers rise to a complexity of squinches. Paintings of saints march along the base of the plinth of the raised choir. Down in the crypt is the tomb of St. Hripsime, a Christian woman from Rome who, escaping from the persecution of Emperor Diocletian, attracted the attention of the Armenian King Tiridates III. This occurred before Armenia adopted Christianity, and Hripsime, rejecting the advances of the pagan monarch, opted instead for martyrdom. A chapel was built around her tomb, and then replaced by the present church.

The row of cars parked outside belonged to a wedding party. Taped to the sides and bonnet of a white Volga were pink carnations; a doll in bridal whites wobbled on the bonnet. Inside the flesh-and-blood bride and groom were standing beneath the crossing and enduring the lengthy blessings of the priest. They then advanced towards the altar. Coronets were placed on their heads, but the bride's fitted oddly on top of the broad-brimmed summer hat she was wearing. The couple faced each other, then faced the priest as they drank from a goblet. The ceremony was over and the newly married couple accepted the congratulations and kisses of their relatives and friends.

I asked Arman whether such church weddings had been common during the Soviet period. Among ordinary people, he said with surprisingly snobbish condescension, they had been, but anybody with an official position or a Party post who married in church would have been asking for trouble. Such people did so occasionally, but secretly.

The cathedral, set within spacious precincts, was founded in the fourth century, although little remains from that period. It dominates an ecclesiastical complex which includes gardens, a large seminary and the residences of the clergy, as well as the palace of the Catholicos. Between the gateway and the cathedral seedy-looking photographers, as if recycled from an English seaside town in the 1950s, awaited tourists and pilgrims. The first side of the cathedral one sees from the gateway is the vaguely neoclassical treasury extension to the east end of the church; but the cupola and belfries are evidently older. The porch and belfry are lavishly decorated with twisted rope motifs not unlike Manueline work in Portugal, as well as with more traditional Armenian geometrical forms along the friezes. Open turrets over the north and south transepts give the cathedral a surprising lightness. On either side of a small door on the south side the masonry blocks have been grooved by the tongues of penitents, but this slightly unsavoury practice is no longer common.

Entering the cathedral requires some skill, because the pious leave the church in reverse. My nose detected a welcome smell of incense and candlewax, a rich bouquet of liturgy and ceremony. Yet the interior is a disappointment, despite the imposing cupola. The walls and piers are mostly painted cream, and some areas are frescoed in dark patterns; framed paintings in a slightly naif style hang from the walls. The effect is shabby rather than magisterial. There are two thrones for the use of the Catholicos: an elaborately carved wooden throne, and, beyond the choir rail, another used only during mass on Sundays, made from mother of pearl and sheltered by a canopy swirling with baroque fancies.

Most of the contents of the treasury date from the previous two centuries: croziers topped with dashing serpents' heads encrusted with gems, stoles and chalices and crosses, silver crowns and mitres. Silk stoles of blue and red are sensuously embroidered with portraits of saints in gold thread. There are older items, reliquaries and a crucifix studded with semi-precious stones and filigree work, some gold metalwork from 1300, and illuminated manuscripts of high quality. The oldest item I could discover was a powerful ninth-century wooden relief of the Descent from the Cross.

South of the cathedral the baptistery is set within a long range of buildings; with its robing room and two fonts, it has the air of an ecclesiastical processing plant. A clutch of babies were showing the usual signs of displeasure at having to undergo such ritual humiliations. Their outrage might have been greater had they been sharing the fate of the sheep I saw outside another of Echmiadzin's churches. St Gayane, named after Hripsime's wet nurse who also endured martyrdom, was founded in 630 but rebuilt a thousand years later. Its broad five-bay porch now shelters a number of tombs. A large cemetery surrounds the church, and many of the tombs are casket-shaped, reminding me of Moslem burial grounds. A priest in the forecourt was blessing sheep and pigeons which had been brought to him; he sprinkled salt over the heads of the animals and touched the heads of their owners with his crucifix. At the church gates you could buy pigeons for 50 roubles a pair, as well as bubble gum and religious paintings. Sometimes the pigeons are released, but sheep are less fortunate. Some are taken home to be butchered at leisure, but most people take advantage of the facilities provided in the compound. I peeked into the slaughterhouse, but cut my visit short when I saw the floor covered with gleaming entrails. The meat, Arman assured me, was usually distributed to poor relatives or others in need.

On the way back towards Yerevan, we stopped at the ruins of Zwartnots, which in the seventh century had been the site of a cathedral and the palace of the Catholicos. Three hundred years later the complex was destroyed by an earthquake and it was only excavated in the early twentieth century. This must have been an extraordinary structure, quite unlike any other building surviving in Armenia: a domed three-storey church on a polygonal site, raised on a platform and surrounded by flights of steps. A ring of columns remains, the capitals decorated with interlaced patterns, and a single tall column bears a splendid eagle design on the capital. There are similar columns lying on the ground. An apse has been reconstructed, and beyond the cathedral some old foundation walls of the palace have been refaced. There's an ancient winery, equipped with shallow stone basins, very similar to Portuguese *lagars*, in which the grapes would have been trod, and next to them the deep pits into which the juice would have been drained off for fermentation.

We returned to Yerevan for lunch at the hotel, where Yura had been skewering a blend of beef heart and lungs, served with noodles. It tasted better than it sounds, which was just as well, as it was to become a staple feature of the menu. Mineral water, previously in abundant supply, was no longer available. Apparently there was insufficient transport to bring the crates into town. Coffee, usually provided at lunchtime, was no longer on offer.

I lingered after lunch, as Mr Zakoyan was bringing a writer to meet me. It sounded as though he had bagged a trophy, a fine specimen of a Writer. Artem Haroutyounian certainly looked the part. He was a large, flamboyant man, with a long expressive face, swept-back greying hair, and a valuable collection of gold-capped teeth. He was an artist in the very grandest manner, Wildean without effeminacy, fond of expansive gestures, visionary declamations and pithy formulations all expressed at top speed in curious but articulate English. He was a poet and academic: a university lecturer in English and American literature, specialising in an unlikely trio of American poets: Robert Lowell, Allen Ginsberg, and Theodore Roethke. Artem had translated Joyce's *Dubliners* and Eliot's *Four Quartets* into Armenian and was now writing a novel about his student days in Moscow during the Brezhnev years. His favourite British writers were D.H. Lawrence – 'rural England, wonderful, sexual relations, everything, balance of forces, very wonderful, romantic perhaps but there are also lines of gold' – and Dylan Thomas, whom he quoted at length with the original rotundity.

He had been sufficiently in favour with the authorities to have attended a literary festival in Newcastle in 1984, and had briefly visited London. 'I liked London, I like big cities. In strange cities all connections are lost, but sometimes a god can enter your soul.'

The once all-powerful Writers Union, Artem told me, had dwindled in importance. Although it had an undoubted ideological role and controlled literary activities, it would be wrong, in his view, to say that all writers in the Union were arm-twisted by the state. Many writers, by the subtle employment of symbolism, had expressed themselves relatively freely.

'With freedom in Armenia, these are now the best of times to be a writer. But I must also say that Marxism had its positive side. There was an emphasis, a value on spiritual renewal, which writers could express in their work, but of course there were also the negative aspects, the repressions.' I found it hard to think of many approved Soviet writers who had been known for their spirituality, but I let it pass. I asked instead about the character of the Armenian language.

'It has a huge vocabulary and is full of religious expression. It is a language of mystery, of sound and fury, and although it has tremendous historical roots it also absorbs contemporary words well. Less well, of course, than languages of cultures that are more technologically sophisticated.' Artem rattled on, talking about 'a volatile basis' and 'man in this world who is inside this process' and I often lost him. He, however, never wavered. Zakoyan was looking on approvingly, rather like a parent who has brought his child to play with another child and is relieved that the combination is a success.

Was there something nostalgic about Armenian literature, given both the tragic history of the country and the revival of nationalism?

'Yes, many writers do look back, now that totalitarianism is behind us. There is a search for national and religious values, and some writers are reviving our former vocabulary, trying not to lose what their ancestors had created. But the best writers are careful about dwelling too much on the past. It's easy for a writer to be swallowed up by the past if he lacks vision. It's also true that literature is being used to arouse nationalist sentiments, and there are voices full of vistas, but this can harm creative expression. It's not a good idea to give too much thanks to the monsters of the past, to our patriotic literature. It can be good for educational purposes, for informing people of our history, but the individual voice can get lost. In America a writer like Saroyan could come from the past but at the same time he could grasp the future too.'

'Are writers valued in Armenia?'

'Definitely. For Armenians, writing is a public event. That is why the political views of writers can have value and are respected. But I think societies that are better knit, like yours, have less dependence on writers. Some writers here try to be sages, but in the face of real dangers they fall silent, as such a situation demands a political response.'

I asked Artem what changes had struck him most forcefully over the recent past.

'Freedom comes internally first, but of course it is an illusion that freedom is total. The Soviet system achieved tremendous industrial successes, but now we see that it was not all so successful, and shortages come upon us like a lion.'

'How long will it be before patience runs out? Nerves are understandably strained here.'

'People are stoical now, but this will not continue indefinitely. That is why we need new politicians, men like Ter-Petrossian, and we also need to retain our connections with the Russians, if only because they are the only other Christian nation in the region.' (The Georgians had been overlooked, or lumped with the Russians.) 'The rise of Islamic fundamentalism is very worrying to us. Most Armenian intellectuals live here in Yerevan, and I feel that perhaps we should be dispersing to the borders, just as the Israelis did with their kibbutzim. But I am confident that Armenia will survive all these difficulties. Remember that we are part of the belt around Russia, and Russia needs us too, psychologically.'

Artem pricked up his ears. Across the table, he informed me, Arman and Mr Zakoyan were fiercely debating the quaint topic of premarital sex. This was still a live issue in Armenia, where the sexual revolution had never happened, and Zakoyan was arguing strongly that young women should enter the marital state with their hymens intact. Whether the same discipline was to apply to males was less clear. Artem told me that Armenian men could be very strait-laced and, on visits to vice-ridden Moscow, could be taken aback when offered 'French love'.

'What's that?'

'When woman takes penis in the mouth. French love.'

15 Art without Patrons

Arman drove me out to Echmiadzin again to hear the Sunday liturgy. I offered to take the bus but he looked horrified at the suggestion. Near the meat market, the traffic ground to a halt, and the impatient driver in front drove his car across the grassy verge which separated the two carriageways and up the incoming lane. I waited for the sound of crashing metal and the screams of the freshly amputated, but heard nothing. Along the highway shepherds were loitering with their flocks, some of which were being slaughtered on the spot, their carcases slung over boughs and offered for sale. A petrol station was open for business, but because of a power cut the pumps weren't working. A queue had formed in the expectation that the electricity would soon be restored.

The cathedral choir was dominated by women, dressed in cream cassocks and white headscarves, but the powerful voices of the blue-cassocked men behind them seemed to have equal weight. A long golden curtain in front of the apse was drawn aside to reveal the clerical cast, headed by a priest in a dark purple mitre with a matching raised collar. Acolytes kept hold of staffs to which were attached metal plates with bells; when shaken, these emitted a sound like the clatter of a tambourine. The clerics processed with shaking plates and censers through the cathedral, and the faithful pressed forward to kiss the hem of the banners and the priest's crucifix. A few old women pitched forward on their knees and held this uncomfortable position for some minutes.

The music was a disappointment. Two male voices chanted in unison, reminding me of the chanting at St James's Armenian

Cathedral in Jerusalem, but the rest of the music was thickly harmonised and plangent with minor keys, and the sound, although often impressive, seemed Italianate, too crudely emotional. It was a far cry from the complex and searching sonorities of the Georgian Orthodox tradition.

Arman always took great pleasure in citing how prices had been rising, and as we drove back he talked about cars. A new Lada should cost no more than 18,000 roubles (Sandro in Georgia had quoted half that sum), but they are never available, even if you've been on the waiting list for years. As new cars come off the production line, they are sold for about four times their list price to brokers, who then distribute them for even higher prices. Thus the black market has taken over the ordinary market, but in this case the 'ordinary' market is a phoney one which has not kept up with economic realities. The same situation prevailed with tyres. Notionally available for 80 roubles, they are obtainable only on the black market. They had cost 400 or 500 roubles each a year ago; today they would cost 1500 – if you could find them.

Arman looked back to the time, not much more than a year earlier, when government shops were still functioning; because prices had been controlled, private farmers were dissuaded from charging extortionate prices at the market, since customers could always patronise state shops instead. Now government shops are empty – a few grubby cabbages and wormy apples apart – and there is a free-for-all, with constantly rising prices, uncontrolled by any forces except greed.

I commented that the theory had to be that prices would eventually stabilise, because, with the exception of essential purchases customers could refuse to buy overpriced items. 'Price rises are exacerbated because of shortages and the blockade, but when the situation becomes normal once again, prices should stabilise.' I can't say I had a great deal of confidence in my arguments, given that 'normality' had become as remote as Xanadu. Just a month later the liberalisation of food prices in Russia sparked off sharp inflation from which Armenia would not be exempt. The sums Arman had been quoting would by 1992 be looked upon as bargains.

Perhaps I misread his views, but it seemed that Arman believed the present instability vindicated his earlier reliance on the Soviet system. Contemptuous of many new members of Parliament, whom he regarded as ignorant and indolent, he extolled the experience of those such as Kevork Ghiraghosian who had held power during the Communist years and managed to retain it. Ghiraghosian was undoubtedly experienced and probably highly competent too, but that didn't make him typical of the breed. It was not for nothing that Alexander Yakovlev, Gorbachev's dour but highly intelligent adviser, had remarked that the democrats now in power in the former Soviet Union were paying the price for the incompetence of those who preceded them.

As it was Sunday I encouraged Arman to return to his family. I lunched alone, then took a walk down the former Karl Marx Avenue, and turned off through the narrow park that leads towards Republic Square. Leaves, dessicated and discoloured, still clung to the branches. Every item of street and park furniture looked as though it had been untouched in years. Railings and benches were losing their paint and showing wounds of rust. Some railings had pitched over and were left where they had fallen. Broken lamp bulbs had not been replaced. Steps, bins, paving stones, provided originally with municipal largesse, were decaying at their own pace; if they crumbled or broke, they stayed that way. The curtains in the windows of office buildings had been gathering dust for years, and window-dressing consisted of one or two cacti peeking from tin cans placed in an aluminium doily. The sky was not just grey but flecked with the darker charcoal of smoke and dirt.

The façade of the Armenia Hotel on Republic Square was concealed behind hoardings, but renovation work had come to a halt. The square is actually a circular piazza, embraced at each corner by concave buildings of mottled pink tufa, each with huge arcades and stylised floral capitals. Above the arches a row of colonnades cantered along, as stumpy as Egyptian pylons, screening the top two storeys. Lenin's statue, erected in 1948, had been gone since 13 April 1991, but the empty plinth remained. The 'singing fountains' were empty.

Opposite the park and slightly recessed from the square is the building which houses most of the city's major museums. Inside, gaggles of old women sat about doing nothing, but when I asked a member of the fourth gaggle to show me the entrance to the art museum, she kicked up a fuss because I didn't have a ticket. I didn't have a ticket because the ticket counter was unstaffed, but eventually a crone appeared to relieve me of a rouble. It was only four in the afternoon, but the day was so grey and moist that the light was miserable. Naturally, there was no lighting in the galleries themselves, but then it would hardly be worth illuminating the halls for a single visitor.

The exhibits began inauspiciously with eighteenth-century Armenian paintings, religious in inspiration and crude in execution. The highlights of the nineteenth-century collection are the numerous portraits by Hakop Hovnatanian, precise and delicate, showing timid women wearing lace-trimmed finery and clasping their hands nervously. The heads appear larger in scale than their bodies, emphasising the feminine frailty of their slim figures. A succession of immense and dull seascapes and romantic landscapes came to a welcome end with pointilliste turn-of-the-century exercises in quasi-orientalist eroticism by Vardghez Sureniants.

Paintings by Armenia's best-known twentieth-century painter, Martiros Saryan, are profusely displayed. His work blends the angularity of a Cézanne with the colouring and sense of line of a Matisse, while lacking the grip of either. Too often it seems merely decorative. Saryan is acclaimed for his splashy flower paintings, but I found his bold, strongly drawn portraits far more interesting. Given that his artistic career spanned over seventy years, lasting almost until his death in 1972 at the age of ninety-two, there is remarkably little development in his work, as though he had fashioned a style in his youth and kept plugging away at it until he dropped. (A later visit to the Saryan house museum confirmed my earlier impressions. In 1969, he was still painting an idyllic Armenia which vanished long before. Right through the Stalin years, Saryan continued to produce his amiable landscapes and flower paintings, though it was probably dangerous to attempt anything more programmatic. But neither was there any recognition that the Soviet Union was at war for four terrible years, the sole reference being a self-portrait of 1941 which incorporates a framed picture of a young man in uniform.)

Many halls are filled with copies of mediaeval frescoes. The oldest were painted in Aroutj in the seventh century, but survive only in fragments. Other fragments, from the cathedral at Echmiadzin, were executed a thousand years later, but give no sign that experience brought artistic improvement. Easily the most risible frescoes were nineteenth-century examples from Megri. The best work was from the thirteenth century, and came from Achtala in northern Armenia. These include statuesque saints of immense height, and I wondered what kind of church accommodated them. An adjoining room was devoted to copies of saucy Indian cave paintings, a most peculiar and unexplained acquisition.

As the gloom deepened, I stumbled through the historical museum, past armouries of arrowheads and scraps of pottery and mosaic. My interest revived as I encountered copies of *khachkars* and carved wooden doors of great splendour, fine glazed pottery while showed Persian influence, seventeenth-century furniture from mother-of-pearl, and musical instruments. Jewellery, most of it heavy despite the filigree work, took the form of chains and belts and necklaces which must have weighed more than a horse. I was surprised that the genocide was lightly handled, and came across few of the graphic photographs that make a visit to the Armenian Museum in Jerusalem so disquieting.

A steady drizzle curtained the city and left its mark the following day. The moisture had spread the dirt around and the streets were covered with a film of filth. The flanks of every car had been blackened. I seemed to be walking through a haze of blue exhaust. Budapest and Prague and Tbilisi could be foul-smelling on a dank day, but this was worse. To escape the miasma I followed the road that leads down into the Razdan gorge. The Razdan river separates the eastern from the western parts of the city, and the gorge has been preserved as an extended park, free from housing but cluttered with weirs and a children's railway and other pretexts for sociability. Down here the air was better, and the roar of tumbling water swamped the growls and shrieks of the traffic.

After my walk, Arman took me to the banks again. We learnt that they were now free to set their own exchange rates for foreign currency (this information later proved incorrect) but the new rates would be similar to those just abolished. No transactions were possible yet. Arman then drove me to a large block of studios. Although shabby and discoloured on the outside, inside they were spacious and well-lit, resembling double-height flats with balconies. This cooperative block was the first of its kind in Armenia, paid for by the artists who occupy it. Like loft apartments in an American city, these studios were bought as shells and then adapted to suit individual requirements.

Van Soghomonian and Nona Gabrielian have constructed an internal balcony which overlooks their studio. Here they stored their work – mostly ceramics – shelved their books, and entertained visitors. On a shelf behind the couch where I was invited to sit was a collection of rusty old steam irons, their lids opened and resting on the bald pates of small busts of Lenin. Van is a stocky man in his mid-fifties with greying hair and beard, while Nona, a blonde with a lively sense of humour, could hardly have been more different. These differences in temperament seemed reflected in the ceramic reliefs they produced. His were sombre, with human elements, such as hands or faces or breasts breaking forth from the ceramic straitjacket, whereas hers were more playful, slightly reminiscent of late Picasso in their angularity and fondness for profiles.

This was not an easy time for Armenian artists, they told me. Private customers are sparse, especially for abstract pieces, and the best clients, museums and ministries and the Union of Artists, all of which used to commission work, can no longer afford to buy much. Nor were there any private galleries that could display and sell their work. The basement gallery on Mashtots was no more than a salon catering to popular taste, which explained the insipid quality of its offerings. The union system is fading out and is likely to be replaced by looser associations of like-minded artists. Armenia still needed to find a way, said Van, to organise the tremendous artistic talent that existed in the republic, but the present isolation was complicating matters.

When I asked why Armenian artists didn't establish their own galleries, he and Nona replied that if they offered their works at realistic prices only foreigners could afford to buy them, and these days nobody was coming to Yerevan. There were such galleries in Moscow and St Petersburg and Riga, all of which were more likely to be visited by dealers and art-loving tourists. Van added that he has been successful in selling his work to museums throughout Europe and America, but both their careers have been hampered because ceramics are less portable than prints or paintings.

I asked whether the large diaspora helped disseminate artists' work, but they could think of very few Armenians abroad who were involved in the art business. Until recently, said Van, Armenian artists were not regarded primarily as Armenians, a fact confirmed by a diploma on the wall from an Italian art festival which identified Van Soghomonian only as a citizen of the USSR.

Despite all the difficulties, Van and Nona, who were well known both within Armenia and beyond its frontiers, could earn a living from their art – just. As Henrik Igitian had established in a different context, art is highly valued by Armenians of all social levels, not just by an educated élite. A sculptor who joined us around the coffee table sadly confessed that he was less fortunate. No individuals commissioned sculpture, and official commissions had also dried up. Not, he added, that these had necessarily gone to the best artists.

Our party moved upstairs to the studio of Samvel Ambartsou-mian, a slight but self-assured man of about forty. His studio was laid out quite differently, with many doors and partitions and curtains which provided separate zones. The balcony and lower areas were reserved for sculpture and printmaking, while the easel stood on the balcony. Samvel's paintings, executed with a thick oil technique, consisted mostly of contorted nudes in movement, sometimes with exaggerated breasts and buttocks, often truncated or gashed. Samvel, like Van, enjoys a privileged position among Armenian artists, since he has had a number of one-man shows in Europe and North America. He seemed suspiciously modest, declaring that he sold only a small proportion of his output, since he had no wish to acquire a car or a country house. He only wanted to earn enough to feed his family, and any profits he made from sales within Armenia he usually gave away. For paintings and prints there was a small domestic market of collectors, and he was one of the more sought-after artists. For Samvel, the major problem was not selling his work but acquiring good materials. He had just laid his hands on some excellent French paper for his prints, but often he has to adapt his techniques to the poorer quality materials at his disposal.

I was left to my own devices for the third afternoon and evening in a row. I certainly didn't expect to be entertained and accompanied every day, but it was hard to find anything to do in Yerevan. I had taken walks each day, but one street lined with decrepit houses and apartment blocks was much like the next, and the foul quality of the air diminished the pleasure of the exercise. After dusk, which fell early in December, walking was impeded by dim lighting and by pavements either nonexistent or wrecked, forcing me to walk in the road, a high-risk strategy in Yerevan. There was no Rustaveli Avenue on my doorstep. Here I had little option except to stay in my room, with fitful transmissions of CNN for company. I had been sternly requested to dine no later than seven-thirty, and dinner was swiftly over.

At least I had the daily visit to the bank to look forward to. There was a foreign exchange desk at the Hotel Ani, but when we arrived there the next morning it had run out of cash. Officials were still awaiting news about the new exchange rates; until they heard from Moscow it would be impossible to change money. Perhaps there would be news tomorrow. I pointed out that this had to be a unique occasion: the former Soviet Union was refusing to accept hard currency in exchange for roubles.

The driver took us next to the school attended by Arman's

children. Electricity cuts led to cancelled classes, so Arman had to collect his son and take him to his grandparents' flat, where he could be looked after for the rest of the day. The instability of the school system was worrying many parents, complicating their lives as they rushed about trying to cope with sudden closures. We continued to the Friendship Society, where I had the impression, not for the last time, that my hosts were at a loss to know what to do with me. I still had a long list of things I wished to do and people I wished to meet, but few appointments were materialising. Arman hit the telephones for half an hour, but the results were not encouraging, although he did manage to set up an appointment with a joint venture company.

Micrograf was established three years ago as a British–Armenian enterprise. It imports technical components from other parts of the Soviet Union and from countries such as Singapore, and assembles computers and telephones. The firm occupied a new building on the outskirts, a rare example of modern architecture in Yerevan. The office of the director, Mr Papikian, was far better equipped than those I had seen at ministries. He had a portable phone, a Japanese answering machine, and other up-to-date technical equipment. Since it was difficult, occasionally impossible, for people to telephone each other across Yerevan, I asked Papikian whether poor communications hampered him. Not at all, he replied, as they had fax and telex facilities in all their offices. They also lease their own plane, so they are not dependent on the vagaries of Aeroflot.

I rudely asked why anybody in the West would want to buy their products. The answer, of course, was cost. How about parts and servicing? Well, if a large quantity of goods was being exported by Micrograf they would open an office in the country of destination to provide servicing and would dispatch specialists to install the equipment.

I mentioned that in Britain the image of Soviet workmanship was fairly abysmal. Ladas, the most visible Soviet import, had spawned an entire breed of jokes – 'What do you call a Lada convertible?' 'A skip.' Wasn't this a problem? Yes, but they encourage clients to come and see for themselves, and then their doubts are swiftly dispelled.

'Do you receive any help from the Armenian government?'

'No. Only the extension of credit, which is given to us only because we are already successful. We don't want favours from the government. We will leave them to get on with politics, and we will get on with our business transactions.'

'Is bureaucracy a problem?'

'No worse than in European countries.'

'You should try changing money this week.'

Taxes on hard-currency earnings were about half those levied by the Georgian government, and they were imposed on profits, not on revenue.

Micrograf was one of four or five companies of comparable size now operating in Armenia, but others were being formed. Papikian acknowledged that one of the main problems was persuading foreign investors that Armenia's instability was temporary. In his view foreigners' caution had no real basis – in Arman's old-fashioned Soviet formulation, 'a wrong way of thinking' – since there were excellent possibilities for investment, given the low cost of raw materials and labour.

Mr Papikian showed me round. The conference room was luxuriously furnished in mogul style with items acquired from Spain as part of some other deal. The vulgar mirrored light fittings had been produced here, though why a hi-tech firm was manufacturing gaudy light fittings remained unclear. Like many offices in the building, the room was equipped with large television sets tuned to SuperChannel. Another expensive toy was the Volvo which is put at the disposal of potential clients visiting Yerevan. In the demonstration room computer equipment was set out on metal desks – another Spanish import, but reassembled here. Below the offices were the assembly lines, recently imported from Singapore, all of them unused. At first I was told that the production lines were idle because the cold had temporarily closed down the factory. Later I heard a different explanation from Mr Papikian: the factory could be heated, but only when orders were received that justified taking on additional trained staff. Evidently those conditions were not being met right now. Micrograf's workers would, when eventually employed, be making good money by Soviet standards: between 1500 and 3000 roubles per month. I was puzzled that Papikian could be so enthusiastic when no production was actually taking place. This, he insisted, was a temporary matter. Why, the company had only just received a huge contract from the Ukraine to manufacture millions of telephones.

It was snowing, but that bastion of privilege, the Razdan Hotel, still had no heat and no hot water. The maids' room on my floor was warmed by portable bar heaters, and I asked whether it would be possible to provide my room with a heater too. They did so, to my great joy, but after I went out they removed it and I never saw it again.

Arman arrived in good humour: he had found a politician for me to talk to. Well, not exactly a politician, but Garnik Badalian, the press officer at the foreign ministry. We talked about Karabakh, and he gave me the familiar line of the Armenian government, adding that he hoped both Turkey and Iran would try to act as peace-brokers, as indeed they subsequently did. I asked Badalian whether he could arrange for me to visit Karabakh. He pointed out that the only access was by helicopter, and helicopters were occasionally shot down. In short, no.

I changed tack, and asked how the government perceived the process of moving towards full independence. He stressed the government's diplomatic efforts. At that very moment the foreign minister, Raffi Hovannisian (curiously, an American lawyer in his early thirties and the son of the historian Richard Hovannisian), was visiting five European countries to ask for economic aid and diplomatic recognition. (Those efforts proved remarkably successful. By April 1992, eighty-six countries, as well as the United Nations, had officially recognised the republic. The United States set up a temporary embassy in the Razdan Hotel, and Armenia dispatched ambassadors and chargés d'affaires to major Western capitals.)

'Is is true that Armenia wants closer ties with its old enemy Turkey?'

'Turkey is no longer our enemy.'

'But the psychological perception of Turkey is that of a historical enemy, surely.'

'Yes, but that is an obstacle we must overcome. The response of both Turkey and Iran has been encouraging, so we hope for better relations.'

'I can see why you need better relations with them, but do you trust them?'

'Yes.' Then a smile. 'But then we have no choice. But we also know that Turkey is anxious to join the European Community and become a civilised state. There are obstacles and problems, but Armenia has survived worse difficulties in the past.'

'Just.'

From the ministry we drove through the slush to suburban Yerevan to visit the 360-bed Children's Republican Hospital in Furmanov Street. The hospital had some heat, so we warmed up in the office of the director, a plump kindly man named Albert Khachatrian. It soon became apparent that this was one of the best hospitals in Armenia. It is the principal children's hospital in the republic, as well as a teaching hospital, specialising in kidney ailments. Although medical treatment is still free, the authorities were thinking of introducing low charges for outpatients to augment the hospital's resources. Some doctors were already charging patients twenty roubles for a consultation.

There was no electricity that morning. Usually the hospital was spared power cuts until mid-afternoon, allowing surgeons to work all morning without interruption, but there had been some rupture of supply today. The main problem, according to Dr Khachatrian, was either the lack of gas or very low gas pressure, which affected not only the heating but the kitchens and laundry too. A generator kept the ten dialysis machines (provided by Swiss and Belgian charities) in operation whenever the electricity supply was cut off, but its power was limited. Although the hospital was given priority as a recipient of supplies of energy, the system was evidently fallible. The blockade was also limiting the availability of medical supplies and spare parts, which had been reduced by about one-third. Republics such as the Ukraine had been important suppliers, but as the republics moved towards independence, all such arrangements would have to be renegotiated. Supplies transported by road through Georgia were sometimes delayed or robbed.

In the intensive care unit the monitors were not working because of the power cut. On the other hand the wards were small, they were clean and there were plenty of playrooms to keep the more mobile patients entertained. Children confined to their beds were brought crafts and other activities to keep them amused and stimulated.

The hospital had inaugurated a kidney transplant programme in June 1991. The organs had been flown in direct from St Petersburg, a process which had taken no more than ten hours. Now organs had to be flown to Armenia via Moscow, lengthening the delivery time to thirty hours, a delay which jeopardised the future of the programme. It enraged Dr Khachatrian that these essentially political squabbles were playing havoc with the lives of children.

'We will go to Ashot's office.'

I had contacted Aram, my acquaintance from the meat market. He took me to the Institute of Philosophy where he worked. He had asked some of his colleagues to join us. Ashot, who ran a new research institute in the social sciences, was one of them, Vladimir another. Vladimir, a debonair figure, tall and slender and well groomed, spoke excellent English. He was an educational sociologist with a number of books to his credit. It was a relief to be among these amiable intellectuals, especially since their company could be enjoyed without the presence of an intermediary.

Vladimir was surprisingly gentle in his attitude towards the former régime. Although he evidently harboured little nostalgia for Marxism-Leninism – he had never been a Party member – he believed there had been greater liberty in Armenia than in most other Soviet republics. Many Armenians had viewed the Communist system as a kind of game. No one took ideological issues too seriously, and the authorities were not zealous about monitoring the boundaries of what was acceptable. He remarked that when he had wanted to pursue postgraduate studies in Moscow, he was rejected because he was not a Party member. But there had been no such requirements in Yerevan, where university entrance had been determined by open competition, not ideological conformity. Even the Karabakh Movement had been able to pursue its aims without undue censorship, and when repression did come, it came from Moscow.

As for the Karabakh dispute, Vladimir insisted that it was more than a local territorial spat. He saw the dispute as a clash of values, with Turkey and the Moslem world backing Azerbaijan, and the United States and democratic values supporting the Armenian cause. This sounded too pat to me, partly because I doubted that Western countries were as impassioned in their support as Vladimir believed. 'Turkey would like to reestablish its old empire, and in that scheme Armenia is a small nuisance that can't be bypassed. If we give Karabakh to Azerbaijan, then they will demands two-thirds of Armenia, claiming it's part of their ancestral lands. This is a strategy that has been worked out not in Baku, but in Ankara. That's why this is not just an inter-ethnic dispute. It's a symbolic clash of mentalities and cultures and values, of Christian respect versus the less tolerant culture of Islam. Armenians believe that the only model of development is the Western one, which is democratic and progressive.'

I was not the only one in the room who found this interpretation a touch too conspiratorial. I then asked whether freedom had brought in its wake an artistic revival.

'There has been an awakening,' said Ashot. 'Books that were once forbidden are now being published, though, as Vladimir said, the Communist grip was never as strong here as elsewhere. Some books slightly critical of Marxism were also published here under the Soviet régime.'

'I find,' said Vladimir, 'that I am reading less English literature than I used to – I have read everything by D. H. Lawrence – '

'And I've read almost everything by Graham Greene,' added Aram.

'– but now I am reading more Russian books, because at last it is possible to read what used to be banned. Here in Armenia we have new newspapers, theatre companies and so forth, but, to be honest, it's very hard to assess their quality.'

'And despite this cultural awakening,' said Aram, 'I cannot get my detective novel published. No publisher rejects it, but all say that at present they cannot afford to take it on.'

The steep rise in the cost of living must have taken the shine off the movement towards independence, and I wondered whether Armenians viewed true independence as an attainable goal.

Vladimir replied: 'For Ter-Petrossian, independence is a process, but nobody is clear about how far it will go. I think there was a time when our politicians over-exploited the idea of independence. But the euphoria has passed as people see the extent of our problems.'

'Are there people who look back to the good old days under the Communists, when food was cheap and there was heating in every apartment?'

'Some,' admitted Vladimir. 'For a few people it may be tempting to look back on those days as a time of stability and predictable prospects. Of course nobody *believed* in Communism. It was just a set of ideals people paid lip service to. But most people realise that our present hardships are unavoidable, and they have to be optimistic – we can't look back. We're talking about our future, our survival. There is no other course. The only other possibilities are to surrender and die or to emigrate. That is why the Karabakh problem is so important.'

It was growing very cold in the room as dusk fell. It was time to end the meeting. Vladimir, like Yeranos in Leninakan, regretted that Armenia lacked institutions such as British pubs where we could sit and continue our talk. He and his companions insisted they would accompany me back to my hotel, and I was soon glad of their company. The streets and paths, even close to the centre of town, were so ill lit that without an occasional guiding hand I might easily have stumbled. Uneven pavements and the contours of potholes were imperceptible in the gloom. We walked through the underpass beneath Mashtots, and the steps at the other end were half buried under a scree of rubble. Two-thirds of the way up the slope, the steps petered out and the only way to regain street level was to take the bank of hardened mud at a run. Aram murmured, 'Symbol of our situation.'

Near the Dvin Hotel I left them, since I assured them I knew my way back perfectly well. I stopped at a stall to buy some red wine. When the vendor became aware that I was not Armenian, which took a long while considering that I addressed him in a mixture of sign language and bad Russian, he became quite agitated. I handed him the price in roubles, but he kept repeating 'Dollar, dollar, stairlin, dollar', as though I had cheated him by not paying in hard currency.

In my room some cockroaches had come out to play, and took up audacious poses on my desk and among the bristles of my toothbrush. They were, by American standards, small, and I experienced a few pangs of conscience while wondering what to do with these little chaps with cutely twitching antennae. Then I killed them.

16 Looking Truth in the Eyes

'How about a little banking this morning, Arman?'

'Yes, we shall try.'

The teller said she actually had some money. When she quoted the new tourist exchange rate, I felt embarrassed. The rate now was almost three times more favourable than it had been two months earlier in Georgia. I had been rich in Georgia, but now I was monstrously rich. Later that day I tipped Surik five dollars. Converted into roubles that was now the equivalent of a month's salary. Perhaps he would use this money to continue building his country house. He told me he hoped it would be completed by the summer, and he gave me an open invitation to come and stay with him. Surik may have been a mere chauffeur, but his skill and loyalty must have been well rewarded. Joe, the telephone engineer, had a driver who had to get by on 250 roubles a month.

Surik drove west in the direction of Echmiadzin, then turned off along a good road which led towards the Turkish border. The original plan had been to visit Lake Sevan, with its old churches and celebrated *khachkars*, but the snowy weather had forced a change of itinerary. We passed vineyards planted on the valley floor, but the vines were packed beneath small banks of earth to protect them from the harsh winter. Apricot trees stood bonily in large orchards, sheep grazing beneath the bare branches. To the north I could see the four idle stacks of the Medzamor nuclear power station idiotically sited here. It had been closed after the 1988 earthquake as an environmental hazard which did not meet even Soviet safety standards. The power station had supplied not only Armenia but parts of Azerbaijan and Georgia with electricity. Now the government had begun a costly refitting operation with the intention of reopening Medzamor in 1994. But Parliament had insisted that the final decision should be made by popular referendum. It's not an enviable choice to have to make: reliable energy supplies and a risk of nuclear catastrophe, or more freezing winters.

Before long we reached Hoktemberian. Its name is under threat, since it commemorates the glorious October revolution. This hideous town is filled with clapped-out factories, all of them closed because of the fuel shortage. Workshops and building sites spill out beyond their walls, and piles of industrial debris encroach on to the adjoining farmland. Melted snow and burst water mains had turned some of the roads into carpets of mud. Apartment blocks showed the same makeshift adaptations as those in Yerevan; balconies sagged drunkenly. On the ground floor plate-glass windows rose to the height of the storey to illuminate shops either closed or empty. Many panes were missing, and a random assemblage of plywood boards patched the gaps. Rags were stuffed into the holes to provide rudimentary insulation; those panes that remained intact were too grimy to allow much light to penetrate.

Houses crouched behind low walls and corrugated metal fences. Shrivelled grapes still clung to vines which trailed along the trellises between house and wall. Along the main roads, empty boxes of American cigarettes were tucked over the branches of trees to advertise that somebody within spitting distance of the kerb was offering them for sale. As in Yerevan, boxy Ladas sported Mercedes hubcaps in a pathetic aping of status symbols. Western culture was perceived primarily in terms of consumer goods: Germany was the creator of the Mercedes logo, Britain the source of Scotch whisky, while the United States was a gigantic cigarette factory.

Arman, of course, had a friend here, so we spent over an hour trailing from factory to deserted factory trying to track him down. Failing to find Hovig, we continued on our way to Sardarapat, one of the most famous sites in Armenia, where a great battle put a stop, in the nick of time, to Turkish expansionist ambitions. Had Armenian forces lost the fight here on 22 May 1918, in all probability there would no longer be a place on the map called Armenia.

The site is robustly celebrated by a reddish-brown tufa monument with stylised winged oxen and eagles and a lofty bell tower. A lovely view opens in one direction across the plain until the slopes rise towards the Ararat range, the hump of Ararat lording it over the rest of the peaks. In the other direction I could see Mount Aragats, its fussy little peaks pushing up from the great mass of the mountain. Recent snowfalls had forced the white line down the slopes to a few hundred metres above the valley floor. Wispy white cloud snuggled among the Ararat peaks, and in the bright midday light it was hard to tell where snow ended and vapour began.

Close to the monument, and built from the same reddish tufa, stands the ethnographic museum designed in 1978 by Rafael Israelyan. A handsome square block, its design emulates a mediaeval fort with corner turrets, without succumbing to pastiche. Like many traditional Armenian churches and houses, it is lit from above. Just two small windows poke through the massive exterior, and they are deliberately placed to provide views on to the two mountain ranges. The interior is surprisingly light. Four courtyards provide natural light, as do the skylights. Such skylights – known as *hazarashen*, which literally means a thousand steps – have that layered-beam structure which diminishes in size as the rafters pile up towards the aperture.

The museum is remarkably good, far better than the modern crafts museum in Yerevan. An English-speaking guide used the occasion of my visit to perfect her English, stumping me with questions about the precise difference between 'transport' and 'transportation' and the legal definition of a charter. The exhibits began with a stark reminder of Armenia's dimunition, a topographical map of 'upland Armenia' which made it abundantly clear that present-day Armenia occupies a mere tenth of its former territories, the rest subsumed within Turkey and Iran. The oldest exhibits – menacing headless statues and phallic stones, agricultural implements such as butter urns, and ceramics and jewellery up to 4000 years old – are, strictly speaking, pre-Armenian despite their local provenance. A culture identifiable as Armenian was in place here by the sixth century BC, and there is no shortage of exhibits from this period too. A second-century stone wine press intrigued me especially, and the mediaeval ceramic ware is of first-rate quality, which is not true of the *khachkars*.

I tend not to linger over agricultural implements, but my excellent guide would not let me hurry. She pointed out a device for shoeing oxen, consisting principally of a wooden pole to which the blacksmith lashed the feet of the animal to discourage it from distracting movements. She showed me an awesome spiked collar worn by hounds to dissuade wolves and other predators from sinking their teeth into the dog's neck. A muzzle made from hedgehog skin was attached to the head of a calf to prevent it from sucking so much milk from the teat of its mother that none would be left for humans to drain off. Along one of the galleries I saw comprehensive displays of costumes and musical instruments and modern ceramics, among which I recognised Van Soghomonian's work.

Close to the monument there were two restaurants to choose from. One had lit a fire, so there was no contest. We began with cold *khash*, which resembled brawn in jelly, as well as the usual cold vegetables and cheese, followed by excellent pork shashlik and boiled lamb on the bone.

After lunch Arman resumed the search for his friend Hovig. We found his house, and his children informed us he would be back in twenty minutes. To pass the time we visited the town's shops. First we strolled through the mostly hollow shell known as the local department store. On the ground floor were some shoes – deplorably made plastic moccasins costing 142 roubles which wouldn't last ten minutes on an Armenian street – and plastic bowls. On the first floor were a few awful clothes, mostly nylon, and cosmetics in reasonable quantities. Toys of shoddily made plastic were thrust into grubby transparent bags; stationery items included a two-year-old calendar and leaking ink bottles. Most of the shelves were bare, despite the cheerful signs above them alluding to the wonderful sporting wear or children's clothes on sale. The building was spartan, with bare stone walls and stone floors; there was no lighting.

Next door a greengrocer offered filthy deformed carrots, potatoes and watermelons. The dried apricots were a bargain at 7.50 roubles per kilo, but they were so blackened that even the hag behind the till admitted they were inedible. A meatless butcher was selling hunks of hard flaky cheese with a dangerous-looking green whiskery mould. A stationer, known as a cultural goods shop, was well stocked, and I bought two large notebooks for just under a farthing each. Next door a shop sold chickens, not the small scrawny corpses usually seen at the market but large blotchy creatures, brutally plucked, victims, no doubt, of accidents on the streets of Hoktomberian. There was a rarity for sale at another shop: sugar. The catch was that this shop was reserved for war veterans, and the door was barred until Arman convinced the gatekeeper that we only wanted to look around. Goods were no cheaper than in other shops, but at least some scarce items were occasionally available.

We returned to Hovig's house. Grandma was apologetic, he was still not home. We were welcomed in anyway and shown the garden with its small oval swimming pool and fruit trees and vegetable patches. After a few minutes of polite conversation we left. Just as I was opening the car door, Hovig and his wife Garine returned. We were now committed, and trooped back into the house. Hovig was a finely featured man, about forty, with great personal charm. He was the deputy director of an electrical engineering factory, but the energy crisis had severely curtailed its operations. Many workers had been laid off without pay, but managers such as Hovig were more fortunate. He told me he was about to resign to start up his own business. He said that bribery and corruption still persisted and he had had enough of it.

Despite the modest façade the house presented to the street, there was every sign inside that Hovig had been well paid for his disquiet. Not only was there a pool, but the floors were laid with attractive parquet and a wide wooden staircase led to the upper floor. Spacious verandahs overlooked the garden. Garine apologised profusely for the discomfort of their home. Heating was just about nonexistent; they were attempting to run their central heating system off coal, and that too was hard to find. Electricity cuts usually lasted up to six hours each day, but there had been no power for twenty-four hours. Without gas, cooking was impossible, but they had installed a small electric burner in the living room so that Garine could at least prepare simple hot dishes – when there was electricity.

None of this diminished the outpouring of hospitality. Bowls of nuts and fruits culled from the garden soon appeared, as did a box of chocolates. There was cognac for Arman and me, vodka for Surik and Hovig, and cherry juice for Garine and the children. Not satisfied with the first bottle of perfectly drinkable cognac he had opened, Hovig fetched another and proposed to bring me some of his oldest wines as well until I dissuaded him. His daughter ran next door and soon returned with cups of excellent dark coffee clattering on the saucers.

A venerable gentleman, half-bent with age, now made an appearance, a cigarette conjoined to his lower lip. He was introduced as a great authority on winemaking. Would I be interested to know his methods? Certainly. First, he recommended that if you take young red wine and boil it and then put it in a sealed container, it will keep very well. Did I want to know how they made sweet wine? Definitely. Well, while the wine is still fermenting, you add spirit to stop the fermentation, and then to make sure the brew is even sweeter, you add grape juice concentrate. Fortunately I was not given the opportunity to taste the results. I asked whether he required a licence before poisoning the population and the answer was that under the Communists a licence had been necessary, but now you could do whatever you wanted. Arman added that it probably wouldn't be long before the new régime came up with a licensing system too. For once, this struck me as a good idea.

By 5.30 it was growing dark. The children lit a kerosene lamp, which the family had been lucky enough to acquire when they were still affordable. As the light filled the room with a Victorian glow, Hovig revealed that it was his birthday. I congratulated him, concealing my alarm that the festivities would now be almost unstoppable. Once again he invited me to empty his cellar. He had a special mulberry vodka, even a bottle of Scotch. I almost sank to my knees to dissuade him from opening the latter, pointing out that I could drink Scotch like water when I got home to England. Here, I said, I would much rather drink the excellent Armenian brandy. Hovig had another scheme: we should stay the night. Definitely. He would not even discuss it. They had plenty of room upstairs for us all. He then outlined a vision: by the romantic light of the lamp we would continue with our toasts, then at eight we would nibble on some snacks, and at ten he would get a fire going and we would all gorge ourselves on shashlik. No matter that the house was cold and there was no electricity! We could celebrate until long into the night, and first thing tomorrow morning – he promised – I would be on my way back to Yerevan.

I said I couldn't consider it, I had work to do at the hotel, I had phone calls to make, letters to write. Arman supported me, but with no great vigour, and singlehandedly I had to fend off Hovig's supplications, which were persistent, almost wheedling, for a full half hour. Eventually we worked out an honourable compromise: I promised that if I returned to Armenia with my family, we would stay with them.

What if I had said, after Hovig first extended the invitation, that I thought it was a wonderful idea. Would that have been a faux pas? (When I put the question to Arman, he didn't doubt for an instant that the offer was seriously intended. But for him to have questioned Hovig's sincerity would have put his friend in a bad light.) There was only one way to test the matter, but I couldn't risk it.

At 6.30 we were on our way. Surik, despite a heroic consumption of spirits all afternoon, seemed in command of the car, although the bonnet was still making unpredictable leaps into the air. I asked Arman what my programme would be for my last two days.

'Whatever you want!' he replied grandly, which left me dumb-founded. At his suggestion I had twice presented him with lists of requests and only a few of the items had materialised. The often promised cultural programme had consisted of nothing at all. I expressed amazement that so many doors seemed closed to me. Arman shrugged. He too was surprised. I had no way of telling whether he had tried and failed, or whether he really hadn't tried that hard in the first place. And if it were the latter, was it because of indolence or incompetence, or were there unspoken political motives? Perhaps he was not that keen to introduce me to representatives of the new Armenia; perhaps he lacked contacts. It was impossible to know. All I knew was that I had been stumbling about on the periphery for two weeks. That night my frustration began to invade my dreams.

Sleek and bulbous, the plump dead rat, its tail elegantly curled behind it, made a striking addition to the street furniture outside the Razdan. No one had bothered to remove the disembowelled night runner and its intestinal smears, so I stepped gingerly past it and into the car that would take me to the offices of Sujian Lazar. Mr Lazar was being offered as a compensation for my failure to encounter any of the wizards of Echmiadzin. He was the vice-chairman of the department for religious affairs, and presented a rosy picture of the status of the Armenian Church.

'In the twenties and thirties many churches were closed, but in the more recent period the government was tolerant of the Church. Not long ago our parliament passed a law ensuring freedom of conscience. Although most Armenian believers belong to the Apostolic Church, this freedom of conscience applies equally to all religions.'

Armenia, he continued, was enjoying a religious revival. More churches were open for worship and more men were training for the priesthood. At Echmiadzin, the numbers enrolled at the seminary had increased from thirty-five to over one hundred. Other religious organisations were active too: evangelical groups, the Krishna movement, the Mormons. The Jews were reestablishing their synagogue in Yerevan, and his department was helping the Jewish groups to recover the community's original buildings.

I wondered whether, as in Georgia, there were strong links between nationalist sentiments and religious revivalism. Mr Lazar replied that the two feelings often flourished side by side, but religious leaders discouraged any overt links between them, as they didn't wish to give the impression that the conflict between Armenia and Azerbaijan was primarily religious. 'After all,' he added,

'Armenian communities have flourished in Moslem countries for centuries.'

The Armenian Apostolic Church is famously split, and has been since 1441. In those days the Catholicos was based among the Armenians of Cilicia, and when some clerics decided to revive Echmiadzin, where St Gregory founded the cathedral in 303, as the historical base of the Church, the Catholicos declined to go along with their plans. So the Echmiadzin lobby elected their own Catholicos, and the two patriarchs developed separate spheres of influence, with the Cilician Catholicos continuing to rule not only the Armenians of Cilicia but the substantial communities throughout the Levant. The system worked reasonably well until 1956, when the election of a new Cilician Catholicos became politicised, and hopes for a rapprochement receded. The disagreements intensified as the Cilician see declared that it regarded Echmiadzin as the episcopal seat of Soviet Armenia alone, and expanded its jurisdiction to Armenian communities in North America and Greece. According to Lazar, negotiations between the two sees had been taking place for some time, but without agreement. The split is seriously absurd. In Niagara Falls, New York, for instance, two Armenian churches stand side by side in needless duplication, especially since no major doctrinal differences divide the two branches. Their principal beliefs include the denial of the existence of purgatory, baptism by triple immersion, and the division of the priesthood into two classes. One half is celibate and eligible for elevation to the episcopacy; the other operates only at parish level, but is entitled to marry.

Diaspora publications such as AIM (Armenian International Magazine) had revealed that the Armenian Church, especially the western diocese under the leadership of Archbishop Vatche Hovsepian, had been sitting on $1.4m, mostly from America, donated to help the earthquake victims. Some of the money, it was claimed, had been used to found a university rather than for its declared purpose. The eastern diocese had collected $7.8m, but had spent less than half of this in the two years following the disaster. I asked Lazar whether he could shed any light on these matters. He was vague. The Holy See, he told me, had agreed to oversee the reconstruction of the Stepanavan region, and Armenian-Americans had collected money to this end and had sent over technicians to assist with the rebuilding. Unfortunately, poor communications and the blockade had made it difficult to accomplish all the plans.

'But it's been three years since the earthquake. That's an awfully long time to be stalled. The British and Italians and other contributors have managed to complete their projects.'

'So what are you proposing?'

'I'm not proposing anything. I'm just passing on the observation that tens of thousands of people in Europe and America gave money to assist the earthquake victims and their donations are apparently still sitting in bank accounts.'

Lazar admitted that he was none too sure of the facts, as his department had no control over such matters. Personally, he thought a government commission should look into the matter.

'Forgive the impertinence, but is your department really necessary? Aren't churches and other religious bodies perfectly capable of looking after their own interests? In the old days the function of your department was to control religious expression, which is surely not required now.'

'Our role has never been to control the Church, and indeed, Moscow used to criticise the Armenians for allowing the Church too much liberty. It's true that some other republics have closed down their religious affairs departments for the reason you give, and perhaps Armenia should do the same. But our Parliament expressed the view that this department should be used to enforce freedom of conscience. Our role is to promote and defend all religious rights. Even the leaders of the Church are defending our department.'

Arman was looking at his watch. We had an appointment at the Institute of Foreign Languages in suburban Yerevan, where 2000 students spend up to five years studying a number of languages. Russian was of course the most popular some years ago, but it had now been overtaken by English, and the directors were keen to persuade more students to study French and German too. Some years before most students had been able to travel to Europe or

America to pursue their studies, but this was no longer possible. Teachers I met spoke to me about the happy months they had spent in Oxford or Manchester, but such opportunities were a thing of the past.

In an upstairs room some twenty-five students, mostly female, sat on hard chairs around the walls. Bundled up in cloth coats, scarves round their heads, gloves on their fingers, they were doing their best to ignore the chill. A small bar heater glowed ineffectually in a corner.

I asked the students whether there was any disillusionment after the initial euphoria of independence. Now that it was clear that the immediate future was not going to be filled with sweetness and light, was there any regret or bitterness about the path chosen?

A young bearded man spoke up. 'We nearly lost our heart,' he began, his idiom all the more direct and poignant for its faint inaccuracies. 'We didn't expect all this to happen. Every day brings something unexpected. We have talked of independence, but independence is only a philosophy, and the reality that we must live with is worrying. But we know this is how things are. We have to look truth in the eyes.'

His eloquence suggested that he had not really lost heart. Other students echoed his view. One young woman said, 'We have to be optimistic, we have to accept, we have to try to make our life interesting despite the problems.'

I asked them whether they, or their parents or friends, were expressing regrets about the new direction Armenia was taking. Was anyone looking back longingly to a time when there was heat in their flats and food in the shops? Someone replied that one did sometimes hear such longings from older people, but in her view, and the view of most people, the situation would have been bad even without independence. 'Everyone knows we had been living in a world of lies.'

Another girl added that most young people knew that the present course was the only one feasible – 'even if it takes fifty years. This is our fate. It is written on our foreheads.' It was not only a question of introducing new economic systems; psychological changes were required too. For decades people had been paid to perform specific tasks; how well or how badly they performed them had been irrelevant. 'However hard you tried to do your job well, it didn't help you get further in your life. The system was closed, it did not encourage people to think for themselves. These attitudes are changing, but very slowly. We know we can do it, because we see that Armenians in the West have worked hard and become rich and successful.'

The students were less forthcoming when I asked them what careers they envisaged for themselves. Whether this was because the future was so uncertain or they were simply shy about disclosing their ambitions in front of their peers, I could not tell. But the young bearded man spoke up eagerly: 'I want to travel. I want to travel everywhere! Perhaps not in space – well, why not, yes, to Mars too!'

When I had asked more official contacts whether many Armenians were anxious to emigrate, the response was an aghast 'Definitely not!' The truth was more complex. One of the engineers in my hotel offered to introduce me to a pretty young Yerevan woman who was eager to make contact with Westerners, presumably trading her favours for the opportunity to escape. The students admitted that many people had considered emigration as an option. Some argued that those who had wanted to leave had already done so, but others claimed that many people still longed to go.

'Because of our circumstances,' said one young woman, 'I do not think it is possible to sit in judgment on such people. Myself, I will never leave. I will travel, yes, but I will always return to the motherland. Life here is difficult,' she said, resuming the patriotic mode, 'but it is our destiny.'

I asked them how they felt about the prospect of closer ties with Turkey and Iran. 'Mixed feelings?' I ventured.

There was an immediate murmur of response. Although they accepted that it was prudent to seek better relations with their neighbours, they could never in their hearts trust Turkey. A teacher explained: 'For generations of Armenians the problem has been that Turkey has suppressed its guilt by refusing to admit that the genocide took place. This for us is a great problem and it makes it very difficult for us to trust them. We do not hate them, but there is an instinctive distance between us and them. That Turkey now seeks closer ties with Europe is a hopeful sign for us too.'

The students confirmed that the religious revival in Armenia was widespread and welcome, and my question prompted one of them to ask me whether I had accepted Jesus Christ. I had to disappoint her.

Nevertheless, the next morning I made a brief visit to the large church close to the road bridge which crosses the Razdan. It was an icy morning, and I gratefully warmed my hands against a bank of flickering candles. Worshippers kept arriving to seek advice from the priests, who were more shabbily gowned than their counterparts at Echmiadzin.

I continued on my way, crossing the bridge and passing the dark-grey fortress-like Yerevan winery. Far below the rushing Razdan charged through the sparsely wooded ravine. From the other bank a path led down the slope to an informal property exchange market. People were holding up handwritten notices offering flats in exchange for other premises. I was looking for the weekend market which usually took place nearby, but a police road block warned approaching motorists that the market had been moved outside the city because of the excessive traffic congestion it had been causing.

As I walked back to the main road, two young women came up to me and one of them, smiling broadly, greeted me in English. This was more like it. Natalie had been one of the students in the class I had met the previous day. I had not recognised her, even though she was exceptionally pretty, because of the voluminous clothing she had been wearing in the frigid classroom. Now her gleaming black hair was pulled back beneath a broad white band so that the morning sunshine could illuminate her flawless dark complexion. She introduced me to her friend, a less comely woman called Diana. They too had been intending to visit the market and were now walking back into town. They would be pleased if I would accompany them.

Their non-Armenian names were clues to their origin. They were refugees from Baku, and with their families had fled from there two years ago, leaving behind memories of their comfortable flats and their pleasant lives along the shores of the Caspian Sea.

'It sounds as though you miss Baku.'

'Oh, yes. It was very cosmopolitan. Most of the people were Moslem, but there were also Armenians and Jews and Russians. All that has changed now. We also find it very much colder in Yerevan.'

Natalie's mother was an English teacher, now working in a kindergarten, and her father an engineer. He too had found a job in Yerevan, but it was unrelated to his professional skills. They hadn't been able to afford a flat in the centre, but were happy enough in the suburbs, although the abysmal public transportation system was a constant frustration. More often than not Natalie was late for her classes. She was amazed by the high prices of food and other goods in Yerevan, and by their shoddy quality. With a student's grant of 150 roubles a month, she had no choice but to live, like her fellow students, with her parents. For her, as for other refugees from Azerbaijan, the main problem was linguistic. There had been no Armenian schools in Baku, so she had never learnt the language. She had been given a special dispensation by the Institute to allow her to use Russian rather than Armenian in class. Her English was excellent, slow but precise, but Diana spoke no English at all. Diana's mission this morning was to trade in her gloves for a pair in a more becoming colour, and to this end we visited a number of private shops. She could not find anything that satisfied her.

I walked back to the hotel for a late lunch. The waiter ignored me completely, and then sat down at a table to drink vodka with some friends of his. He was a stumpy little slob whose waistcoat protruded a few inches over his belt. I caught his eye, and spread my hands to suggest that after half an hour I'd appreciate some food. He looked back at me with supreme indifference. Eventually the one waiter with whom I had some rapport appeared, and he soon brought me three courses – simultaneously. He told me there was neither lemonade nor mineral water, yet minutes later he brought bottles of both to neighbouring tables. Here in the best dining room in Yerevan, there were classes and categories of which I was completely ignorant, and I was at the bottom of the hierarchical heap.

Joe joined me at my table. He asked how I was getting on, and I confessed to considerable frustration. He nodded sympathetically. During his many months in Armenia he had run into countless Westerners who had arrived with high hopes but who found themselves snarled in bureaucracies and immobilised by the mysterious inaccessibility of the very people they most needed to see.

17 Great Train Journeys of the World

Aram and I jumped on a bus that took us to the now familiar surroundings of the Institute of Philosophy. Ashot was waiting in one of the offices, which was surprisingly warm. He explained that they habitually used one of three offices, depending on which was warmest at the time. Soon Vladimir arrived with his wife Armine. Brought up in Beirut, she had migrated to Yerevan in 1978. Like many Levantine Armenians, she spoke not only Armenian and English and presumably Russian, but Turkish (acquired from her grandparents) and Arabic.

An expert on mediaeval Armenian architecture, she worked at the Academy of Arts, but she feared its days were numbered. Under the Soviet system Moscow had provided 80 per cent of the funding, but once Armenia declared independence, the Soviet government, logically enough, saw no reason to maintain these subsidies. The Academy would, in the local euphemism, be 'reorganised'.

As she talked, she unpacked the contents of a sturdy carrier bag, hauling out sandwiches and pickled vegetables. Aram contributed a bottle of brandy. Ashot, acclaimed as a coffee maker unparalleled, was put to work at his craft. When Armine asked me if I would be returning to Armenia for Christmas, I replied that this was out of the question, if only because any such proposal would not be welcomed by my wife.

'Wives are always angry when their husbands are not at home,' muttered Aram the bachelor. And when Ashot placed some candles on the desk in preparation for dusk in a building without electricity, Aram, never lost for a laconic observation, remarked, 'In Armenia, the difficulties are so romantic.'

The philosophers philosophised. Vladimir maintained that little had changed, structurally speaking, in the country. 'In order to change society,' he declaimed, 'it is necessary to change mentalities, ways of thinking.'

Aram demurred. In his view, in order to change ways of thinking, it was first necessary to change society. 'It is like the story of the dragons who terrorised the people. Many brave men sought to kill the dragon, and eventually one of the knights succeeded. Once he slew the dragon he found that he too was transformed into a dragon, and the cycle of tyranny continued.'

None the less, I said, there had been dramatic changes. The fact that we could meet unhindered and speak freely among ourselves was one of them. I recalled that when I visited Moscow in 1979, such a meeting would have been highly risky. When, some months later, a Russian publisher I had met and liked in Moscow had come to London with his boss, I had been asked to meet him. My impulse had been to greet him warmly, but his glance – swift acknowledgment followed by blankness – informed me unambiguously that I must not let it be known that our contact had been anything other than frostily professional.

The brandy was poured and Aram was appointed *tamada*. 'There are four things that are important to me: literature, nature, women, irony – oh, and travel.' My own toast was to the Yerevan central market, where my chance encounter with Aram had led to this succession of meetings. As we raised our glasses the electricity supply was unexpectedly restored. Ashot rushed over to the electric heater and placed a coffee jug over it. After ten minutes the jug, unprompted by jog or shudder, tipped over, spilling a third of its contents on the floor. Aram looked at me sagely. 'In Armenia,' he fabricated, 'to spill the coffee is the symbol of a good journey.'

We talked of English literature, but I knew little about the writers they were familiar with, except for Graham Greene. I could find little to say about the work of J. B. Priestley, Colin Wilson, and H. E. Bates. Had I read Iris Murdoch? Yes. Aram, just to annoy us, declared that women were incapable of writing fiction. Vladimir said that it was increasingly difficult to keep up with modern literature and scholarship. There had been a time when he could order British and American books from Moscow. It had been slow and expensive, but it had been possible. No longer. The inter-library loan system was moribund, and the price of foreign-language books had skyrocketed; it was no longer possible to build up a good library of foreign books. It was, he declared, one of the many ironies of the present situation that Armenia, in gaining independence, had in some respects increased its intellectual isolation.

In the early evening, our little party broke up, and we walked back to the Metro. I asked Armine about cultural life in the capital and, almost as an afterthought, asked her whether the theatres and the opera house and concert halls were closed. Not at all, she replied, they were open most evenings, although audiences, deterred by the cold and by poor transportation, were thin. Until that moment, I had assumed that the 'cultural programme' promised me by the Friendship Society had been abandoned because of theatre closures. Now I learnt that the places I wished to visit were not only open but that tickets were easy to obtain.

Although it seemed ungracious to complain about the Society's hospitality, I felt manipulated. At Sardarapat most of the day had been spent hunting for Arman's friends and drinking with them. Most days only began at eleven, so I spent the mornings taking aimless walks to pass the time. My own stated interests had been largely ignored. Perhaps I should have been more demanding, but Arman always had a postponement or an excuse. Nothing I wanted to happen was going to happen unless my hosts wanted it to; at providing meals and making travel arrangements Arman had proved enthusiastic and expert, at enlightening me about his country he had been ineffectual. There had clearly been a moment when the Society had given up on me as a nuisance.

Vladimir had struck me as cynical in his insistence that despite all the reforms and brave words, little had changed in Armenia. Now my experiences appeared to confirm his view. The mental processes of trusted functionaries such as Arman had scarcely altered with the transition to democracy. Vladimir had been politely dismissive of the changes which had taken place because he felt they were merely skin-deep; Arman was more subtly dismissive because, it seemed to me, he wanted to prove that democracy and freedom and all those other fine words couldn't transform Armenia overnight. I could tell, from his stilted toasts to friendship and good relations between nations – the identical formulae I'd heard trotted out on countless occasions in 1979 – that he was steeped in the old Communist hypocrisies.

The next day it was time for the parting ceremonies. I sat in the frigid bar with Arman and Mr Zakoyan, who asked me to translate dosage recommendations from packets of American pills in his possession. As soon as we moved into the dining room for dinner, Zakoyan walked off and sat down at another table among, presumably, more interesting company. Rafik the driver wandered in to join us. A bottle of vodka was produced so that Arman and I could exchange insincere toasts. A platter of trout arrived, and Zakoyan made a guest appearance at our table, not to eat but to propose a toast. Our glasses drained, he returned to his pals at the other table. I was past caring, but I couldn't help thinking that as an example of international manners this rated fairly low. It confirmed my feeling that my hosts had written me off some time before.

I fetched my luggage from my room, said a final farewell to Mr Zakoyan, who made a dash from his smoke-wreathed table for the occasion, and set off for the station. Seated in the back of the Volga with Arman, I asked him outright why my 'cultural programme' had never materialised. Ah, he said, that's because this week is the anniversary of the earthquake, and special events had been scheduled in the north.

'You mean nothing has been going on in Yerevan all week?'

'There was a concert in Yerevan yesterday morning.'

I said nothing. It was just the kind of event I would have wished to attend. If it had been a fundraising event, I would have gladly contributed. It was too late to complain, so I remained silent.

When we arrived at the railway station I didn't recognise it. Apart from a single feeble street lamp in the forecourt, there was no illumination. The scene resembled a wartime blackout. Arman went to investigate and came back with the not unexpected news that my

8.45 p.m. train to Tbilisi was now scheduled to leave at 11.30 – 'maybe, maybe'. We drove back to the Razdan, where I sat in my room reading until 10.30. Returning to the station at 11, we heard more encouraging news. The train would be leaving tonight. Every fifteen minutes Arman shuttled from car to booking hall to glean the latest information. (There was no information.) I accompanied him on one of these expeditions, and watched as hopeful travellers tugged luggage around a booking hall lit only by the vestigial street lighting outside.

He proposed that we drive over to the train depot. I could board my carriage in the yards, which would save us hanging about at the station. We drove to the depot gates, then bumped along water-logged ditches between the tracks, the headlights lurching up and down. Arman vanished into the darkness and sludge around the tracks, while steam engines hissed around us.

He returned. He had spoken to the chief guard on the Tbilisi train, who had identified my carriage. It was all right for me to board now. I said I was worried about sitting alone with my luggage on a darkened train in a deserted siding. No, no, he assured me, I would not be alone and there was no danger. We drove further down the ditch, the car sinking perilously into the sludge before heaving itself out again. With considerable difficulty we carried my luggage towards the steps of the carriage, moving carefully from steady plank to rooted stone, avoiding troughs of slime on the one side and piles of soft rotting rubbish on the other. Inside the carriage we were greeted by a woman so swathed in thick cloths that it was impossible to make out her features or her age. She was obviously friendly, so when Arman offered to stay on the train until it left for the station I urged him not to. We said goodbye.

The cronelike woman turned out to be a cheerful soul who soon brought me worn but clean linen and made up my berth. I explored. The toilet was a swamp even before the journey began. My two-berth compartment was equipped with storage bins beneath the seats and reading lights that did not work. The overhead lighting – two panels, one working – was too dim to read by.

After an hour the train crawled into the station and was noisily boarded by passengers with as much luggage, string-tied boxes, carrier bags and sacks as they and their well-wishing relatives and friends could carry. By 2 a.m. we were on our way. There was no heat on the train, so I slept fully clothed. During the night I heard the steady loud droning of Lancasters on their way over Germany to puncture a dam, but more wakeful investigation established that it was the snoring of the plump Armenian in the other berth. All through the night the train tottered and shuddered along the tracks like an old lady picking up her skirts as she treads unsteadily home after a night of gin. In my half-sleep I visualised the train jolting across bridges which everyone knew would one day collapse in the most exciting circumstances.

I raised the blinds. We were in Alaveran, an industrial town of unsurpassed ugliness strung out along a valley between snowy mountains. For miles I could see a succession of smokestacks, scrapyards, steaming pits, concrete structures that served no obvious purpose, piles of planks and discarded building materials, oil drums scattered about on their sides, muddy plots and empty huts, and piping as thick and tangled as ventricles. Overlooking this somnolent industrial cloaca were apartment houses, subtly positioned to enjoy the full benefit of the miasma beneath, though the poisonous potential was temporarily abated because of the fuel shortages. Nevertheless what seemed to be a storm cloud coming over the mountains turned out to be the wafting discharge of a chimney spouting thick black smoke which the wind was puffing back into town for the inhabitants to enjoy.

By ten we were still in Armenia, following a valley studded with small towns and villages composed of houses with rickety verandahs over more solid stone bases. From time to time the valley narrowed into a canyon, the rim hundreds of feet above almost vertical cliffs. The Lancasters had been joined by reinforcements. I did my best to bring them down with improvised flak: I talked to myself, slammed the compartment door, left the door open so that my companion would be disturbed by the bustle of the corridor. After an hour he stirred, slowly shuffled off the coat that had served as a blanket, put on his socks and tied his boots, rubbed his eyes and asked me for a cigarette. I had none, so he stumbled off in search of a smoke. He returned and sat heavily on the seat opposite mine. Taking out a matchbox, he used the splintered matches to clean first his nails and then his ears.

By noon we were among rolling hills rather than high mountains, but still in Armenia, still following a boisterous dirty-olive river. Slowly we emerged into a softer, more fertile and verdant landscape. The change of script on station platforms signalled that we were at last in Georgia. Large farms and vineyards patterned these lowland valleys. At stations kerchiefed girls tugged milk urns on trolleys along the platform.

The village houses looked more prosperous amid well-tended gardens patrolled by troops of chickens and turkeys. The tortoise-shell tufa and the sagging verandahs of the Armenian villages gave place to square houses of mellow grey stone embraced by large airy porches, but public sites, such as factories and workshops, were no lovelier than their Armenian counterparts. Half-completed walls had been erected from misshapen blocks of concrete, with most of their corners chipped off. Gaps in the walls were plugged with smaller stones and mortared. Had these makeshift constructions been stuccoed or whitewashed the effect might have been tolerable, but in no-frills economies such raw masonries were left in all their brutal ugliness.

The train crawled on, its stops unrelated to the presence of stations. I set my watch back an hour to match Georgian time. By 3.00 we were drawing into Tbilisi, and I calculated that the fourteen-hour journey had been accomplished at an average speed of 20mph. There was no sign of Svetlana at the station, so I phoned her at home. She told me she and Soso had waited at the station from eight until one, when they were informed (falsely) that the train was still not on Georgian territory. It was not the lateness of the train that was so appalling but that the authorities refused to give out pertinent information. It seemed inconceivable that there was no way to get a message from Yerevan to Tbilisi informing the stationmaster that the train would be five hours late.

*

Walking with Erekle and Levan down Rustaveli Avenue I realised how pleased I was to be back in Tbilisi. We wandered through an autumnal drizzle – even that was welcome after the persistent wintry dankness of Armenia – to the Mardjianishvili Theatre across the river. Koté Mardjianishvili had been a distinguished director until the 1930s, when Stalin had ended his career in the traditional draconian manner. The small theatre was now reviving one of his most celebrated productions, *Uriel Akosta*. Written by the German dramatist Gutzkow in 1846, it examines the crisis within a mediaeval Jewish community when the young scholar Uriel pursues an independent line and is denounced for heresy. He loves Judith, who is betrothed to another. Uriel is forced to choose between his love and his intellectual freedom; inclined to recant, he changes his mind. Judith, on the brink of marriage, realises Uriel still loves her and chooses poison rather than wedded misery. Uriel arrives in time for a poignant scene of farewell, and then goes off and shoots himself. A Jewish elder addresses the audience and blares out the moral of the piece, condemning religious dogma and exalting freedom of choice.

This was bold stuff, perhaps, just before the revolutions of 1848, and bolder still in Stalinist times, but it seemed dated now. Mardjianishvili's production had been meticulously restored – sets, scratchily recorded music, and all – but I found it ludicrously hammy, full of gesture and posturing, dramatic entrances and leaping exits, fists shaken at the heavens. The actor playing Uriel seemed to have stepped out of a biopic about Rasputin. I couldn't take any of it seriously, but the audience stood and cheered.

I'd rather have gone to the Rustaveli Theatre, but Erekle advised me that there was nothing of particular interest being staged that week. That was too bad. One of the most exhilarating theatrical experiences I can recall was Robert Sturia's production of *Richard III* which the Rustaveli Theatre brought to London some time in the late 1970s. Its excitement derived from its inventive theatricality, the brillance of the staging, with the crippled king whizzing about crouched on a small trolley like a legless Indian beggar, and Bosworth field represented as an immense backdrop flag, hacked into shreds by opposing swords.

Walking back towards the hotel, Levan and Erekle told me about developments in Georgia during my absence. In some respects the situation had improved. Soviet newspapers and television broadcasts were now permitted, although the latter were being rationed, allegedly as an energy-saving measure. Some Opposition newspapers were being published, but their appearances were irregular and restricted to the capital. Tengiz Kitovani was still sitting out at the Sea of Tbilisi with his troops and with Tengiz Sigua, but few took him seriously any longer, except for Zviad Gamsakhurdia. None the less, support from the local population kept Kitovani's forces well supplied with food, enabling them to stay put despite a lack of electricity and other services.

Back in my room I learnt from the BBC that Russia, Byelorussia and Ukraine had agreed to form what would soon become the Commonwealth of Independent States, and that Armenia was considering joining this new Slavic federation. This seemed like an attempt to manoeuvre Gorbachev out of office; that the stratagem would succeed within weeks no one could foretell, but it was obvious that Gorbachev's union treaty was a dead duck.

It was like old times outside the Parliament. A barricade of buses blocked my approach the next morning. I toiled up the steep hill to a side entrance which would give me access to the press office, and since I had to climb the slope anyway I decided to call on Mr Gabashvili at the foreign ministry and renew my accreditation. At the entrance the guards were busy emptying their Kalashnikovs and comparing bullets. On the fourth floor, I found the minister's office bare. I recalled that his chinless assistant had an office on the floor below. I went down, tapped gently on the door and opened it. Putting my head around the door, who should I see behind the desk but the large, potentially genial figure of the deputy foreign minister.

'Mr Gabashvili!'

No response.

'They've moved you! I'm glad I found you.'

An owlish blink from the Bunter of diplomacy, but no verbal comment. I approached. Gabashvili hauled himself upright and allowed me to shake his hand. I reintroduced myself and he seemed to recall that I was one of the troublemaking journalists who plagued him from time to time. In his high soft voice he asked me to take a seat and I settled in for our usual exchange of dismay and banter.

'Tell me, Mr Brook, what are your impressions?'

'I'm afraid I don't have any. I only got here last night.'

'You know, it is a very strange thing. In Kazakhstan, Mr Nazabaev is the only candidate in the presidential election, and Kazakhstan is hailed by the Western press as a model of democracy.

They come to Georgia, where we have had democratic elections, and they write such foolish things, comparing the president to Saddam Hussein. Can you tell me why?'

Well no, I couldn't, and he should direct his questions to the authors. I hadn't yet printed a word. He asked me why I had chosen to write about Georgia and Armenia. I explained.

'And why did you not include Azerbaijan?'

'That's a good question, and the honest answer is that I thought I would have a tricky time there, and that I would not have been granted sufficient freedom of action.'

'I think you are right. I speak to correspondents who have been there, and they tell me of surveillance, of restrictions. Here everything is open to you. Our president has made himself available on an almost daily basis to correspondents, answered their questions, and still they write such stories about Georgia. I think the president has had his fill of correspondents.'

'What a pity. I was hoping to see him.'

'I doubt that will be possible. But you must speak to the press office.'

He brought my old accreditation up to date, then limped slowly out of the room to have it typed up. When he returned he made an important phone call in Russian, and on another line he took a call in Georgian. Three other phones, all in different colours like playblocks, lay as yet unused on his desk. I was hoping for a full five-phone cadenza, but it was not to be.

He asked me whether I found things changed. No, I said, Parliament was still blocked by stupid barricades. That is because of the Chanturia trial, he explained. In Gabashvili's summary, the charges against Chanturia consisted of his failure to register the National Democratic Party, and his contravention of the Georgian constitution. He was specifically accused of organising barricades and disturbances. The trial, after two previous postponements, was scheduled to start today.

An aide came in with a letter from Amnesty International. As he read it, the minister shook his head and chuckled, more in sorrow than in anger.

'Good news?'

'If you want, you can read it.' Ta. The letter had come from Denmark and concerned someone called Abzianidze who had been arrested and charged with the possession of firearms; according to the writer, proper procedures had not been followed, and there was reason to believe he had been framed. I didn't know the case and neither did Gabashvili, but he said it was absurd to claim that all prisoners were political. Amnesty would do better to send its representative here rather than send these pointless letters. Yet they were clearly not so pointless if they were reaching the deputy foreign minister.

'What will you do with the letter?'

'We will reply.'

I couldn't help it, but I had developed a soft spot for the bruiser. What seemed odd was that, unlike so many of the president's entourage, he was a highly educated man, yet seemed incapable of understanding what almost every observer of the Georgian scene found so disconcerting about political developments in the republic. He unswervingly attributed unfavourable reports about his country to bias; that observers might be genuinely appalled by what they saw and heard never occurred to him.

At the Parliament the courtyard was almost deserted although two tanks still stood in position. I tracked down Gamsakhurdia's press secretary and requested an interview with the president. To my surprise, he said he would see what could be done. It did not materialise.

Walking down Rustaveli I noticed that the wine shop closed down during the prohibition phase had reopened, though prices had risen. Grocery shops stocked only a few items, all packaged, but in abundant quantities. Yet it was not the marginally greater availability of provisions that struck me most; it was the condition of the buildings. By Western standards the modern offices and apartment blocks of downtown Tbilisi were heavy and bland, but after the peeling, stained walls of Armenia they seemed positively chic. The restoration of the church opposite the Parliament was well under way and the university buildings were receiving a new coat of paint.

Evergreens brought splashes of colour to the street, as did the often fashionable clothing worn by the well-turned-out young women strolling through the university district. After Yerevan, Tbilisi looked less down at heel, less angry, less downtrodden. Not that all was well in Tbilisi. There were still bread queues a hundred long and public transportation remained erratic and overcrowded.

Since it was International Human Rights Day, the Opposition organised a rally that afternoon in Victory Park. No sooner had they made the announcement than the government decided it too would celebrate the day with a demonstration. Its timing seemed somewhat unfortunate, with the political trial of Chanturia about to begin.

Accompanied by Erekle and Levan I made my way to Victory Park. Despite a slight loosening of the régime's grip on civil liberties, the conflict between government and Opposition was unabated. Control of the press had been liberalised, schools and universities and theatres had reopened, and prohibition had ended. Yet Gamsakhurdia continued his rabble-rousing rallies, caricaturing the Opposition as criminals and hooligans. In October the Supreme Soviet had accepted the president's labelling of Opposition activities as a putsch, but had not gone so far as to expel the deputies from Parliament, even though they were now officially tainted with the crime of putschism. According to one story I heard, Gamsakhurdia had accused some Opposition deputies of stealing spare parts for cars and selling them at the markets, though I found it hard to picture Nodar Natadze flogging exhaust pipes from behind a trestle table.

There were familiar faces among the crowd. Rusiko Beridze, still in her uncompromising widow's weeds, admitted that the Opposition had grown weaker over the autumn. I told her how Gabashvili had detailed the charges against Chanturia and she roared with laughter. The registration issue was a nonsense, she insisted, since that law was defunct and no parties in Georgia are registered. Yes, Chanturia had indeed organised the erection of barricades (Rusiko quoted exact dates) but only in response to Gamsakhurdia's barricades put up two days earlier. It was not yet clear whether the trial would be closed; Gamsakhurdia had promised an open trial, but it seemed unlikely that it would conform to democratic standards of justice.

The repression was continuing in other ways. The Mkhedrioni leader Djaba Ioseliani was still in jail awaiting trial and, since Gamsakhurdia had persuaded the Supreme Soviet to increase the period for which a prisoner could be held without trial from nine to eighteen months, he was likely to remain there for some time. In November Gamsakhurdia's men had ordered further arrests, but courageous prosecutors and judges had refused to issue the warrants, and had been sacked for their pains. The chief prosecutor had also refused and had resigned. Nor were there any improvements in the economic situation; planned reforms were stalled and power structures remained unaltered.

As for South Ossetia, clashes between Georgian troops and Ossetians continued on an almost daily basis. Since the Georgians only reported atrocities against their own people, it was hard to work out what was going on. Georgia had abolished the autonomous status of South Ossetia, an action which Erekle defended as within their rights, since he believed that Ossetian separatists were being supported, often clandestinely, by Soviet troops.

By four o'clock the rally had still not begun. Someone yelled out that the electricity had been cut off at the park – 'accidentally'. Everybody laughed. Since the microphones couldn't be operated, the organisers had summoned a car with loudspeakers, but it had not arrived. It was growing cold.

I spotted Natadze and went over to speak to him. He was convinced that the people were beginning to understand what the Opposition had long been saying, and the president's approval rating was plummeting. The present demands of the Opposition were for new parliamentary elections, the freeing of political prisoners and the independence of the media, especially television. Natadze insisted that Parliament still had a useful role to play, if only as a platform for the Opposition, whose views were being transmitted in broadcasts of parliamentary sessions.

The loudspeaker van arrived, and Natadze hurried to address the crowd. He stressed the importance of building democratic structures in Georgia, as this was the only way in which Western nations would recognise the republic. Rusiko's cousin Helen told me that the worst thing the West could do was to recognise Gamsakhurdia's government: 'It would be ruin for us.'

After an hour of speeches, Erekle agreed that we had done our duty for that day, and we slipped away to the marionette theatre. I had done my best to summon up enthusiasm for this outing, although the genre did not greatly appeal to me. I was wrong. The story, loosely modelled on *La Traviata*, was easily accessible to the children in the audience, while the dialogue was sophisticated enough and sufficiently stuffed with in-jokes to give pleasure to the adults. The playlet opens with three down-and-outs with pretensions to learning discussing the merits of Dostoevsky and Freud. Alfredo encounters Violetta first on a park bench, where they neck before going indoors and climbing into bed together – quite a feat for puppets. The dialogue had been recorded, many years before, by some of Georgia's best actors. The actor, now dead, who had recorded the part of Alfredo's father had also been a famous sports commentator. His aria to Violetta was laced with references to Tbilisi Dynamo, an allusion lost on me but not on the rest of the audience.

Erekle told me that this commentator had been famous for his sense of humour, which had often landed him in trouble with the authorities. Commenting one evening on a match between Dynamo and an Italian team, he became more and more lugubrious as it became apparent that the Georgian team was going to lose. The whistle blew: the final score was one to nil. Then he addressed the radio audience in a slightly more cheerful tone. 'Actually, I have a surprise for you. There was another goal earlier on, but I decided to keep it to myself for a while, and in fact the Tbilisi team scored about ten minutes ago. The result is a draw.'

The next evening I exchanged a parody of opera for the real thing. Nunu Gabunia had invited me to see *Un Ballo in Maschera* at the opera house. I have made something of a speciality of attending obscure opera houses, and fondly recall some truly appalling nights at the opera in Prague or in school gymnasia in Boston. I was prepared for the worst.

The Paliashvili Opera and Ballet Theatre is a charming building, with a distinctive cod-Islamic style of interior decoration, revelling in mirrored screens and walls and ceilings painted in deep blue and red. After a fire gutted the building in 1973 it was rebuilt in exactly the same style. The salons were empty, and very dimly lit as an economy measure. Rising from the corners of the balustrade were handsome dripping light fixtures on engraved bronze bases, and similar but slightly less monumental designs adorned the chandeliers inside the auditorium. All this playful theatricality needs a swarm of people to bring it to life, but there were no more than fifty people in the audience.

This was a shame, as the performance was excellent. I was expecting a low-budget production, but not a bit of it: the sets and costumes were not in the most exquisite taste, being variations on the dusty drapes which obscured the windows of shops and cafés throughout the Soviet Union, but they were undeniably lavish. The only jarring note was struck by the ill-fitting wigs of the male chorus, especially since eighteenth-century white wigs don't match twentieth-century black beards. The performance was highly competent, and the Riccardo, Nugzar Gamgebeli, was outstanding, with a firm clear voice which remained steady and strong throughout the range. The opera was sung in Italian, appropriately, since the voices were Italianate rather than Slav, with none of that heavy vibrato that can disfigure Russian soprano voices and none of the weediness of some Russian tenors.

After the performance Nunu took me backstage to meet the principals, most of whom she knew. We were not the only ones in the audience to follow that route. Crossing the stage towards the dressing rooms was half the audience, which suggests that the number of people who turned up simply to see the performance was even smaller than I had originally supposed. Nunu introduced me to some of the other backstage visitors.

'Amelia – her husband. Renato – his wife.'

It is forbidden to export roubles, a regulation placing worthless roubles on the same exalted level as precious icons. I'd been told I could change money at the Hotel Tbilisi, but this was not the case; I was directed to the Hotel Iveria. The Iveria, however, scorned my roubles; it was hard currency they were after. The Iveria sent me to a bank behind Parliament, which I found with difficulty since it occupied the upper floor of a small unmarked building in a courtyard. The staff were friendly and spent a happy fifteen minutes filling out forms. Just as I thought the transaction was complete, I was told to collect the money from another bank, from which a young woman had been dispatched as a guide. When she arrived, we hiked down the hill towards Freedom Square, entered a large building, climbed imposing steps and crossed impressive halls, until we found a teller behind what looked like an enlarged keyhole. The transaction had taken me an hour and a half. Later I counted myself lucky; Erekle, entrusted with confirming my flight back to Moscow, had queued for three hours at the Aeroflot office.

Svetlana was waiting to take me to School No 1, a handsome early nineteenth-century building in Russian neoclassical style which stands next to the Parliament. Founded in 1802, this had been the first European-style classical high school in Transcaucasia. Its unimaginative renaming had taken place, of course, during the Soviet period. A large school with about 1800 pupils, it had processed many of Georgia's best-known citizens. Merab Kostava and the three principal protagonists of the present troubles – Gamsakhurdia, Sigua, and Kitovani – were all graduates, and jokes later circulated that the civil war was simply a belated settling of schoolday scores.

The motherly principal explained that despite its ancient pedigree, School No 1 was not privileged in any way; its venerable traditions, however, meant that sometimes four or five generations of the same family had attended the school. She was proud of the small class sizes: no more than thirty-five, and after the ninth grade as low as ten or fifteen. (Her students, when I mentioned these figures, laughed. Their average class size was not thirty-five but forty-five, they said. Teachers exaggerate.)

The school was officially closed that week. When the barricades once again obstructed Rustaveli, most parents, fearing a renewal of violence, kept their children at home. The street fighting in October, after all, had taken place within yards of the entrance. In addition, the central heating system had broken down. The halls were chilly, but after Yerevan perfectly bearable. Although the children were under no obligation to trek into central Tbilisi just to meet me, a sizeable contingent had gratifyingly done so. Not surprisingly, they were eager extrovert children. They told me that they liked coming to school – 'this is a friendly school, we have good teachers, we like to study' – which sounded too good to be true, but the enthusiasm seemed genuine. One girl wanted to be a doctor, another a psychologist; a young man, adopting the Western name Nick, had recently graduated and was beginning a career as a journalist. Two of the girls attended a special music school after classes.

When I told them about the sparsely attended opera performance, they were not surprised. With so much political turbulence, people have other things on their minds than cultural outings. 'There is no bread, no butter, no sugar, nothing. Everybody worries about finding food. And in the evenings, it is difficult to go out without your own car. The trolleys stop running early, and to walk in the evening is dangerous.'

Mugging, according to Nick, had been almost unknown five years ago. When I recounted how I had been threatened with a knife one night, they were aghast that I had been on the streets at such an hour.

'But I was waiting for a trolley bus,' I explained.

'Never wait for a trolley bus,' said Nick. 'It will not come.'

I was surprised by their vehemence when I asked how they felt about the situation in Tbilisi. Maya Enukashvili, a vigorous girl anxious to answer every question, sounded exasperated: 'We are very tired of this, very tired. There have been no changes, no advances.'

No doubt to some extent they were reiterating their parents' views as they responded to my questions. Their parents were architects, theatrical designers, doctors; these were the children of the intelligentsia.

The teachers reminded them that they should have prepared party pieces to impress their visitor. One class had recently staged Thornton Wilder's *Our Town*, but as only a handful of the cast were here, they would perform a skeletal version. The first segment, a scene between Emily and George, lasted twenty seconds as Emily couldn't remember her lines. Maya and Teya, both fifteen, did rather better in a gossipy scene with lines such as 'if I don't tell you I'll burst', which sounded enchanting in their Georgian accents.

The youngest girl, Tamuna, was keen to put her oar in. She pushed her chair next to mine and confided that she not only attended the special music school but composed her own songs. The older girls, noisier and more extrovert than the studious Tamuna, were dominating the proceedings, but I insisted on hearing her too. She moved swiftly to the piano and sang a song that resembled a 1950s ballad. Despite the bustle in the background, she refused to be flustered. Her encore was a surprisingly soulful song, a remarkable composition for a twelve-year-old. But then Tamuna was a soulful girl, with sad appealing eyes, a shy smile and an admirable determination not to be outgunned by her older schoolmates.

Nino Tseriteli took her place at the piano. She launched into a Scott Joplin rag, followed by a sizeable chunk of the Grieg piano concerto, all played with complete nonchalance. This, she was implying, is just a taste of what School No 1 can do.

I attended a more formal concert later in the day when, after a superb lunch at her home, Nunu Gabunia took me to the conservatory. The director led me to the upstairs chamber music hall, a delightful art nouveau room decorated with lyre patterns. She apologised that because of the short notice she had not been able to rustle up the best students, but the flautist, the baritone, the cellist and the soprano who performed for me were extremely impressive. I bathed contentedly in the music, trying to forget that the streets outside were patrolled by government-hired thugs, and that my hotel was still overrun by police with Kalashnikovs and by plainclothesmen and their molls.

Erekle met me after the recital. An Opposition rally that afternoon in Republic Square had been attended by Tengiz Sigua and his bodyguards, and Gamsakhurdia had summoned a counter-demonstration. While I was listening to Moussorgsky songs, the Opposition rally had moved down Rustaveli and up to the barricades near the Parliament. We now joined the crowd. Buses separated the government supporters from about a thousand Opposition demonstrators. There were sound vans and flag wavers on both sides, but there was no attempt by either side to drown out the other.

A small car hummed down Rustaveli and came to a halt near where I was standing. In the passenger seat I spotted Irena Sarashvili. I walked over and crouched beside the car so that when she rolled the window down we were eye to eye. I asked her whether there was any further news about the trial of her husband, Giorgi Chanturia. In terms of the formal procedures, she said, it was in effect over, although sentence would not be pronounced until the next day.

'In the Soviet period, charges and evidence were fabricated but they were formally correct. In my husband's case there is clearly no proof of the charges made against him. The only question now is whether the judge will be prepared to risk her job. She has surely been directed to find my husband guilty, but there is no evidence and she knows it. Gamsakhurdia told a meeting of students yesterday that he would not release my husband, so we don't know what will happen.' With her throaty laugh, she noted the irony of Gamsakhurdia celebrating Human Rights Day while keeping her husband behind bars. Her suspense was prolonged when the next day the hearing was postponed yet again.

The argument with the Opposition was being conducted from the Parliament steps by Prime Minister Gugushvili, whose words were apparently full of fine patriotic sentiments but empty of substance. After his speech there came a surprise. The chairman of the parliamentary cultural committee, Mr Khoridze, was, he said, standing next to Tengiz Sigua, who had popped up within yards of the president's headquarters in an act of impressive defiance. Khoridze argued in a low voice for forgetting the past and fashioning a new unity among the Georgian people. The government supporters fell silent, puzzled that Khoridze should be standing next to a renowned criminal and hooligan. Sigua himself appealed for the barricades to be removed so that the two sides could meet and form one large united rally. He announced his intention of passing through to the other side, but changed his mind after the crowd shouted that this was inadvisable.

We should have realised that all these gestures were merely symbolic, that the gulf between the sides was too great to be bridged by a stroll across the no-man's-land of the barricades. Nevertheless we held our breath. In Georgia dramatic gestures counted for a great deal. Our excitement mounted when we heard the government side declare that they were ready for dialogue. Not that they were prepared to shift the barricades. No matter, the tone was conciliatory, and soon negotiations of some kind were indeed taking place. Nodar Natadze pressed towards the van where Sigua was closeted with Khoridze and other government deputies. Minutes later Sigua, surrounded by bodyguards with machine guns pointing skywards, emerged to announce that there had been no breakthrough. When he had raised the matter of the political prisoners, Khoridze had denied their existence and told him that he couldn't take demands for their release to the president. The two men were, after all, on different planets.

The flame of hope flickered and gutted. A student leader took the microphone and denounced Gamsakhurdia in familiar terms. The crowd, plunged back into anger and despondency, chanted 'Ceaucescu', its standard expression of frustration. The clichéd response was depressing.

'Illusions,' muttered Erekle, echoing my own view.

The indefatigable Demo now found us and, taking my arm, led me off to meet Giorgi Kvaratskhelia, Kitovani's right-hand man and the tallest Georgian I had ever encountered. My chin bumped against his bullet-proof vest as I asked him whether the National Guard was now isolated at the Sea of Tbilisi.

'Isolated from the government, but not from the people.'

What were the Guard's aims now? The peaceful resignation of Gamsakhurdia, he said. But that wasn't going to happen, was it? Well, if not, then the National Guard would continue to protect the democratic forces of Georgia, as they were doing right now.

Demo also introduced me to Koté Gabashvili, a former deputy minister of education in Gamsakhurdia's government and no relation to the florid deputy foreign minister.

'We have no idea where this country is going,' he began. 'Gamsakhurdia is strongly against Moscow, so we have few relations with the former Soviet Union. Relations with the Moslem countries are almost impossible for us. That leaves Europe, but here too Gamsakhurdia has closed all the options, and rests his policies on an appeal to the lumpenproletariat. But this is not the Georgian way. This anti-intellectual climate goes against the grain, for we are an educated and sophisticated people. All our ideas of the motherland and of our native culture were denied under the Soviets, but Gamsakhurdia is perverting these concepts. His style of government looks back towards what preceded it. Chanturia is being tried in the basement of the former KGB building – can you imagine what resonances that has for us? In the face of all this we cannot stay silent.'

'Yet Gamsakhurdia remains popular.'

'He has hardly any support among the intelligentsia. The workers are still moulded by the Stalinist past and feel comfortable with Gamsakhurdia's authoritarian image and appearance of strength. None the less the Opposition is gaining ground, and some government deputies are switching to our side. After all, the president is doing nothing. There has been no economic reform, no privatisation. Yes, a few joint ventures, but very few. And we have commercial shops, but they represent speculation, not economic activity. But Gamsakhurdia even speaks of closing the shops. He talks of government capitalism. But when people press him it seems to be the same as the socialism we lived under. The president doesn't understand, or doesn't want to acknowledge, that economic freedom entails personal freedom.'

'Does he believe his own rhetoric?'

'I'm not sure. Even fifteen years ago he would find enemies everywhere. Today only the labels have changed. For him to see enemies around him is a normal response.'

I was up early the next morning to take my chances on the Aeroflot lottery. The previous day ninety-eight airports in the Soviet Union had been shut, including all those in Transcaucasia. I was lucky; the airport was functioning the next morning. The other foreign passengers included a group of Australian oil geologists who had been booked on yesterday's flight. On checking our luggage before boarding, each passenger was charged ten roubles, a 'service charge' for the privilege of hanging about in an unheated terminal.

The geologists had, like me, a few hours to spare in Moscow before catching flights out of the Soviet Union. I joined them on a quick tour of the capital. Used to living in the hard currency world – in Tbilisi they had been quartered in the Metekhi Palace Hotel – they lunched at the Pizza Hut, where a simple but satisfying lunch cost us ten dollars each, while outside in the snow Muscovites were queueing for pizza slices at eight roubles each. The Red Flag still flew over the Kremlin, while a short distance away the Russian flag fluttered over the White House, where Boris Yeltsin was planning the swiftest way to remove Mikhail Gorbachev from his Kremlin offices. Red Army troops still mounted guard over Lenin's tomb, now closed to visitors.

I assumed my travels to the Caucasus were over. They were not.

19 Offstage

Those last hours I had spent on Rustaveli had shown me that only a stand-off could result from confrontation between the two opposed political forces within Georgia. Were Gamsakhurdia to feel truly threatened, he would not hesitate to use force and the full machinery of oppression. His active opponents were few in number, had little apparent strength outside the capital, and were backed by a phantom military force marooned far from the city. No doubt seasoned observers were right in believing that the struggle would be decided on purely economic grounds: if Georgia could survive the winter without excessive hardship, Gamsakhurdia would cling to power.

They were wrong and I, agreeing with them, was equally wrong. Nine days after I left Tbilisi National Guard forces attacked the Parliament building. After another Opposition rally, exacerbated by Georgia's continuing refusal to join the Commonwealth of Independent States, fighting broke out on 22 December. Opposition spokesmen explained that in the early hours government troops had fired on demonstrators, which persuaded the National Guard to intervene. Television pictures showed heavy artillery positioned on Rustaveli. Within the first day or so seventeen people were reported killed and a hundred more injured.

Erekle later gave me a detailed account of how the civil war had begun. On 21 December the Opposition had gathered again on Rustaveli. The demonstration took an almost identical form to the one I had attended nine days earlier, but the tension was greater. Sigua, surrounded by bodyguards, had called for the removal of the barricades. Three days earlier Gamsakhurdia had announced that he had a great surprise for the nation, and people should come to the Parliament steps to hear the wonderful news. Government supporters arrived, only to be told to be patient, as an Opposition attack on Parliament was imminent. In the meantime the crowd was entertained with the usual stirring speeches, including some declaring that Gamsakhurdia had been sent by God (no less) to save Georgia from the agents of the Kremlin (the Opposition). There was, of course, no attack, and eventually the announcement was made: Georgia had been recognised by Ukraine! This, according to the government, was a tremendous breakthrough. There was dancing in the streets.

Unfortunately, the announcement wasn't true. All that Ukraine had offered was to discuss the future of its relationship with Georgia. By the time the Opposition rally took place on 21 December, the government supporters were incensed, echoing Gamsakhurdia's view that the Opposition was deliberately stoking up tension to discourage Western countries from recognising Georgia. In Gamsakhurdian logic, this provided further proof of how his opponents were conspiring with the Kremlin against the interests of Georgia. The twenty-first of December happened to be Stalin's birthday, so the Opposition provocatively said they would commemorate the occasion by bringing dictatorship to an end in Georgia that day. Loyalists retaliated by claiming that the Opposition's choice of this day to mount another rally proved they were indeed Kremlin agents.

After more bogus negotiations Gamsakhurdia refused to respond to Sigua's requests. That evening the Opposition moved up vehicles powerful enough to remove the buses and dismantled the barricades. Surprisingly, there was no serious conflict between the two sides after this action. As the situation seemed calm, most people went home, except for a few Opposition supporters who stayed behind to keep watch. Sigua called a meeting for the next afternoon. The next morning at eight o'clock between forty and sixty OMON troops dashed out of the Parliament building and opened fire, seemingly at random, using automatic weapons. Since there was no rally in progress and few Opposition supporters in the plaza, their action seems inexplicable. Three or four people were killed, including two women. Sigua and his bodyguards, concealed near the Artists House, responded by firing into the air; there were no casualties among the OMON troops. At this point Kitovani's patience broke. He had always maintained that his role was to protect the Opposition. This indiscriminate shooting of unarmed civilians was the last straw, and the National Guard came rumbling into the city centre from the Sea of Tbilisi. Quite clearly, the encampment I had visited was not the sole National Guard base; heavy weaponry and tanks concealed in various places now emerged. Government forces, concentrated within the Parliament buildings, made no attempt to prevent their progress into the city.

By 9.30 National Guard artillery opened fire on the Parliament buildings. Sigua declared that if Gamsakhurdia would resign, the Opposition would guarantee his safe passage out of the country. Gamsakhurdia scorned the offers, and the fighting continued. In an interview with the BBC he denied that he was acting dictatorially and described the Opposition in the usual blood-curdling terms as criminals who 'steal cars and drugs from hospitals'. Yet many Opposition leaders openly regretted that the struggle within Georgia was being resolved by violent means.

By 26 December there was no diminution in the ferocity of the fighting, although it was limited to the city centre. Fatalities had risen to either forty or fifty-six, depending on which report you trusted. Both sides were augmenting their weaponry by looting Soviet stores. The Soviet army wisely remained neutral, though it was not above selling hardware to the highest bidder. With the Soviet Union dissolved, the chain of command within the CIS military forces had become more brittle, and some local commanders were indulging in a little arms trading on the side. It was estimated that Gamsakhurdia's troops numbered between 400 and 3000; some reporters believed that Kitovani commanded no more than 600 men. Kitovani had established his headquarters in the Hotel Tbilisi, and his strategy appeared to be the encirclement of the Parliament buildings where the president was holed up in his bunker.

The following day Opposition forces captured outlying buildings, such as the former KGB headquarters. The ordeal of Giorgi Chanturia was brought to a swift conclusion when he and seven other political prisoners, including Giorgi Khaindrava, were released by the National Guard. Fighting spread to the airport, where reinforcements for the government troops had flown in from the autonomous region of Chechen-Ingushetia just north of Georgia. When challenged by some Mkhedrioni, the Chechen troops said they had come here to prevent further bloodshed. The Mkhedrioni suggested this could best be accomplished by going home again, which they did.

There was increasing unhappiness about the violence among more pacific elements in the Opposition. Natadze denounced it as a bad precedent for resolving problems in the fledgling republic. Chanturia too expressed reservations about the resort to force. 'It is a very cruel and senseless war,' he stated. 'We will do everything to finish this as soon as possible. It is important to arrest [Gamsakhurdia] and bring him to justice.'

The president repeated that he was staying put. Despite the fighting, rallies both for and against the government continued in different parts of the city. A truce arranged on 29 December soon broke down. Peace talks were announced but Gamsakhurdia's representatives failed to turn up. Heavy fighting resumed. The Hotel Tbilisi was burning and the rebels had moved their headquarters to the Academy of Sciences near Republic Square. Gamsakhurdia's position continued to weaken as former supporters, such as the deputy defence minister Desik Kutateladze, deserted the government camp, as did the commander of the garrison defending the television tower on Mount Mtatsminda. Gleefully the Opposition began to broadcast, until an unexplained rupture in the power supply silenced them for four days. Gamsakhurdia's supporters continued to broadcast from studios in the presidential bunker.

By 2 January 1992, there were signs of a government offensive; the National Guard retreated after destroying the artillery pieces they had abandoned near the Parliament. This setback did not prevent the Opposition from setting up a military council to replace the besieged government. The council announced that it was assuming power until fresh elections could be held, and its leaders imposed a state of emergency and a curfew and gave Gamsakhurdia twenty-four hours to resign. Gamsakhurdia responded by denouncing the council as a 'junta' and calling for a general strike. He blamed the civil war on Boris Yeltsin and 'a gang of criminals who don't understand how the game is played in a democracy.'

This was rich coming from the autocratic Gamsakhurdia, but even among the Opposition there was continuing unease about the course of events. Natadze and Chanturia were widely respected, and Tengiz Sigua was a former prime minister, but could one really trust men like Kitovani and Ioseliani and his murky paramilitary Mkhedrioni? It was impossible to gauge whether their real priority was the restoration of democracy and sound government or personal aggrandisement.

An article by Mark Almond in the *Daily Telegraph* took a cynical line about the Opposition, worth quoting as counterweight to my more sympathetic view: 'Although some old-style Communist bureaucrats found employment under Gamsakhurdia, many of Shevardnadze's old protégés found themselves out of work after he took over. By cutting all links with the centre at Moscow, the president threatened to terminate their remaining source of influence on events in Georgia where they, like Shevardnadze himself, are less popular than they feel they ought to be. The mafia-type of gangs which have proliferated in Georgia, particularly since 1985, stood to lose easy access to their markets and rackets in the rest of the Commonwealth if Gamsakhurdia took Georgia into isolation. Amid the classic Caucasian tangle of broken loyalties and feuds which have also played their part in bringing Georgia into chaos, the role of the mafia and its connections with the centres of former Soviet power should not be overlooked.' But this was only a half-truth, for one of the criticisms of Gamsakhurdia was that he made too small a break between the Communist bureaucracy and the official ranks of his own régime.

The following day, 3 January, Sigua was appointed caretaker

prime minister by the military council, with Kitovani and Ioseliani occupying the other senior positions. Demonstrations and rallies were banned, and the Mkhedrioni enforced the curfew. At the same time Georgia's political parties were asked to form a consultative committee which would prepare for the new elections. Gamsakhurdia was still in place and reporters confirmed that arms and food were getting through to his stronghold. He did not lack bravado, and cheekily compared his struggle to that of President Landsbergis of Lithuania. He accused the Soviet army of aiding the 'bandits of the Opposition' and said he would 'fight, fight, fight. We are in a position to be able to wipe [the Opposition] out, but we have to proceed slowly to avoid a bloodbath.' By this time Tass was estimating the death toll at 300, though local observers cited lower figures.

Despite the formal legitimacy of Gamsakhurdia's presidency, the rebels, newly packaged as the military council, were having the better of the propaganda battle, until pro-government demonstrations in Tbilisi were attacked by masked gunmen in early January. True, such demonstrations had been banned, but there was no justification for masked men to shoot unarmed civilians. A few demonstrators were killed, and one of the gunmen was captured and almost lynched. The shootings, which the council failed to condemn, provoked another round of fighting near the Parliament.

Giorgi Chanturia spelt out what could happen next: 'It is inevitable that the Parliament will be stormed. The Opposition has a helicopter, and if we want we can pour petrol on the building. It would be in flames within minutes, and not a single person would remain alive in the bunker.' While threatening immolation on the one hand, some members of the council were musing aloud about the possibility of instituting a constitutional monarchy. In the early hours of the morning of 6 January the Parliament took some direct hits and Gamsakhurdia made a run for it. The Parliament was ablaze and the president's whereabouts were unknown. Kitovani mentioned sightings of a three-car convoy heading towards Azerbaijan; others said Gamsakhurdia had been arrested; yet other reports claimed that the story of flight was a ruse and that he was still in

Tbilisi. Later in the day there were more reliable reports that he was on his way to Armenia.

It soon emerged that his escape was not unplanned. The commander of the government forces, Nodar Georgadze, had prevailed upon Gamsakhurdia to leave his bunker, even though Georgadze had himself been arrested by the president for meeting with rebel commanders on 29 December. Georgadze managed to obtain vehicles in which the presidential party of about one hundred could escape. The military council claimed that they had cooperated by opening a corridor from the city centre to the outskirts. The next morning the convoy of three buses and three armoured vehicles was spotted near the border between Armenia and Azerbaijan.

Despite continuing pro-government demonstrations, the rebels now controlled Tbilisi. The situation in the provinces, especially in western Georgia, was more confused. Western Georgia was Gamsakhurdia's power base. Always intensely political, the people of that region were not going to witness the overthrow of their idol without a protest. There were demonstrations; a television station was attacked and railway lines were uprooted. Djaba Ioseliani announced that any pro-government resistance in the regions would be crushed.

It was impossible to feel sorry for Zviad Gamsakhurdia. Carried into power on a wave of overwhelming popular support, he had wrecked a golden opportunity to steer this fertile land, populated with men and women of sophistication and inventiveness, towards a future which could have been enviably prosperous, compared to that awaiting the rest of the former Soviet Union. Instead he had succumbed to paranoia, devoting his energies not to the political and economic transformation the new republic urgently required but to infighting. Intolerant of dissent, he hounded his enemies, taunted the ethnic minorities within Georgia, marginalised opposition and – perhaps most seriously of all – drove Georgia into eccentric isolation.

Opposition politicians were rightly aghast as Georgia slid into economic stagnation. They feared a decline into a closed society which they understandably compared with Albania. Diatribes against his opponents became for the highly educated Gamsakhurdia a substitute for action. Meanwhile Georgia's impoverished neighbour Armenia managed to introduce reforms, in circumstances of difficulty and danger, that were only paid lip service by the Georgian government.

Rather than uniting his people to work for the national rebirth they all espoused, Gamsakhurdia ranged Georgian against Georgian in a futile game of political point-scoring, all directed towards the consolidation of his power. It became clear that he would not rest until his rule was absolute, and only the tenacity of the intelligentsia stood in his way. With no inkling of what democracy was about, Gamsakhurdia believed that the popular vote conferred absolute power, giving him the right to savage his enemies and to treat all criticism as an attack on the nation and on himself as its sole guardian. He squandered his presidency on preserving his vanity. That the conflict ended in violence was a hateful outcome, but one provoked for months by the rhetoric of the president, by his duplicity during the August coup in Moscow, and by the actions of his ill-disciplined militia.

The new ruling council in Tbilisi was taking stock. According to the ministry of health the final casualty figures were 113 dead and 420 wounded; others believed this to be a conservative estimate. Newspapers, once banned, were again free to publish, although practical difficulties meant that publication and distribution would be irregular. Political parties began to organise and recruit. Eduard Shevardnadze voiced his approval of the overthrow of Gamsakhurdia, but kept his distance, aware that his thirteen years from 1972 to 1985 as head of the Georgian Communist Party had not endeared him to all Georgians. Natadze was urging the military council to set a date for new elections as soon as possible, and Ioseliani predicted (over-optimistically) that they would be held within two or three months. Strikes and protests by Gamsakhurdia's loyalists continued in western Georgia. Rural routes were blocked by gunmen and vigilantes, although it was not always clear whom they represented. Public transport had ground to a halt.

Zviad Gamsakhurdia had one more trick up his sleeve. Armenia had agreed to take in the fleeing Gamsakhurdia only if he came unarmed and abstained from political activity. When he flouted these conditions, the Armenians asked him to leave. There had been talk of his going to France or Switzerland, but instead, on 16 January, he turned up in the west Georgian town of Zugdidi. Insisting that he was still Georgia's rightful leader, he urged his supporters to instigate a civil war. Fortunately the grip of the military council was by now strong enough to minimise this threat. Gamsakhurdia may have had many supporters in western Georgia, but they lacked weaponry. It was one thing to demonstrate, quite another to march on Tbilisi and risk losing your life. After initial confusion in the capital the military council dispatched National Guardsmen to western Georgia to try to surround Gamsakhurdia and his supporters. Attempts were made to persuade him to leave the country again rather than cause renewed bloodshed.

Estimates of his military support varied greatly, but it soon became clear that his forces posed little threat. When about 2500 loyalists began marching the sixty miles from Zugdidi to Kutaisi, they were, according to Sigua, easily intercepted and persuaded to turn back by the National Guard. By 19 January the military council was said to be in control of Kutaisi. By 21 January Gamsakhurdia's forces had been forced back to the Black Sea coastline. There had been clashes but little bloodshed. The military council was still offering Gamsakhurdia safe passage out of the country, but the ex-president was nowhere to be seen. Since his return to Georgia he had not made any public appearances. From his hiding place, wherever it was, he continued to issue defiant statements, but his declarations were not translated into action. On 28 January the town of Poti was captured by troops led by Ioseliani, and two days later Zugdidi fell to the new régime. Meanwhile living conditions throughout Georgia were deteriorating fast. Shops were empty except for bread. Proliferating vigilante groups provided cover for unsavoury armed gangs, especially in rural areas. It became highly dangerous to venture out after dark.

Some two weeks later Zviad Gamsakhurdia made a public

appearance – in Chechen-Ingushetia. Although he declared that he was still the head of the Georgian government, his attempted comeback had failed ignominiously, and it was safe to say (insofar as it was safe to say anything about Georgian politics) that his political career was over. With Gamsakhurdia gone, some leaders of the new régime looked elsewhere for a figurehead. Giorgi Chanturia and the Monarchist Party leader Temur Djordjorliani set off for Spain to have a word with Jorge Bagration, the rally driver. They were to return disillusioned. The Georgian prince's primary worry, according to Chanturia, was who was going to pick up the tab for his air fare back to Tbilisi. Bagration was none too impressed by his visitors from Georgia either, and described their visit as 'disagreeable'.

Only one person could confer international credibility on the new government and that was Eduard Shevardnadze. He may not have enjoyed the undying affection of the people he once ruled, but his standing in the West was considerable, where he was regarded, rightly or wrongly, as a principled democrat. On 8 March the former foreign minister of the Soviet Union returned to his native land, where he was offered the presidency of a ruling council that would govern Georgia until proper elections took place later in the year. Djaba Ioseliani was named as his deputy. The state council was to have fifty members and a praesidium which included the triumvirate – Sigua, Ioseliani, and Kitovani – who had headed the military council. The Mkhedrioni, having completed their task in western Georgia, were brought back to the capital to enforce the curfew and to offer themselves for hire as security guards. Shevardnadze argued that armed men had no business patrolling the streets of Tbilisi any longer, but since the Mkhedrioni supported his return to Georgia his protests were muted. Despite Gamsakhurdia's exile to Chechen-Ingushetia, his supporters in western Georgia had not entirely given up the struggle. By the end of March they still controlled six towns and were threatening to march on Tbilisi, so the National Guard was again dispatched westwards.

Shevardnadze got to work immediately. He set up a fund to encourage investment in Georgia by Western nations and companies. The United States announced that it would open an embassy in Georgia; the German foreign minister Hans-Dietrich Genscher paid a visit to the republic. Once diplomatic recognition was underway, economic revival could at least begin. Shevardnadze may have dispelled to some extent the image of Georgia as the unruly adolescent among the newly independent republics, but there was a very long way to go.

Meanwhile Armenia was struggling through a prolonged winter, with industrial production severely reduced. When Yeltsin and other CIS leaders abolished price controls on most foods in January 1992, Armenia had no choice but to follow suit. The winter also saw a deterioration in the situation in Nagorno-Karabakh. The break-up of the former Soviet Union had created a vacuum of authority in the region, and on 2 January 1992, President Ayaz Mutalibov of Azerbaijan introduced direct presidential rule over the enclave, which Armenians understandably interpreted as an attempt to consolidate Azeri authority. Both republics stated their intention to mobilise their own armed forces as Soviet troops began their gradual withdrawal.

Conditions within Nagorno-Karabakh were dreadful. With the airport closed and the road to Armenia blocked by Azeri forces, the only access from Armenia was by helicopter, a journey which entailed considerable danger for the passengers. The Azeris maintained that the helicopter flights were not being used only to transport medicine and other essential supplies but to carry weapons and ammunition, so it was all right to shoot the helicopters down. From the hills around the capital, Azeri troops fired night after night on to the capital, Stepanakert, forcing its inhabitants to cower in basement shelters. Sniper fire made the city equally dangerous by daylight, when a few brave souls ventured forth in search of bread or water or other supplies. The infrastructure was in tatters – water mains and sewers were severely damaged, increasing the risk of disease. Unheated hospitals struggled to treat the sick. Severe cold may have inhibited the spread of disease, but it brought other problems, especially since little fuel had reached the enclave since August 1991. Trees were being cut down in city streets to provide at least a modicum of heating. Schools, of course, were closed.

The fighting was incessant, and villages in the enclave passed from Azeri to Armenian control, and vice versa, with bewildering frequency. As the situation worsened, diplomatic activity increased. In late February the foreign ministers of both republics were at least talking about a ceasefire, and a short while later the Iranian foreign minister Ali Akbar Velayati succeeded in negotiating one. But it lasted only a few hours. The proposal that the CIS should send in a peacekeeping force was opposed by the Azeris, who feared that they would show greater sympathy for the Armenian cause than the Azeri. The Popular Front in Azerbaijan kept up the pressure on Mutalibov to make no concessions to the Armenians, pressure which did not make the efforts of the mediators any easier.

In March the Azeris accused Armenians of massacring a thousand civilians during the capture of Khodzhali, from where the Azeris had been shelling Armenian villages. The figure seemed inflated, but independent observers confirmed that about one hundred civilians, including women and children, had been killed. Naturally there were political consequences after the massacre. The Azerbaijan Popular Front accused Mutalibov of failing to prevent heavy Azeri casualties and demanded his resignation, and a day later Mutalibov, after saying he would not resign, did step down. He later turned up in Moscow, pleading ill health. In purely military terms the Karabakh forces were beginning to notch up some successes as strategic Azeri villages fell into their hands. On the other hand, the Azeris had captured the largest Soviet arms depot in Transcaucasia, ensuring a five-year supply of weapons and ammunition, an arsenal the Armenians could not hope to match. Fortunately the one chemical weapons depot in the region remained firmly in CIS hands.

Velayati's attempts to act as honest broker had ended in failure. Cyrus Vance, as the special envoy of the United Nations, stepped in. On 16 March another ceasefire was negotiated. It didn't last, but the growing participation of the international community in trying to resolve the dispute was, arguably, a positive sign. Armenian officials played down a few articles in the Turkish press expressing solidarity with their Azeri brothers and insisted that the official Turkish government line was more conciliatory. Armenia also argued that it had made a major compromise. Despite a vote in Parliament favouring the reunification of Armenia and Karabakh, it was no longer Armenian policy to demand union or annexation. Armenia would favour any solution which met with the approval of the Armenian majority in the enclave. Any acceptable solution, however, would have to guarantee basic human rights, long suppressed by the Azeri administration. In addition, Azerbaijan must abandon its policy of deportations from the enclave and stop all military action in the region.

Towards the end of March a vague agreement was reached between Armenia, Azerbaijan, and Artur Mkrtchyan, the president of Karabakh, that there should be tripartite negotiations. This would have been an important step forward, but the teams neglected to agree on a time or place for such a meeting. With the mysterious death of Mkrtchyan in Stepanakert a few weeks later, this plan too fizzled out.

On 7 May Armenia and Azerbaijan agreed at talks mediated by Iran to a new ceasefire and an exchange of prisoners. It was all meaningless, as the very next day the Armenians, after heavy fighting, captured Shushi, the major Azeri stronghold in Karabakh. The new Azeri government, formed from Popular Front supporters, reversed Mutalibov's banning of political activity and promised fresh elections in June.

PART THREE

20 Back from the Brink

Dawn slunk across the horizon just as I was curling up on a banquette in the lobby of the Hotel Armenia. I'd arrived at six in the morning to find that my prepaid reservation did not, as I assumed, entitle me to a room. A room would be available by eight. In the meantime I was welcome to make myself comfortable on the banquette.

The journey had been as tiresome as expected. On the plane an Armenian baby had been deposited on my lap while its mother – returning to Yerevan after two years in Paris where she'd acquired *une nostalgie terrible* – sorted through her seventeen pieces of hand luggage before we landed. The baby did not like me, and I did not like it. Only a single passport official was available to check the documents of two hundred or so passengers, and he didn't get out his rubber stamp until we'd been queueing for half an hour.

I spent a day recuperating in Yerevan before undertaking the train journey across the mountains to Tbilisi. Vladimir, Aram and Ashot acted as my personal bearers, lugging my bags on to crowded buses heading towards the station. On the platform Ashot affected to admire the sulphurous smell emanating from the chemical plant located a mile away. Ruminating, he moved away from us and stood on the edge of the platform peering at the tracks.

'Do not stand outside the collective!' said Aram, rebuking him.

'Have you become a Communist in your old age?'

'I was born in this system,' shrugged Aram. 'I am a perfect example of *homo sovieticus*.' Aram enjoyed irony.

My carriage surprised me by being in excellent working order.

Lights, hooks, racks, they all functioned. There was another surprise: the train left on time. We chugged past tiny allotments crammed between workshops and tracks, and once outside the city drew alongside a highway as empty as Canada. We passed small-holdings with plastic cloches over the rows of seedlings, abandoned small factories and storage yards, and the idle smokestacks of Medzamor. An old slobbering beggar came shuffling drunkenly down the corridor, sidling into each compartment with his hand out. I noted how rarely one sees drunks in Armenia, until moments later another one came stumbling through. We stopped for half an hour at a small country station, where fishermen were relaxing on the benches with bottles of vodka. Two geese slurped from the puddles, ignoring the travellers dashing from the train to the water pipes to fill their bottles and splash the dust from their faces. A sultry afternoon had filled the train with clammy heat and the window in my compartment wouldn't open.

Slick with sweat, I slept little, but the return journey some days later was worse. I shared the compartment with a Georgian lorry driver, who, as soon as he sat down, fished out a bottle of vodka. I produced a bottle of wine, and was obliged to match him drink for drink. We toasted Agatha Christie and Conan Doyle, John Major and Eduard Shevardnadze, and I found myself raising my glass after a garbled toast which contained only two recognisable words – 'sex video'. He kept telling me in Russian that he loved me, but this, to my relief, was mere Georgian hyperbole. By the time he finished his vodka, he was exceedingly drunk, suggesting he'd had a few before boarding the train. He rummaged in his bag and pulled out a bottle of wine, which he insisted we drink. I refused to drink any more, which he regarded as an affront. He knocked back a glass, then passed out.

For the next eight hours he snored and snuffled violently, sometimes springing into an upright position while still asleep or slumping heavily on to my bunk, from which I had to dislodge him. He had enough vestiges of coherence to realise he was being a bit of a nuisance: 'Sorry. I love you. Sorry.' Then another round of snores. In the middle of the night two men with machine guns burst in, but as a conductor stood behind them I was not too alarmed. They searched the luggage racks beneath the seat, presumably looking for weapons, as saboteurs had a habit of blowing up the bridges along this route. When my companion definitively awoke, he drank half a bottle of wine for breakfast.

The rolling hills just south of Leninakan were no more ingratiating in May than they had been in December. This landscape, on roughly the same latitude as southern France, could easily be mistaken for tundra. Stone huts were parked on expanses of pale green undulating hills cluttered with stones. The hills, which were not especially high, were still streaked with snow, like the patterned stripes of a cat. Spring seemed a recent arrival, with the freshest of shoots greening the trees. The blockish houses were roofed with corrugated iron that reflected a forbidding dazzle in the sunlight hardly less austere than their incorrigible greyness beneath winter skies. Along the Turkish border lookout towers marched like pylons across the treeless slopes and plains.

Svetlana was out of town for a week, and I stayed with Erekle and his extended family, drinking small glasses of brandy – 'just symbolic, just symbolic' – at ungodly hours with his elderly grandfather, and coping with Zeinab's dismay if I failed to eat a full meal every three hours.

It had been a hard winter, said Zeinab. There were frequent lapses in supplies of electricity, heating and gas. Often there was no bread, and when it was available she'd had to queue for two hours in the cold to obtain a loaf. Prices had risen. Bus fares were now 50 kopeks, the metro 60. Petrol cost 15 roubles per litre. Car tyres, at 8000 roubles each, were as precious as jewellery. Schools had been closed for much of the winter; she and her colleagues at the university had not been paid for a month or more. She had ended the winter with a bout of pneumonia. Svetlana's husband Soso had died suddenly just weeks after he saw me off at the airport, where he gave every appearance of robust health.

Later that day I visited the market near Freedom Square. It was uncrowded. When I saw the prices I understood why. Prices per kilo were 6 roubles for radishes, 13 for potatoes, 25 for cucumbers, 30 for carrots, and 60–70 for tomatoes. Fruit, even now that spring was here, was also expensive: 50 for cherries or apples, 40 for pears, 200 for strawberries. Cheese varied from 120 to 220, walnuts, so beloved by Georgian cooks, were 200. Beef was now 130 per kilo, and a chicken was priced at 250. True, salaries had doubled, more or less, since January, but they had not begun to keep up with the relentless rise in food prices. Transportation costs had risen steeply too.

In 1987, when writing *The Double Eagle*, I had interviewed various Czech dissidents. Three years later the men I had spoken to, usually in clandestine circumstances, had become the new masters. Pavel Bratinka was a member of parliament, Rudolf Slánský ambassador to Moscow, Peter Pitthart prime minister of Bohemia, and Václav Havel president of Czechoslovakia. I had not been quite so effective in Georgia, but many of those I had met at Opposition rallies had done well. Luisa Shakiashvili and Irena Sarashvili were now on the state council, as was Koté Gabashvili. Tengiz Sigua was prime minister again, and had appointed his protector Kitovani as minister of defence. Nodar Natadze had declined to join the state council, but devoted his energies to dealing with the South Ossetian problem as head of a special commission on the region.

The state council had expanded from fifty to sixty-eight members, and additional members could be coopted with the approval of a two-thirds majority. Not all its members were political leaders; some were specialists whose expertise would guide the council in its deliberations. The council was chaired by Eduard Shevardnadze, with Djaba Ioseliani as his deputy. Although the government, under Tengiz Sigua, was a separate branch, many ministers were also members of the state council. The two bodies did not always see eye to eye, and there had been an occasion when tax proposals submitted by the government had been vetoed by the council. After the elections called for October 1992, the council would self-destruct and be replaced by some kind of parliamentary democracy.

I asked Giorgi Gogsadze, a leading light in the right-wing Liberal Democratic Party, whether he expected those elections to proceed smoothly. He worried that secessionist problems, stoked by Russia, could be quite disruptive. I asked him why Russia should bother to destabilise a tiny country such as Georgia.

'Because we are on the Black Sea, we have a fertile land, we look to the west rather than the north. Russia doesn't want to lose its political and economic hold on us. Georgia is the one republic not yet recognised by Russia, because they know that after recognition we would demand the withdrawal of the remaining Russian troops here, and Russia doesn't want that. Once the troops are out of here, it will be easier for us to solve our ethnic disputes with Abkhazia and South Ossetia peacefully, and that too is not in Russian interests.'

The final form of the electoral system was still undecided, but the new Parliament would have 150 seats and would be elected for a three-year term. The largest party was the National Democrats under Giorgi Chanturia, but about forty other parties would be participating in the election. A coalition government seemed the inevitable outcome. After the elections, many political parties would probably disappear or amalgamate. Some are simply vehicles for opinionated individuals or for single issues; few would be likely to survive.

Some political groups favoured a parliamentary democracy, others preferred a presidential system, especially if Shevardnadze could be persuaded to stand for election. The whole matter of the constitution remained hazy, as the present one is based on the outdated social democratic model of 1921. A new constitution is being drafted, but will not be ready till 1993. The thorniest issue is the way in which the ethnic minorities would participate in the political life of the nation.

'It gets very complicated,' said Gogsadze. 'South Ossetia is still a war zone, and the Abkhazians don't trust the Georgians, for a start. What may well happen is that we'll devise some kind of federation, possibly on the German model. The view of my own party and of some others is that all ethnic minorities should enjoy the same rights, with the exception of the Abkhazians. That's because the Abkhazians are an aboriginal people with no other homeland outside Georgia. So in our view they should have a degree of political autonomy that we wouldn't favour granting to, say, the Armenians who live here. Of course there's no separatist or secessionist movement among the Armenians, who can go back to Armenia if they don't like it here. They don't go back, of course, because they know perfectly well that their standard of living is considerably higher than it would be in Armenia.'

I tried to find out what had happened to Gamsakhurdia's ministers, but they had faded away. Even the former prime minister Besso Gugushvili had returned to the obscurity he deserved. This seemed to confirm that Gamsakhurdia's régime had been utterly dependent on his personality, and the competence of his ministers of little account. The ex-president's chief ideologist, Guran Petriash-vili, had resurfaced, and when interviewed on television had been asked about the 'principles' on which Gamsakhurdia's foreign policy had been based. He replied that the intention had been to form some kind of Caucasian federation, scorning the patronising attentions of the capitalist West, which sought only to destroy Georgian national consciousness, and relying instead on the common interests of the Caucasian republics. Since Armenia and Azerbaijan were hardly on the best of terms, and relations between Armenia and Georgia were also a touch frosty, this hardly seemed a sensible basis for a foreign policy. Conceit and unreality walked hand in hand. No wonder the Georgians were prepared to forget the past sufficiently to allow a skilled old hand like Shevardnadze to take control of their present. At first it had seemed curious to me that Shevardnadze, like Gamsakhurdia, was reluctant for Georgia to join the CIS. But by the spring of 1992 the CIS was showing signs of strain, with the Ukraine increasingly obstreperous. Shevardnadze was probably wise in deciding that Georgia should adopt a policy of wait and see.

There were still diehard Gamsakhurdia supporters, especially in western Georgia, and occasional pro-Gamsakhurdia rallies, al-though the continuing state of emergency forbade such gatherings. His supporters were particularly incensed when Shevardnadze, whom they loathed with rare passion, persuaded Hans-Dietrich Genscher to visit Georgia. The loyalists insisted that the distin-guished visitor wasn't Herr Genscher at all but a Georgian actor who resembled him. When, a short while later, the German foreign minister resigned, the loyalists changed their tune. Yes, it had been Herr Genscher after all, but after his visit to Georgia Gamsakhurdia had phoned Chancellor Kohl to let him know how outraged he was that Shevardnadze's government had been given respectability by the German visit, and in the wake of this withering rebuke Herr Kohl had had no choice but to fire his minister. Perhaps these stories are exaggerations but, knowing how tenuous is the grasp of reality displayed by Gamsakhurdia and his supporters, I find them completely plausible.

I asked Gogsadze to estimate the former president's strength in Georgia. 'Probably 20 per cent throughout the republic, 50 to 60 per cent in the west, and 10 per cent in Kakheti and the east. He has no support at all in regions populated by Armenians and Azerbaijanis. Even though social conditions are worsening here, the evidence suggests that Gamsakhurdia's support is decreasing all the time. He himself will be prohibited from standing for office in October, and his followers have little or no personal support. But they will probably continue with their campaign of civil disobedience and terrorism, and with attacks on public buildings and the blocking of railway lines.'

His local influence had been further diminished by the abolition of the prefect system. Their appointment had emasculated local elected councils, which the prefects had the power to disband, and their authority opened them to the temptations of kickbacks and other forms of corruption. They had been replaced by district chiefs, whose role was to ensure that local councils were putting into effect the reforms and laws passed by the state council. Should a council be found acting in ways contrary to new directives, the dispute would be resolved in the courts. The new system did not sound exactly democratic, but until a parliamentary system was installed in October accountability would be unattainable.

Even those who do not fully trust Eduard Shevardnadze were giving him credit for returning to Georgia in the first place. After all, he could, like his master Mikhail Gorbachev, have headed west to enjoy the fat fees and adulation of the lecture circuit. He could even have adopted the final vanity of the retired or defeated politician, a foundation named after himself, stacked with ample funds from wellwishers and with a nebulous programme.

Although for many his reputation was blighted by his period as head of the Georgian Communist Party from 1973 to 1985, even those who recalled those days with little sympathy paid tribute to his crusades against corruption and to his personal courage. He had first displayed this courage in 1977, when a crucial football match had taken place between Tbilisi Dynamo and a Russian team. The rule of the centre affected sporting events too, and it was regarded as unseemly for a team from the republics to defeat a Russian squad. Towards the end of this match the Russians were leading by one goal, but the Georgians were on the offensive and seemed likely to equalise. The referee's whistle blew five minutes before the end of the match, ruling out that possibility and saving the honour of the Russian team.

The crowd was furious. Before long anger had turned into rioting, as fixtures were wrecked and fires were set. Russian troops were alerted, and a short while later Shevardnadze arrived at the stadium with his bodyguards. The reception was unfriendly, but he told his bodyguards to stand back and walked alone into the crowd. The spectators were so taken aback by this dramatic if foolhardy step of quelling a riot by force of personality alone that they became more subdued, discussed their grievances with him, and serious bloodshed was averted.

The following year there had been more trouble, when Moscow announced that Russian would henceforth be the primary language of Georgia, reducing the ancient language of Georgian to the status of a foreign tongue. Huge rallies were organised, to which the Russians responded by mobilising their forces. The turning-point came when Shevardnadze sided with the Georgian people rather than with his masters in Moscow. The plans were dropped.

The council Shevardnadze now chaired was based at the former Institute of Marxism-Leninism on Rustaveli, from which I had watched the frieze of the Marxist pantheon being dismantled some eight months earlier. There was, I suspect, no ironic intention in the choice; it just happened to be one of the few large buildings in the city centre still usable. The Hotel Tbilisi and School No 1 had been gutted, as had other buildings close to the Parliament, and some 250 families had lost their homes and their possessions. One whole side of Freedom Square had been so badly damaged that it had been torn down, though the authorities were hoping to reconstruct and restore the hotel and school. (The barbershop in the square was untouched, so I darted in for a trim.) The cinema and the State Museum opposite the Parliament were open for business and I was relieved to learn that the Gudiashvili House had been spared. The wings of the Parliament had also been gutted and their exterior walls blackened by extremes of heat and smoke, but the portico was in surprisingly good shape. Some of the tufa facing on the columns had been chipped off by the relentless shelling, exposing the reinforced concrete at the core, but not a single pier had collapsed. As Erekle remarked, the Communists built for keeps.

The new régime certainly had its hands full. The infrastructure was shattered and the government was broke. I wanted to know how this was affecting daily governance, so I went to a building near the Mardjianishvili Theatre which housed the ministry of education. The matronly minister, Gucha Kvaratzkhelia, admitted that universal free education was no longer within the means of the government. Private education was being encouraged, even though it was not easy to ensure that standards were being upheld in private schools and colleges. Her ministry simply hoped that competition between these new institutions would force the mediocre ones out of business – eventually.

When I asked whether the encouragement of private education would lead to a two-tier system which would discriminate against the children of poorer families, her response was brusque: 'In Georgia the alternative would be to have children who are completely uneducated. The problem throughout the old Soviet system was everyone wanted qualifications, but nobody wanted to complete the studies necessary to acquire them. The result is that we have too many people with diplomas who are in fact uneducated.'

(An Armenian acquaintance later told me a joke which reflected this situation. A Georgian went to be interviewed for a job, and presented a whole stack of diplomas and qualifications. The employer picked up a medical diploma and asked the Georgian where he had bought this particular item. The Georgian was indignant: 'Bought it! I never bought it! It was given to me as a birthday present.')

The goal of the changes being considered by the new government was that the state system would provide a basic level of education, while the private system would offer a wider curriculum and smaller classes. To ensure that it was not only the children of the better off who could avail themselves of these costly benefits, the government was considering offering financial assistance to poor but motivated students who wished to attend private academies. Nothing, it seemed, was decided. Fundamental changes were necessary, but everyone recognised that tampering with education would have profound consequences, so the discussion was prolonged and intense. Another scheme, still not approved because of the considerable opposition to it, was to give parents an indexed sum equivalent to the sum disbursed by the government on a child's education, and to allow the parents to spend that sum on the kind of education they favoured. Educationalists from Europe and America were being invited to Georgia to offer their advice.

The fears expressed to me by Jumber Lominadze that the continuing existence of the Academy of Sciences would be in jeopardy in an independent Georgia were confirmed by the minister. The present Academy was too large an establishment to remain as it was. It would not be abolished, but it would shrink, with certain areas of costly research being abandoned. 'It isn't practical,' she pointed out, 'for a country as small as ours to conduct its own nuclear research.' What would probably happen was that the old Soviet separation of teaching and research would be abandoned, and there would be much closer links between the Academy and the universities.

Leaving the building I fell into conversation with a dapper, self-confident young man who told me he was soon going to Bristol

University to study international law. I marvelled that a Georgian student could afford to do so, and he explained that he had relatives in Britain.

'Anyway,' he added airily, 'it will only cost about ten thousand pounds.'

Only. While those who had been teaching him at his university in Georgia were earning the rouble equivalent, at current exchange rates, of sixty pounds per year. I wondered whether this personable young man would ever return to Georgia when he completed his education abroad.

21 Shake That Hand

The lobby of the state council building was packed with people. A single hole in the wall functioned as an inquiry desk, and a single telephone connected visitors, if they were lucky, with the office they wished to contact. A small group of elderly women in black sat alongside the guarded doors which led to the offices, and I jokingly called them Shevardnadze's women, recalling the harridans on the Parliament steps who were Gamsakhurdia's most fanatical supporters. Nobody found this enormously funny. The guards were slow and stupid, as tradition demands, but genial enough and, flashing our freshly acquired passes, Erekle and I entered the corridors of power. Here unshaven men in leather jackets were lounging against doorways smoking foul-smelling cigarettes. In anterooms people sat silently on chairs around the wall, waiting to be summoned.

We were here on a fishing trip. Erekle knew most of the government by sight and hoped that if we wandered about long enough, we would eventually encounter somebody worth talking to. In one smoke-filled room we came across David Turashvili, a former student leader who is now a playwright working closely with the Rustaveli Theatre. Despite his veteran status at the forefront of anti-Soviet demonstrations, he was still only in his mid-twenties. His connections proved impeccable and we soon found ourselves in the anteroom to Djaba Ioseliani's office. The status of the official was reflected in two ways: there was carpeting and a colour television set. The extras were the same as elsewhere; enough unshaven men to staff a conference of *banditti*. A few minutes later I was shaking hands with the second most powerful man in Georgia. With his record as former criminal, man of the theatre, militia boss and political prisoner under Gamsakhurdia, I had expected someone with very rough edges. Not a bit of it. Ioseliani was well dressed in a dark blue suit and a button-down shirt. He had rippling thin grey hair and a pair of aviator glasses, a rarity in the Caucasus. There was a canniness to his smile, and a hint of fleshiness around an otherwise firm jaw. He had acquired an executive aura.

I began by recalling how some Opposition leaders had welcomed Gamsakhurdia's downfall but deplored the violence used to unseat him. What was his view?

'Such people,' he replied calmly, 'are either uninformed or have the wrong information or are fascists. Were they better informed, they would have known that the Opposition tried its best to use peaceful means against Gamsakhurdia: demonstrations, meetings, petitions, hunger strikes. Gamsakhurdia arrested and locked up a hundred people, shot at his own people. In December the Opposition repeatedly offered him the chance to leave office peacefully, offers he always refused.'

'But wasn't the violence a bad precedent? After the October elections, what's to stop another group saying the new government doesn't suit them, so it's all right to attack them with military force?'

'It was a bad precedent, but there was no other way. Our famous poet Erakli Abashidze, who died not long ago, put it this way. I go to the market, buy a cucumber, and take it home. When I begin to eat it I discover it is rotten. Am I obliged to eat the cucumber to the end because I chose it at the market? Anyway, Georgia is not the only country that has had to get rid of a dictator.'

'What will happen to your Mkhedrioni? Will the militia be disbanded after the elections?'

'Perhaps before the elections.'

'Will they be integrated into Georgia's new army?'

'Possibly. It depends on how stable the country is. There are still some pockets of resistance in the west, but we're talking about very small groups of saboteurs, including many criminal elements.'

When I asked him to clarify his nefarious past, he remained

vague, saying only that he had been in prison in the 1940s and 1950s on criminal charges. But, he added, he had been a very young man.

Soon after the overthrow of Gamsakhurdia, Ioseliani had been sympathetic to the idea of constitutional monarchy. Support for the idea seemed to be dwindling fast and I wondered whether he had changed his view.

'In the past I was in favour of it, yes. Many nationalist politicians here were self-seeking and did not always put the interests of Georgia first. I regarded the monarchy as an institution that could stop this political infighting and become a symbol of the entire nation. If we'd had a monarch last year, I feel sure we would have rid ourselves of Gamsakhurdia by peaceful means. But today I think the creation of a monarchy would be a backward step. Still, if there were ever another threat of dictatorship, I might return to the idea. I'm definitely not in favour of a presidential system. That brings back bad memories.'

I returned to the building shortly before a meeting of the state council was due to begin. David Turashvili took me straight up to the landing outside the council chamber. I watched many familiar figures from the former Opposition filing in, and Erekle pointed out others I had not recognised, including Temur Djordjorliani, the leader of the Monarchist Party (arrested in November 1991 for organising a hunger strike to demand the release of political prisoners), and Chabua Amireghibi, a skinny old man in a mud-brown suit who was one of Georgia's best-known novelists and had spent seventeen years in Stalin's camps.

'Look,' said Erekle, as an alert-eyed, white-haired man slowly crossed the landing, 'he goes without bodyguards.'

Erekle was recalling, as was I, our rare encounters with Zviad Gamsakhurdia, who never went anywhere without a pair of gunmen, while here was Eduard Shevardnadze strolling about seemingly unguarded.

We were both surprised when, instead of walking straight into the chamber, Shevardnadze came up and ceremoniously shook our hands. Naturally he had no idea who we were, but his politician's instinct told him that it could do no harm to be amiable. I asked

David whether, with his infinity of good connections, he could book an interview for me with the great man, but even David was unable to achieve that. Everybody in Georgia with a problem – political, business, judicial, family – was keen to see Shevardnadze in the hope of a miracle cure. The queue was too long for there to be any realistic chance of my jumping it.

Inside the chamber, the councillors sat on either side of a boomerang-shaped table, but the pillars of the hall obstructed the view from one end to the other. A few chairs were set out for visitors at the sides of the room. Shevardnadze and Ioseliani sat more or less in the centre. Although it was broad daylight outside, the curtains were drawn, and the councillors had to contend with television lights beaming on to their faces. The meeting proceeded slowly, with some remarks about whether representatives of the ethnic minorities should be coopted on to the council, followed by a lackadaiscal discussion about private colleges. The steady drone of comment from one end of the table would be politely curtailed by the fruitier tones of Shevardnadze's intimate growl. I caught the eye of a well-groomed young woman with sleek hennaed hair and large dark doe eyes. I had been observing her for some moments, but only when she looked up at me did I recognise her. It was Irena Sarashvili, who no longer resembled the pale, exhausted, somewhat bedraggled figure I had met in December.

After an hour a young woman stepped silently into the chamber carrying a glass of tea wrapped in a pink napkin. She made her way behind the long table and placed the glass beside Shevardnadze, then tiptoed out again. It was clearly going to be a long meeting, and I followed her out.

I walked past the main post office (where the price of a fax to London had risen from 100 to 450 roubles in six months) to the Rustaveli Metro station. Here it looked like the old days, with a hundred policemen standing about, their buses parked awkwardly by the sides of the plaza. Two armoured cars were stationed here too, and when I photographed one of them a sharp hoot from a police car rebuked me. Mutters from one or two people made it clear that the supporters of Mr Gamsakhurdia had wanted to stage a rally here, but were being prevented from doing so by the police, who were enforcing the emergency regulations.

I had dinner that evening with Sandro Taktakishvili, who had taken me to Borjomi the previous September. Although he came from a family of distinguished musicians, all four generations shared a rambling flat in the university district. His wife, the beautiful film actress and pianist Lika Kavzharadze, was ill and absent, but Sandro introduced me to his mother Nana Dimitriana, a concert pianist, and his eighty-year-old grandmother, an opera singer with the curious distinction of having entertained Stalin, Churchill and Roosevelt at the Tehran Conference in 1943.

Sandro and his associates, all physicists, were continuing to develop their business, and had signed contracts both with other republics and with the United States. Gamsakhurdia had done everything possible to discourage such ventures and many Georgian businessmen had moved their operations to Moscow, where some of them had prospered greatly. Earlier that day Ioseliani had told me that Georgia wanted to encourage foreign contacts both in business and culture, and Sandro confirmed that the new government had jettisoned the worst features of Gamsakhurdia's isolationism. Taxes on currency brought into Georgia had been reduced from 80 to 20 per cent, and other taxes had been lowered to nominal levels to stimulate trade.

Sandro still shuddered when he recalled the Gamsakhurdia régime. 'I myself didn't participate in the fighting, but I had many friends, who are the last people you would describe as wild gunmen, who didn't hesitate to fight just to get rid of that terrible man who was ruining our country. Everything he did was so divisive. As you know, antisemitism is unknown in Georgia, but under Gamsakhurdia there were attempts by his men to extort money from the Jewish community here and I know that some businesses were dissuaded from having commercial contacts with Israel. Really, under Gamsakhurdia I was for the first time ashamed to be a Georgian.'

*

The day before, when climbing the hill towards Erekle's flat, we had walked behind two women carrying between them what appeared to be a tub of washing. The younger, with long black hair, was Tamriko Chkheidze, a historian by profession and a leading light in the nationalist Ilya Chavchavadze Society. She was first arrested as a dissident when she was seventeen, and had been an early associate of Gamsakhurdia but they had fallen out as long ago as 1982. By an appalling irony, she had been the driver of the car in which Merab Kostava had been killed. Swerving to avoid an obstacle in the road, she had caused the car to overturn, which killed two of the passengers. Despite the trauma, she had remained politically active and was now a member of the state council.

After Sandro, unwilling to entrust me to the muggers' paradise which Tbilisi after dark had become, had driven me back to the flat, Erekle asked me whether I would like to visit Tamriko that evening. Her home was just a few doors away and in these quiet streets we could safely ignore the curfew. When she opened the door I saw before me a very slight pale figure, intensely nervous, knotting and unknotting her fingers. She invited us in. Each time I asked her a question she would furrow her brows deeply while considering her response. It took a while for her to relax slightly, and it was half an hour before she ventured a flash of a smile that gave her gaunt face a wisp of charm. She spoke precisely in excellent English, and I had the impression that she said exactly what was on her mind and had no intention of tailoring her answers to my expectations.

I wanted to know whether the return of Shevardnadze gave her more confidence about the future.

'I am more optimistic,' she said slowly, 'but I am still uncertain. I do not fully trust Shevardnadze.'

'Because of his past career in Georgia?'

'Not only because of that. He is a distinguished man, but I worry that he may be acting with the agreement of Russia. He must justify his reputation with actions as well as words.'

I wondered what the atmosphere had been like when she began to oppose the Communist regime in the 1970s, when the penalties for dissent were so great.

'It was very bad, of course, but the atmosphere was worse under Gamsakhurdia, even though it was far more dangerous in the seventies. I say this because Gamsakhurdia precipitated a greater national catastrophe, and the possibility of national conflict was realised. His rule was a kind of fascism.'

'When he attacked his opponents as KGB agents and drug addicts and so forth, did he really believe this rhetoric or was it pure calculation intended to arouse populist support?'

'I believe his stance was mostly calculation.'

'So it was purely cynical?'

'Also comical.'

In the 1970s she had participated in one of a small number of tiny nationalist groups which organised meetings, put up posters and engaged in other illegal activities. These dissident groups were essentially nationalist, but it was clearly impractical at that time to demand independence, so they focused their demands on human and national rights. The crime for which she was jailed for two years in 1983 was the organisation of a meeting to demand the release of political prisoners and the disruption of traffic. In 1987 she helped found the Ilya Chavchavadze Society. Merab Kostava had been associated both with that group and with Gamsakhurdia's circle, and his aim was to unite the two. This proved impossible due to Gamsakhurdia's personality. I asked why she had fallen out with Gamsakhurdia.

'I didn't trust him. Even in those days he was calling anyone who disagreed with him a KGB agent. I also didn't like his contempt for Western democracies.'

Did she agree with Ioseliani and others that there was no alternative to the violence in December?

'The Society was against it, but I can accept that nothing would have changed had it not occurred. It was clear that Gamsakhurdia was moving towards ever greater repression and something had to be done.'

'And yet a large section of the population didn't seem to mind that their liberties were being eroded. Why not?'

'Because seventy years of repression had changed their psyches.

Gamsakhurdia exploited the bad side of people by inciting ethnic conflicts. He used nationalist feelings to create divisions, to create both internal and external enemies. And the sole purpose of this was to consolidate his own power. He was a man with no moral sense whatsoever, no political principles. Before Gamsakhurdia such ethnic hatreds played no part in Georgian nationalism.'

To avoid any repetition of this authoritarianism, she wanted the widest possible representation in the new Parliament. The Society, now a political party, would campaign for more private enterprise and a more rapid introduction of an independent currency. 'The government has been too timorous on the economy, not radical enough. I want to see real privatisation, but the government keeps saying how poor we are and how difficult it is to make changes. But I don't think we are as poor as they want us to think. I am sure there are possibilities that are not being pursued. We have to create a real market with real industrial production to allow us to generate the wealth we need to cope with the rising prices forced on us by Russia.'

'Coming here twice from Armenia, I can't help noticing how fertile and luxuriant Georgia is in comparison. Given time, Georgia could be extremely prosperous, surely.'

'Yes, but we need stability. The government is not being firm enough in dealing with sabotage. We should allow political meetings to proceed without hindrance, but be much stricter about cracking down on sabotage.' Easier said than done, I suspected, with the dissolution of the Soviet apparatus of security forces. Despite the nightly curfew, it was difficult to prevent small armed groups from wreaking havoc in parts of the country still sympathetic to the former president.

As a reminder, we heard through the open windows of the flat the crackle of rifle fire, followed by a second round a minute later. Tamriko shrugged. This was nothing out of the ordinary in Tbilisi. (In mid-June a car bomb, intended to incinerate Djaba Ioseliani, left him intact but killed four passersby.)

With as much tact as I could muster, I asked her about the accident that had killed Kostava. Was it really an accident?

'There are many doubtful aspects, but we will never know for sure. Merab's removal was certainly politically useful for some people. He made no secret of the fact that he found Gamsakhurdia's methods unacceptable. Conflict between them was inevitable. Merab Kostava was not interested in political power as such. He wanted a Georgia free of Soviet troops – that was his aim.

'There was another suspicious factor. A few weeks after the accident, in November 1989, Gamsakhurdia worsened the situation in South Ossetia by mounting an expedition to Tskhinvali. Kostava had opposed this expedition as provocation. After Merab died there was no other opposition to Gamsakhurdia's adventurism. Some of his men remained in South Ossetia and provoked terrorist acts. Before that time, there had been good relations in South Ossetia, with little tension and a good deal of intermarriage with Georgians. But Gamsakhurdia exploited the presence of a few ethnic leaders with extremist views to inflame the problem. He could easily have negotiated with the minorities to preserve the national rights of the Georgians in those regions, but he wasn't interested in that. Interestingly, the other person injured in the car crash, Zurab Chavchavadze, had been negotiating quite successfully along these lines. Zurab had been badly injured but was gradually recovering and then, suddenly, two months after the accident, he died in hospital. Gamsakhurdia said that Zurab was an agent of Ossetia and ordered people not to attend his funeral.'

We were dwelling on the minutiae of the past, but these were living issues for the Georgian intelligentsia, the issues which had shaped their political consciousness. Zviad Gamsakhurdia had taken on demonic status for many of his opponents, and it was hard not to sympathise with their view. Even after his flight he remained a dominating presence.

I was seated in a typical Georgian living room which had been compelled to serve too many purposes. There was a small bed in one corner, a grand piano, an ironing board, maps pinned to the dingy wallpaper, assorted chairs, piles of clothing. Across from me sat the philosopher Mikho Naneishvili, the thoughtful leader of the Liberal Democratic Party, which was modelled on classic nineteenth-century European liberalism. Jammed into his broad mouth crammed with teeth that resembled a New England colonial graveyard was a cigarette holder. From a neighbouring flat I could hear the sounds of Chopin being practised on the piano.

Like Tamriko Chkheidze, he had reservations about Eduard Shevardnadze, in his case because he was still in contact with the former Communist bureaucracy in Georgia. 'Those people,' Naneishvili said, 'are no great lovers of capitalism. They may wish to think progressively, but they simply aren't trained to. The best we can say for them is that they are utterly devoted to Shevardnadze himself. Shevardnadze may wish to use his immense influence for the nation's benefit, but our other prominent politicians are more interested in power than principle. The ministries are full of unworthy people who have no expertise and can't be relied upon. I understand that Shevardnadze is limited at present in the choices he can make among his officials, but after the elections we'll see what he can really do.'

Naneishvili thought that a presidential system would prevail, despite the reservations of Ioseliani and others. He believed a majority would grant Shevardnadze the powers any leader needed to push through the reforms necessary to reverse the damage inflicted by Gamsakhurdia. He was not unduly worried about the emergence of another dictatorship. 'Fortunately our politicians fear dictatorship because of their experience.'

'You had that experience for seventy years and that didn't stop you choosing Gamsakhurdia.'

'That's because no one had any real understanding of what democracy was. In the late 1980s the dictatorship of Communism was seen as less of an issue than our occupation by Russian troops. People wanted freedom from the Russians above all, and they didn't give enough thought to how Georgia should be governed. This opened the door to Gamsakhurdia and the extreme nationalists.'

The government had to do all it could to stimulate economic cooperation with the West, he said. Indeed, the evening before, in a televised interview with Valery Kvaratzkhelia, Shevardnadze had said he was keen to speed up both privatisation and foreign investment, yet even if he succeeded it would be another two or three years before the Georgian economy would improve.

Many factories were still idle, but Georgia had traditionally been competitive in such fields as textiles, food processing, chemicals, metallurgy and machinery. Those markets had to be captured once again. Gamsakhurdia had never been interested in cooperation with Western companies, as he feared the loss of control a market economy would imply. Brought up with the old centralist pieties of Communism, he found it impossible to envisage a looser structuring of the economy.

As for land reform, with which the new government was trying to press ahead, good intentions had foundered on practical difficulties. First, it was not always clear how the land should be distributed, especially in the case of large families with multiple claims. Gamsakhurdia had raised the fear that any redistribution of land would favour non-Georgians, notably Armenians and Azerbaijanis, who had been working some of the best land for decades. The greatest obstacles to land reform, however, were those erected by local officials, especially heads of collectives who feared losing their power and their perks.

'All these problems can be solved, but we need competent people to put these reforms into practice.'

'If the old-style bureaucrats are being obstructive, why not fire them?'

'Because there's no new generation to take up the reins. It's only the old bureaucrats from the Soviet days who have any experience of running things.'

The economics minister, Roman Gotziridze, confirmed that mediocrity and corruption at the municipal level were huge obstacles to reform, but the government would push ahead. A slight, dapper man with small dark eyes, Gotziridze had been a member of parliament under the banner of Natadze's Popular Front. As a professional economist he had the expertise to initiate reforms, and as a member of the state council he had, he hoped, the political influence to set them in motion.

He did not want to exaggerate the progress made thus far. 'The administrative and legislative structures necessary for reform to begin are now being put in place. We have set up a separate tax department and a committee to supervise budgetary matters that will be subordinate to the new parliament after the elections. We have set up commissions on land reform, on the use of state assets, on privatisation. We have put an end to the practice whereby bodies such as the militia and the state prosecutor's office could interfere in commercial matters.'

Prices, except for bread and milk and services such as electricity, had been liberalised. Trade had been completely deregulated during the spring. Georgia now had very low import and export controls, and extremely low import taxes, as well as tax incentives to reward foreign investment.

I asked whether the liberalisation of prices was leading to speculation rather than the restoration of productivity. 'We're not just talking about speculation,' he replied. 'This kind of free trading activity is necessary in itself. Gamsakhurdia liked to say that business worked against the interests of the people. We completely disagree. Without freeing prices, it will be impossible for us to stimulate production. We have also begun to free the land. About one-quarter of the land has now been given to those who work on it, and we will soon begin to dispose of larger units such as tea plantations and orchards. By the autumn of 1992 collective farms will also have been abolished, and flats will have been given to their occupants. Shops already operate without government interference.

'These are preconditions for stimulating productivity, but industrial revival also involves factors not in our control. There is a lack of raw materials and an energy crisis. Transportation is difficult. What we've done is to retain government ownership of our industries but to free those industries to manage their own affairs. I realise this is not yet privatisation, but it is the necessary first step. All our factories are working once again, though industrial production is still a third less than it was in 1985.'

Gotziridze was in no hurry to introduce a new currency. 'We'll introduce it when we think it's necessary. By the end of the year the bills will have been printed, but bringing them into circulation is not top of our agenda. Much will depend on the Russian economy. What we want is a currency adequate for the situation we find ourselves in. Of course in time we will have to introduce our own currency, if only because it's a political issue too. No country can claim to be truly independent without its own currency.'

Georgia's dependence on the Russian economy meant that it had been unable to escape soaring inflation after the liberalisation of prices in January. In the first four months of 1992 inflation had been 1000 per cent, whereas for the whole of 1991 the rate had been a more trifling 700. The minister was predicting a total inflation rate of 1200 per cent for the whole of 1992, and confidently believed that the worst of the price increases was over. 'We can't be completely certain in our forecasts because no one can predict all price movements. Russia has just increased petrol prices by a huge amount. Obviously that will affect us too. The only way we can control inflation is by bringing in extreme measures, such as closing our borders and imposing restrictions on the free exchange of goods. But such measures would weaken the reforms we are undertaking. If we can continue to implement these reforms, Georgia will be in the forefront of the reforming republics in the old Soviet Union. Our movement towards privatisation is faster than that of Russia. But it's not a race. We know that we can't accomplish all we want to do until we have the right people in place to implement them.'

The dispute with South Ossetia seemed profoundly unnecessary. Its seeds had been sown a century ago, when the tsarist government encouraged Ossetians to settle on Georgian lands, a policy continued by Stalin. Even in the 1920s there were very few Ossetians living in the newly created South Ossetia, and none at all in the present capital of Tskhinvali. The Georgians maintained that although the Ossetians were welcome to live where they did, that did not entitle them to political autonomy. Ossetians had mixed well with the Georgians, and there was a high rate of intermarriage. There had indeed been Ossetians of extreme views who favoured the region's secession from Georgia, and Gamsakhurdia, by advocating the abolition of the region's autonomous status, had played into their hands. He had gone out of his way to inflame the situation rather than resolve it, and his sole policy had been to use force rather than negotiation.

The irony was that the Ossetians living in North Ossetia, which is part of the Russian Federation, have never enjoyed the cultural liberty accorded their kinsmen within Georgia. Schools, theatres and newspapers in the Ossetian language had been permitted in South Ossetia, but not in North Ossetia. The Georgians were convinced that Russian forces within South Ossetia were just as much to blame for perpetuating the conflict as Gamsakhurdia's provocative rhetoric. The new Georgian government wanted Russia to recognise the republic and thus to recognise its international borders. Once this was done, there would be no more talk of reuniting South and North Ossetia. Shevardnadze, in the course of his television interview, had noted the absurdity of Russia's alacrity to recognise the fledgling Yugoslav republics of Slovenia and Croatia when it was so reluctant to recognise Georgia. The only interpretation the government could offer for that reluctance was Russia's wish to exercise influence by prolonging the conflicts in the Caucasus.

As Nodar Natadze had been assigned the tricky task of resolving the problem, I asked him what he thought the basis for a solution could be.

'First there must be a stop to Russian intervention in the region. By that I mean a stop to Russian arms and advisers. South Ossetia is an artificial region. We cannot have the principle of granting autonomy to diasporas. Otherwise the Algerians could argue that southern France should be called northern Algeria. The Ossetians have their own land in North Ossetia, and the claim that South Ossetia is also their land is false. Remember there are 160,000 Ossetians living in Georgia, but only 60,000 live in South Ossetia. The 100,000 who constitute the majority here are claiming no national privileges. The South Ossetians can have cultural and economic autonomy, perhaps some political autonomy, but not territorial autonomy, as they are living side by side with an indigenous population of Georgians.'

'What practical steps are you taking to deal with the crisis?'

The answer was uncompromising. 'We must have more militia posts and better road access to the nine Georgian villages that have become isolated.' Not a word about discussions and negotiations at this stage. (By June 1992 a sharp increase in fighting and casualties suggested militias on both sides were out of control.)

I asked Notadze what governmental system he would like to see in place.

'I do not want to see a presidential system. Until Georgia becomes a civil society again, it will be inevitable that any president will eventually become a dictator. Perhaps in ten or twenty years' time we will be ready for such a system. Until then we must have a parliamentary system.'

I reminded him of his view that the use of violence to overthrow Gamsakhurdia had set a bad precedent. Did he still hold that view, given that the situation now seemed more stable?

'I am hopeful, I am optimistic, but my judgment is the same as it was. It was a bad precedent that no other means were used to persuade Gamsakhurdia to go.'

'Many, perhaps most, in the Opposition say there was simply no choice.'

'There was a choice, there was a choice.'

22 Just Like Paris

The winter had been so bad in Armenia that even the loquacious Vladimir was reluctant to recall it. Six-hour power cuts were routine, and a lack of candles meant that many hours were spent sitting in the dark. Schools and kindergartens were closed; as in Georgia, salaries went unpaid for weeks or months. Postal services between Armenia and Europe had more or less collapsed. Moreover, the winter had been unusually protracted, with the last snow falling on the fourth of April. A doctor told me that in Armenian hospitals you might find excellent diagnostic equipment but no elementary supplies such as surgical spirit. Bronchial and viral complaints had multiplied over the winter, and botulism had made alarming appearances.

Prices had risen steeply, as elsewhere in the former Soviet Union, and although salaries had also been increased living standards were falling. A three-room flat in central Yerevan could now cost two or three million roubles; yet there were some who were able to afford such prices. For the overwhelming majority no such aspirations were possible. Having survived this winter, my Armenian friends were already worrying about the next: the supplies and preserves that fed their families through the winter had been used up; and inflation meant they could not afford to replace them.

Public transport was worse than ever, and not helped by the strikes of Metro workers, who, with remarkable selfishness, were insisting that their monthly salaries – which at 2–3000 roubles were far higher than most professional people's – should be raised further. Petrol prices had increased tenfold to over thirty roubles a litre and many car owners could no longer afford to use their vehicles. The rises generally were even steeper than in Georgia. At the central market apples and meat were now about 100 roubles per kilo; eggs had trebled in price. Butter cost 200, oranges 150, coffee 400. A bottle of decent Georgian wine was 60; Armenian Areni was half that price, but the one bottle I bought was merrily fermenting and barely potable. Bread was 3 roubles if you were prepared to queue for it at state shops; loaves from private 'cooperatives' were double that price. Some former state shops had been leased to private traders and were stocked with cigarettes, jeans and vodka. Private shops were clearly thriving, and offered an excellent choice of German biscuits, electronic calculators, make-up kits and cosmetics, and Havana cigars – for the rich. Yet there were fewer beggars on the streets of Yerevan than in London. Despite their meagre earnings – I heard of families of four with a combined monthly income of 1300 roubles, barely sufficient for food, let alone for clothing or luxuries – many families supplemented their incomes with what is collectively known as 'business', though what that business consisted of they were reluctant to say. Either the activity was murky and best not discussed, or it boosted the morale to allude to some entrepreneurial exercises which may not have existed.

I joined Vladimir and Aram at their offices and we set off for Vladimir's home. We passed a cinema which, according to Aram, now showed pornographic movies, though the billboards did not suggest that anything too shocking was on view within. Vladimir, uncompromisingly highbrow, was more disapproving. He had deplored the closure of Russian-language schools in Armenia, many of which had been among the best schools in the country, and the consequent downgrading of Russian to a foreign language like any other. Those who had argued successfully for doing this had maintained that by supplanting the Russian language with the Armenian, a renascence of Armenian culture would inevitably take place. In Vladimir's view nothing of the sort had occurred; instead, what had replaced the discredited Russian culture was the worst of American offerings. I suspected he was being over-censorious, as Aram told me about the British and American films currently being shown at cinemas and on television, and they were hardly inferior to those shown in the West.

As we were crossing Republic Square, two police cars screamed into the large oval space in front of where Lenin's statue had once stood. This space was a no-go area for pedestrians and cars alike, and the police were upbraiding a few young men who had been strolling across it. The youths resisted arrest, police reinforcements arrived, the youths threw a few punches and the cops wielded a few truncheons. It was difficult to take the fracas seriously, but Vladimir took a sterner view. While acknowledging that the offence was trivial, he observed that more and more people were exploiting the growing breakdown of order in the country, and such token arrests conveyed to those who found all rules and regulations a huge joke that a line could and would be drawn somewhere. The men were taken away in the police cars, and no doubt, after paying a small fine or, more likely, making a personal gift to the arresting officers, they would be released.

Aram was not surprised that the police took the easy option of arresting erring pedestrians. 'If you walk around with a gun in your hand, no policeman will stop you.'

In the afternoon sunshine we toiled up Abovian Street, which gets progressively steeper. We passed an outdoor café and Aram exclaimed: 'See! Yerevan is just like Paris.' This had been his favourite haunt as a student, so we paused for coffee and some exceedingly dry pastries. Upending my emptied coffee cup, Aram said he would read my fortune. A woman in a mantle would change my life (nothing to do with sex, he added), I would live to the age of seventy, and in general, he concluded with great perspicacity, 'everything will be all right.'

All along the main streets traders were still operating from small tables which had contributed to the Armenian vocabulary. The Armenian for 'table' is *seran* and street trading had become known as '*seran*isation'. Traders needed to register, to obtain a licence from the city, and to pay a daily rent of about 250 roubles for their patch. But the system was essentially corrupt, with city officials taking money in exchange for granting a particularly favourable spot or for giving traders access to goods intended for distribution in different ways. Every worker from Western aid agencies had stories of how some goods destined, say, for the earthquake zone, had ended up on a *seran*. 'We had this kind of speculation in Communist times too,' remarked Vladimir coldly, 'and the only difference now is that it's legal.'

When the road began its steep ascent to the modern suburbs known as the 'massifs', we joined the other Yerevanites trying to hail a taxi or private car, since the buses were hideously overcrowded. Aram stood fearlessly near the middle of the road, and after twenty minutes his efforts paid off. We were dropped off close to a patch of wasteland which provided a short cut to the stained apartment block where Vladimir and Armine lived. The path was strewn with dogshit and industrial debris. Outside his block two men were grappling with pieces of mismatched fencing which they were attempting to place around a patch of earth.

'These are my neighbours,' explained Vladimir without enthusiasm. 'They have taken over this piece of land which does not belong to them and brought in topsoil. They will presumably plant vegetables on it, and now they are fencing it in.'

'Doesn't this land belong to all the tenants here?'

'It belongs to nobody. That other patch of wasteland over there was dug up because somebody wanted to build a garage. They gave up, but what was once a pleasant lawn where children could play is now destroyed. There is no law and order any more. Everybody does as they please, and if it disturbs the neighbours, that is too bad. Even though there is supposed to be a severe shortage of building materials, everybody is building, adding on to their houses, creating shops in basements, and so forth.'

'It is a theatre of the absurd,' contributed Aram, and Vladimir added, 'Yes, but all of us are the actors.'

The flat was small but comfortable, with space carefully divided among competing interests, such as two small daughters and Vladimir's collection of English novels. Before supper I washed my hands from a jug, since water flows from the taps for only six hours a day and the residents fill their tubs with water during the gushing hours. When we arrived we had found Armine watching Turkish television. Russian and Armenian broadcasts only begin at seven each evening, but Armine understood Turkish. The programme she was watching was a dubbed Venezuelan soap opera; Russian television offers a rival Mexican series, *The Rich Also Cry*, in the evenings. We sat down to an early supper, featuring the delicious Lake Sevan fish called *sig* and home-made pickles, and with our tea, a very sweet but delicious syrup made from rose petals.

Vladimir asked whether I felt Armenia had a future. Yes, I replied emphatically, though it would inevitably be some years before any economic recovery would become evident. Armenia would be aided by its contacts with a large and loyal diaspora, and by its highly educated population. My hosts were not convinced. A survey had shown that 30 per cent of Armenians would emigrate if they had the chance, and 25 per cent were undecided. The undeclared war and the privations of the blockade had worn people out. Many had relatives abroad, which gave them the opportunity to find sponsors to underwrite their emigration. Some of the most talented and educated people had already left. Vladimir and his colleagues had studied for up to ten years, they were experienced researchers and teachers, and yet they earned one-third of a bus driver's salary. Under such circumstances, the temptation to emigrate could be overwhelming, and there was no stigma attached to those who made that decision. But who would be left to take Armenia into a new golden age?

The Communists were no longer in power, but many of the structures and bureaucracies they had created were intact. There was still a tendency for the top jobs to go to the old *nomenklatura*, simply because these were the people who knew how to do things, even if most of them did it badly. Vladimir knew from his work as an educational sociologist how difficult it was to change habits of mind and working methods acquired over seven stultifying decades of Soviet rule. A newer generation flush with good qualifications and innovative ideas but poorly connected to the old networks of power stood little chance of securing the important jobs. No wonder many were waiting for their chance to go West.

That evening, back in my hotel room, I had further confirmation of the despair of the intelligentsia. There was a knock on the door; I opened up and saw a diffident man in spectacles. When he addressed me by name, I assumed he was a friend of a friend and asked him in. My assumption was wrong. He had simply gone to the front desk, asked if there was anybody at the hotel from England, and, having obtained my room number, had sought me out. His motive was not sinister; he merely wanted to find someone who could post some letters, already emblazoned with English stamps, on returning to Britain.

My visitor was not an indigent pensioner, but a brain surgeon and a member of the Academy of Sciences. As in Georgia, the Academy was tottering and the government was unable to guarantee funds to keep it going the following year. His qualifications entitled him to a salary of 600 roubles per month. The cost of living in Armenia was said to be two or three times that amount. No doubt, like many other middle-class Armenians, he survived by cramming as many salaried members of his family as possible into a single flat. Finding me a willing listener, he felt compelled to tell me that he was baffled by the European indifference to Armenia's struggles.

'We are the front line of Christianity. On either side of us we have the Moslem world that has consistently been hostile to us. You Europeans have forgotten how three centuries ago the Turks advanced through Europe to the very gates of Vienna. If the Turks triumph over Armenia once again, the same fate could await you.'

Perhaps it was little comfort to the surgeon, but in its battles against its Moslem foes Armenia was doing rather well. By mid-May Azeri troops were being chased from their last strongholds inside Karabakh. There were skirmishes within Nakhichevan too, although Armenia repeatedly said it had no territorial claim against this Azeri enclave tucked between Armenia and the Turkish border. Azerbaijan was claiming that Armenian forces were attacking Azeri troops within Nakhichevan, but it was hard to see why they should want to do so. Nevertheless the town of Sadarak had been shelled by Armenian forces on 18 May, causing casualties and refugees. The accomplished Nakhichevan leader Geidar Aliyev and Levon

Ter-Petrossian had agreed to stop this pointless fighting, but neither seemed able to control their trigger-happy troops.

I walked back to my old haunts above the Razdan gorge. The wasteland behind the Dvin had been turned into a building site. Austere round-arched houses of basalt or some similar stone were rising from the rubble. The Hotel Dvin, its coffee bar closed, looked even more uninviting than it had in the winter. At the Razdan, American and French flags fluttered over the entrance, marking the location of the newly opened embassies. I descended the hill towards Mashtots Avenue and continued to Abovian to say hello to my hosts of the previous year.

I timed my visit well. Men and women in folkloric costume were making their way up to the offices of the Friendship Society, where they were presumably about to engage in some culturally uplifting performance. I found Kevork Zakoyan in his open-doored office, but somebody else was seated behind his desk. I asked him how he was, and he said so-so, but would not elaborate. Arman was now working elsewhere. Zakoyan was clearly surprised to see me, and his only question for me was: 'Who invite you?' 'Nobody,' I replied, which puzzled him. He soon spotted some more important guests and went over to greet them; it was clear that I had been allotted as much time as he cared to give me. More costumed dancers were entering the premises, so I moved swiftly to avoid being enmeshed in their performance, just as in summers in England I would go to great lengths to stay out of Dorset for fear of being subjected to Morris dancers.

With the brief spring making way for the torrid Armenian summer, the theatres, closed for five months during the winter, were back in business. Khoren Abrahamian has run the actors' union for four years, and did not welcome my suggestion that such unions were the poodles of the political establishment. That may have been true of other artists' unions, he said, but not of the actors', which had never been government-regulated or government-subsidised. His job was to look after his members' professional interests and to organise festivals and tours. The government does subsidise the theatre, but Abrahamian felt that such subsidies, by keeping the price of theatre tickets down to about fifteen roubles, helped to undervalue the theatrical experience. Theatre, as in Georgia, was a revered institution, with a tradition, much interrupted, that went back two thousand years. The theatre gave continuity to Armenia's cultural life, even when there was no Armenian state; it had helped to preserve and unify the nation. When I referred to the Georgian passion for Shakespeare, Abrahamian disdained to be upstaged by his unruly neighbours. Armenians, he insisted, were performing Shakespeare long before the Georgians had a theatre to perform in.

'A former Catholicos once said that the theatre was as important as the Church in terms of its value to the nation. As soon as a community was founded in the diaspora, its leaders would open first a church, then a school, and then a theatre. It's always been a popular rather than an élitist art form. But I can't deny that our theatrical life is not very healthy at the moment. We live under great stress, and people have to spend all they earn on food, on survival. People who want to come to the theatre find it impossible to get home in the evenings because of the poor transportation, so our audiences are shrinking.' The Georgians, I had noted in Tbilisi, were responding to the same problem by replacing sparsely attended evening performances with matinées.

Abrahamian was no bureaucrat but a much respected actor. With his fine large head, deep-set eyes and fleshy lips, his white cropped hair and beard, he resembled the older Hemingway, and even in the privacy of his office he relished the dramatic gesture, the pregnant pause, the alternation of sweetness and ferocity. He was proud of the success with which Armenians reinterpreted the classics of other cultures as well as their own, and a leading company had just won great praise in Oslo for its mastery of Ibsen. Abrahamian, not above a touch of self-promotion, could not resist mentioning to me that Vanessa Redgrave had told him he was a finer actor than her late father. (Redgrave, in her autobiography, recalls a visit to Yerevan in which she too failed to see any live performances, but, like me, was handed a video cassette of a fine production of *Coriolanus* starring Abrahamian, which she greatly admired.)

Overseeing artistic life in Armenia was the new minister of culture, Hagop Movses, a writer. Abrahamian's desk had been superbly messy, piled with papers and scripts and ashtrays. The minister's was more controlled, and garnished with the most splendid modern switchboard I had so far seen in the Caucasus. Unfortunately it didn't appear to be in working order.

The government, he told me, was doing its best to continue its funding of the arts despite the country's economic crisis. The discontinuation of central funding from Moscow was only a minor blow, since most of that money had been earmarked for propaganda purposes rather than for worthwhile cultural endeavours. The old unions, which had rewarded compliant artists with work and privileges, had been set adrift, though some might survive in the form of associations financed by subscriptions and sponsorship. Like Abrahamian, he attached great importance to cultural exchanges and wished the government could afford to underwrite tours by Armenian artists and troupes to festivals around the world. The cost of travel ruled out most such proposals, but the diaspora organisations were helping out. His ministry was working towards closer ties with the West; an Armenian-German cultural centre was about to open, and an Italian firm had plans to take over the running of Armenia's cinema network. He confirmed that lack of opportunity was prompting many artists in all fields to emigrate; it was the biggest tragedy in Armenia's cultural life, but the government, despite some direct patronage of the arts, was powerless to stop it.

The country had managed to retain some decent dancers, to judge by a performance of Khachaturyan's *Gayane* that I later saw at the Spendiarov opera house. It was far better attended than the opera in Tbilisi the previous December. The ballet is of the kind best described as colourful, with the simplest of plots and ample opportunities for virtuoso dancing. As the curtain fell after each act, a brigade of little girls, each clutching a bouquet, dashed on to the stage to hand posies to their favourite dancers. After the second act – 'Is it over?' whispered Ashot, hopefully – on scampered a child with a bunch of carnations. The prima ballerina stepped forward gracefully to receive her tribute, but the child ran straight past and handed the flowers to a secondary dancer. That made the whole evening worthwhile.

It was dusk when we emerged on to the streets. There was no street lighting, but the outdoor cafés were crowded as Yerevan did its best to forget its deprivations. A balmy spring evening could induce a brief but refreshing amnesia.

The next day I strolled over to the park which had so depressed me the previous year. It was still decrepit. The fountains remained drained, and some lamp posts still looked as though they had been hit by a drunken driver, but it was pleasant to sit in the coolish shade of oak, chestnut, willow and plane. Rose bushes awaited a last burst of heat before unfurling their buds. Grass had spilt from what had once been flowerbeds on to the paved paths, pushing up between the slabs. In another part of the park a carousel was creaking round, and pingpong tables gave clipped wooden cries as paddles pounded the plastic balls into them. Pony traps and mechanised boats were taking small children for rides. Most promising of all, some benches had been repainted park-bench green. At an open-air arena old men in hats were snoozing, reading the newspaper, chatting to neighbours. Girls in embroidered woollens snuggled up to their boyfriends. Only the small children on a school outing were brightly dressed, though their clothes rarely matched and gave every sign of being random hand-me-downs. Like children of that age anywhere, they played tag and skipping games, except for one girl who was sure she was a bird and pranced around the circumference flapping her arms and singing. When I returned to the park a few days later, the fountains were working, although those in Republic Square remained dry.

I went back to my hotel room and sat on the balcony reading in the late afternoon sunshine. I looked up and gave a start. To the south the snowy peak of Ararat was floating above a band of haze. This was my first clear view of the mountain since my return to Armenia, and it had never been visible through the December fug. Ararat is a mesmerisingly beautiful sight, rising alone from the horizon, apart from its single attendant conical companion. Viewed from Yerevan there is no range for Ararat to jostle with. It dominates the plain, so it is easy to understand how it became such a potent symbol of the Armenian nation – poignant too, ever since the great peak slipped tantalisingly from their grasp across the Turkish border. As dusk fell, shadows tumbled into the crevasses, outlining the contours of the peak with ever greater clarity.

I dined at the hotel, where the food was perfectly acceptable. There were a few groups staying at the Armenia, so the management laid on music, which took the form of deafening popular songs from a four-piece band. The Armenians clearly enjoyed it, and rose from their tables to dance. Their feet moving nimbly, they raised their hands in front of them and flapped them sinuously in rhythm, displaying a gracefulness I was always surprised to discern among these often harsh people.

The music made no impression on a large group of young Russian women who were also staying at the hotel. They sat impassively at two long tables, puffing smoke into each other's faces. Instead of expelling the smoke in complex conjunction with talking and coughing, as Caucasians do, the Russians lifted their noses into the air and exhaled all at once in a fierce lofty stream from the mouth.

Back in my room I was preoccupied by one thought: how to get to Nagorno-Karabakh? I had asked my acquaintances in the government to get me there; they said they would try, but I didn't believe they would try very hard. Jenny, a young Armenian-American woman working for an aid agency based at the hotel had offered to put me in touch with a military man who might get me on a helicopter, but that too seemed unlikely to materialise. I would have to reconcile myself to a rather dull weekend in Yerevan.

23 The Road to Karabakh

At the Hotel Tbilisi I had grown used to the presence of heavily armed men wandering the corridors, but nevertheless I was slightly taken aback when Kamo came strutting into my room with a packed holster strapped over his shoulder. This was Jenny's military man. She had spotted him in the lobby and had brought him to my room to meet me. Kamo would be accompanying a convoy from Yerevan to Stepanakert the next morning over the newly opened road to Karabakh. There might be room for me to accompany him.

The difficulty was how to persuade Kamo that I was worthy of joining the expedition. Before the road linking Armenia and Karabakh had been opened just four days earlier, supplies could reach the enclave only by plane or helicopter. Kamo had been in charge of monitoring this traffic from Yerevan airport, determining priorities on each flight: medical supplies, flour, journalists, politicians, wounded soldiers. He was no functionary; he had recently participated in the fighting and a gouged scab on his nose had been bequeathed by an Azeri bullet during the battle for Shushi.

He was not a pretty sight. Short and stocky, he hadn't shaved for a week. His eyes were bloodshot and fierce. He was a case of walking aggression. He wanted to know how long I could spend in Karabakh. The weekend, I replied. He became blustery. Even Armenians, fluent in the language and steeped in the culture, could derive little from a whole week in the enclave! The inhabitants of Karabakh were mountain folk; they were closed and uncommunicative, even with fellow Armenians. They were a prickly lot; for four years they had borne the burden of their self-defence and they did not take kindly to outsiders swanning about now there was a lull in the fighting. How much, he asked me, could I expect to learn in just a couple of days? Very little, I had to reply, but so long as I wouldn't be in anybody's way I still wanted to go. Since I would have to write about Karabakh in any case, I would do a better job if I went there than if I didn't. Kamo pondered, glowering. He was also making short work of most of a bottle of wine I had pushed towards him. I hoped that by accepting my hospitality he would feel some obligation to offer me his. Reluctantly, he did.

Armen was a suave man in his early thirties, polite and helpful. His English was excellent, which was just as well, as I had hired him for the weekend as my interpreter. After attending university in Yerevan he had studied the interpretative arts in Moscow before returning to Armenia. His real passion in life was dealing in art, and he had helped organise two shows in Europe which exhibited the work of younger Armenian artists. Now that the air fare to Paris was 40,000 roubles, not to mention the other expenses of conveying works of art safely across a continent, he had shelved his plans. Moreover, some of those artists had managed to settle in Europe and had less need of an intermediary. He and his brother also owned a shop, and had started a small business as outfitters of private shops. To fill any spare time remaining, Armen was taking business studies courses at the newly opened Haigazian College. Judging by the hard bargain he drove with me for his services, he would go far.

We waited in the hotel lobby until Jenny arrived with a driver who would take us to where the convoy was parked. These four kerosene tankers would travel first to the town of Artashat where they would fill up with fuel before continuing to Stepanakert. I clambered into the cabin of the first tanker, which had the word Artsakh – the Armenian name for Karabakh – crudely painted in Russian script over the radiator. By the time we reached the outskirts we had managed to lose the fourth tanker, which did not surprise me at all, since there are hardly any signposts on Armenian roads.

Since 1988 the single road linking Armenia with Karabakh had been closed to through traffic. This road crossed the strip of Azerbaijan which separated the two regions, so the Azeris were no doubt entitled to close it, but the economic consequences for Karabakh were dire. Encircled by Azerbaijan, Karabakh could reach the outside world only by air, and Azeri troops had often shot down planes and helicopters. On 19 May 1992, Karabakh forces, with Armenian backup and supplies, had captured the Azeri villages along the road, thus opening it to Armenian traffic for the first time in four years. Almost immediately, the Armenians began organising convoys such as the one in which I was none too comfortably riding. When the first of these arrived in Stepanakert, townspeople gathered in the main square and wept with the relief of knowing their years of isolation and suffering were, for the moment, over.

In Artashat soldiers were hiring themselves out as weekend construction workers to build an addition to an old house. At the fuel depot there was intensive inactivity. Only the superintendent was authorised to permit the loading of the tankers, and he was nowhere to be found. Armen and I sat in the sun and waited. After half an hour Kamo tore into the compound in his jeep. The party had grown. Among his passengers were Jenny, of course, and two other Armenian-American women, Vartouhi and Anoush. Vartouhi was a western Armenian, whose family had left Beirut for California during the 1970s. She was now teaching English at the American University of Armenia. Despite her Levantine upbringing, Vartouhi had an American amplitude, a wide grin, an abundance of good humour, and an enviable collection of brown curls. She told me that the great majority of students at AUA were pursuing get-rich business studies, and the other courses on offer, industrial and earthquake engineering, were undersubscribed. Some students felt frustrated acquiring sophisticated skills which could never be applied, at least not for some time, in technologically antiquated Armenia, where it often took thirty attempts before a phone call across town was correctly connected.

The situation was far worse in the high schools she had visited. Admiring the small classes which compared favourably with Californian schools, she soon discovered the explanation: chronic truancy. Many of the kids, their education severely disrupted by closures, had concluded that participating in some family scam was more worthwhile than study. The rhythms of education had been lost, and discipline in those schools was almost nonexistent.

Anoush was a monumental woman of indeterminate middle age. She and I got off to a bad start when I asked her which organisation she worked for.

'Why do people always assume you have to be with an organisation or group to come to Armenia?'

'Because the majority of Westerners are.'

She sniffed and said nothing. I tried again, rephrasing my question by asking what she did. She replied that she was a magician. This was a tease, and I found it tiresome. If she didn't want to introduce herself to someone whose company she would have to share all weekend, I would resume talking to the well-informed Armen. Then Anoush admitted she was being difficult and said that she was an artist. But she talked little about her art, since she was so wrapped up in being a born-again Armenian who had come to live in Yerevan indefinitely. She was a patriot and, although her command of the language was limited, she identified wholeheartedly with Armenian causes. She also found the starkness of her ancestral land a great relief after 'plastic America', though I was beginning to long for such manifestations of plastic America as a slice of pizza.

After two hours in Artashat Kamo lost patience. The tanker drivers would have to wait for the superintendent, but in the meantime we would press on in his jeep. He and Jenny clambered into the front with Renig the driver, who resembled a much diminished version of Sean Connery, while Armen and I piled into the back with the other two women. Both Kamo and Renig were armed, and a machine gun lay alongside the gear stick.

Anoush, thankfully divorced, was no great admirer of the male sex, and considered Armenian men particularly unregenerate in their treatment of women. But, she went on, this was typical of Middle Eastern countries. This intrigued me, and I asked her whether she regarded Armenia as Middle Eastern.

'Of course!'

'Maybe you're right, but the Georgians just across the border clearly consider themselves Europeans.'

'Europeans!' she snorted. 'Armenians had a civilisation when the English were still eating grass.'

It was becoming clear that Anoush and I were not going to get on. I later put the matter to Vladimir and Aram who replied, evenhandedly, that Armenia had a foot in both camps.

We were speeding through the hills southeast of the Ararat valley. Here farming land was more sparse, but peasants, taking advantage of their newly privatised land, were tending the soil in the few spots, mostly near the riverbank, where it would respond to cultivation. Some hillsides had collapsed as the result of soil erosion, which Armen attributed to the neglect of the land over many decades of collective ownership. We climbed through a pass at snow level, then descended through a beautiful gorge, thoughtfully provided with a picnic area, where we paused for lunch. Kamo bought shashlik of the most tender young pork from a roadside stand, and the rest of us pooled food we had bought at the market that morning.

Kamo, hacking away at the *basturma* (air-dried beef) I contributed, revealed new sides of his character. This bullet-headed, red-eyed, flamboyant soldier was, in civilian life, a clothes designer, and in more tranquil moments could be found sewing clothes for his wife and three children. He also ran a sock factory in Abovian, a new Armenian town where many of those who had fled from Karabakh had settled, and a cheese factory in Karabakh. Both were closed because of a shortage of materials.

He was a soldier of considerable experience, having spent two years in Afghanistan. In July 1991 he and other *fedayeen* had been captured by Russian OMON troops in Karabakh and turned over to the Azeris, who had kept him in Shushi prison for a month, beating him so severely each day that he had become temporarily paralysed down one side. Still, he considered himself lucky. Had the Azeris known his real identity they would, he told me, have killed him without further ado, since there was a price on his head. Despite his devotion to the Karabakh cause, he felt no hostility towards Azeris. Indeed, he had many Azeri friends and often met up with them on trips to Moscow. In his view the local Armenian and Azeri population were more victims than antagonists. 'I know many

Azeris who are my friends and who even today would fight alongside Armenians if they believed the cause was just.'

He recalled many occasions when both sides had agreed to brief ceasefires and then got together for a beer or a smoke. According to Kamo, whose dramatic style would have permitted a good deal of exaggeration, during the recent political upheavals in Baku, Azeri troops in Karabakh loyal to Mutalibov had turned their fire on troops loyal to the Popular Front, and had requested the Armenians to hold off for a few days while they settled scores among themselves. Probably apocryphal, but in Stepanakert I did meet a sergeant who assured me he had fraternised with his opposite numbers from the Azeri trenches.

After lunch we drove on, passing through the monumental arch that marks the border of the Zangezur region of southeastern Armenia. Range after range of snowy peaks leaned back into the horizon. Swarthy men walked along the side of the road carrying strings of freshly gathered mushrooms that would probably be offered for sale to the few passing motorists. It was cold up here in the mountains, and the women generated some heat by singing patriotic and revolutionary songs from a songbook Anoush had brought with her. Cheerfully, they sang anthems from the turn of the century about how they would turn Istanbul into a sea of blood.

By late afternoon we were approaching Goris, a country town beautifully located between cliffs studded with caves. It had clearly been a prosperous town once. Its hilly streets were lined with handsome stone houses, ornamental grilles of varying designs covering the windows. Kamo decided to visit a friend here. I was keen to press on so that we would reach Karabakh in daylight, but I knew that such visits had their ceremonies which could not be rushed. While food was being prepared for the unexpected visitors, we sat around the edges of the living room on broad couches, Arab-style, and tried to work up some interest in an inaudibly dubbed American television movie with a mock-oriental setting.

Our host Gagik, as tradition demanded, wanted our party to stay the night. Anoush thought this was an excellent idea: we would continue to Stepanakert early the next morning. I was adamant: that would mean turning back within minutes of arriving in the capital. I wanted to get to Stepanakert tonight. Fortunately, Kamo shared my view, and we pressed on after stuffing ourselves with excellent *dolma* and vegetables. At dusk we came to a roadblock which marked the border between Armenia and Azerbaijan. Kamo was recognised by the guards and we were waved through.

'Here,' remarked Armen, 'you don't need a passport so much as a pistol.'

We were in Azerbaijan, although the territory for about four miles on either side had been in Armenian hands since the battle earlier in the week. We could soon see, on the far side of the valley we were about to cross, the two villages of Latchin and Zaboukh, both ablaze. Many houses had already been gutted, others were smouldering, others concealed behind a wall of flame. When I asked Kamo why these villages were being burnt, he replied that the Armenians wanted to plant flowers in their place to commemorate those who had suffered and died as a result of the four-year closure of this road. This was touching stuff, but it was also rubbish. There may well be an intention to plant flowers as a memorial, but that was not why the villages were being burnt. They were being razed as a pure expression of anger. The triumphant Armenians were ensuring that never again would these villages enjoy their former strategic importance.

There had been international remonstrances against this invasion of Azerbaijani territory, but I found it hard to lecture the Armenians. No territory should be required to submit to the kind of strangulation imposed on Karabakh, and if the only way to break that strangehold was to capture the road, the Armenians were justified in making that attempt. It had proved easier than they had expected. On 9 May Shushi, once an Armenian town but more recently an Azeri fortress overlooking Stepanakert, had fallen to the Armenians. From Shushi Grad missiles had rained down day and night on the capital; once it had fallen, the Armenians could implement their plan to capture the road. On 18 May Karabakh forces had approached Latchin and Zaboukh from the hills behind, leaving a corridor along which the civilian population could and did make its escape. By all accounts the Azeris offered scarcely any resistance, and the three hundred Karabakh soldiers, backed by Armenian supplies and communications, had suffered a grand total of one dead and two wounded. The 1300 Azeri soldiers had fled, most before a shot was fired, abandoning many of their weapons and artillery.

As we approached Latchin we could hear sounds of detonation. This was not rifle fire but the explosion of munitions the Azeris had stored in the houses now being torched. Along the hillsides cornets of smoke were rising from the orange cores of the flaming timbers. In the crepuscular light the image was eerily beautiful, a hellish *son et lumière*. Beyond Latchin lorries were carrying furniture steadied by the hands of entire families stationed around the edges of the load. Kamo said these were families returning to their villages in Karabakh, a migration undoubtedly taking place, and Armenians removing furniture from a local factory before it too was set on fire.

Like the touching flower story, this was too good to be true. It was perfectly clear that there was looting going on, which accounted for the surprisingly heavy traffic along the dusty road. Less mobile families had loaded hand-pulled trolleys with anything worth taking from the abandoned houses. Since the houses were being destroyed in any case, I couldn't work up much indignation over this petty looting. The pickings would be sparse.

Near Latchin we had crossed a bridge which to Kamo's amazement the Azeris had failed to blow up as they retreated. 'If they'd demolished it, it would have slowed us down considerably, but they were in too much of a hurry to run away.' Some miles farther down the road, however, the Azeris had blown up a bridge, having first ignited three tanks and armoured vehicles and tipped them over the edge into a gully, where with the help of the jeep's searchlights we could make out the treads and mangled metal below. Azeri casualties had been heavy here, and Kamo had seen the road strewn with corpses. By the roadside I found dozens of discarded boxes that had once contained 100-kilogram Grad rockets.

We had now crossed into Karabakh. There was no other traffic on the long winding stretch of potholed road between the border and Stepanakert. Not even the skilful driving of Renig could prevent frequent jolts and spine-wrenching bumps. We drove through Shushi in the dark. Perched on a hill that dominated the surrounding countryside, Shushi – the Armenian name for a town also known as Shusha – had been an Armenian stronghold and trading centre since the twelfth century. There was still a fortress here, and the prison dating from tsarist times where Kamo and other captured soldiers had been held. From the sixteenth century it had been a Moslem town, but by the nineteenth century it was once again predominantly Armenian, a sophisticated place with, it is always said, eighteen different newspapers. In the 1920s a massacre of Armenians led to an Azeri majority in the town.

The Grad launchers based at Shushi had punished Stepanakert severely. The Karabakh forces had longed to capture the town but its height (about 1000 metres up) and its location made access exceedingly difficult. For a month the Karabakh officers planned their assault, and on 9 May attacked. Only 400 soldiers were involved in the main assault, although 600 were needed to secure the surrounding villages. They were pitted against Azeri forces variously estimated at 1300 and 2500, well equipped and with ample supplies of artillery and tanks. Burnt out tanks still lay like foot-crunched bugs by the roadside, yet casualties had been light, with only about fifteen Azeri dead.

Tigran, a commander of one of the Karabakh fighting units, had been incredulous. 'We saw thirty tanks come rolling out of Shushi towards us and assumed we'd have a real fight on our hands. We destroyed one of the tanks, and the other twenty-nine promptly retreated. A while later they emerged again. We counter-attacked, and the Azeris simply fled. We saw some of them climbing out of the turrets and running away. We captured one of them who hadn't run for it and asked him why he'd stayed behind. "Because I'm from Baku, and I have no idea where to go." The Azeri commanders had dumped a lot of inexperienced troops here, and they had no will to fight. At the first sign of action, they ran for it.'

Kamo said that although the Karabakh troops were fewer in

number and less well equipped than their opponents, they were more committed and intensively trained. 'I won't go into battle with inexperienced men. Those are the soldiers that get killed. Our units know exactly what they're doing and that's one of the reasons why our casualties have always been low. The people who are injured and killed here are the civilians – 1200 people have died in Karabakh during the last year, and 1000 of them were civilians.'

A few minutes later we passed the spot where the sealed road had ended, about 100 kilometres from the Armenian border, and we traversed the outskirts of Stepanakert. It was midnight but even now men and women were tugging looted household and structural items from abandoned houses in Shushi to their homes. Renig drove into the driveway of a former restaurant just outside town, which now served as the offices for military liaison with Armenian forces. After the noise, dust and joltings of the jeep, it was wonderful to clamber out, stand in the grounds and gaze up at a sky filled with the crisp pinpricks of uncountable stars.

Kamo made himself at home behind the one and only desk, but his occupation of the spot was short-lived. The front door burst open and a sturdy man in a black leather jacket came storming in. The colonel was none too pleased to see a bunch of visitors making themselves comfortable at his headquarters. He yelled at his soldiers, glowered at the civilians, and thrust himself moodily into the chair Kamo had swiftly vacated. Jenny turned on the charm and before long he seemed mollified, calling for vodka and bread and tea for us all. Raising his glass, he said to me, 'May God help you to write the truth about our struggle.' But I wondered whether Armen had been too diplomatic in the translation and whether the colonel had in fact said, 'God help you if you don't write the truth about us.'

The colonel downed his vodka – home-made, he assured me, as he topped up my glass – and proudly showed me his American knife and compass, and a mean stubby pistol indistinguishable to me from any other mean stubby pistol. Kamo took the women off to stay at his mother's house for the night. Armen and I stayed behind with the colonel. He was astonished that Karabakh's right to independence had not been recognised by the rest of the world. One day, he hoped, their struggle would be acknowledged as a just one. 'All we want is to live on our own land. We have no desire to occupy anyone else's.'

'But you talk of self-determination for Karabakh, as does the Armenian government. What does that mean to you?'

'It means to be with Armenia. Most of us here hope for eventual reunification. This doesn't mean we want to get rid of the Azeri population here. This is not a war that the local people wanted, and we're perfectly happy to have Azeris living among us – so long as they accept that this is Armenian land.'

'You may find local Azeri villagers who would go along with that, but I can't see Baku doing so.'

'I don't think it's likely that Baku will ever accept it.'

'So are you expecting Azeri retaliation?'

'Not for a while. Their troops are in a shambles right now, and there's too much political turmoil in Baku. But that won't last forever. We're aware that taking Shushi was only a temporary victory. The real victory will be our independence and security.'

A government official had told me, despite my scepticism, that it was perfectly feasible for Karabakh to exist as an independent nation, a kind of Lesotho of the Caucasus. Did the colonel agree?

'Personally, I can't envisage Karabakh without Armenia.'

Our talk was interrupted by the arrival of a gun-toting soldier. There had been a skirmish at a nearby depot where a special patrol had intercepted two men attempting to steal petrol, a growing problem in a region where fuel is virtually unobtainable. He was followed by Serge Sarkissian, the head of the Karabakh Defence Committee. The colonel slumped on a bunk and settled down to watch a Charles Bronson film on television. But Sarkissian was happy to talk. I asked him to what extent the mood had changed since Shushi had been captured.

'It has changed, unfortunately.'

'Unfortunately?'

'Because most people seem to think the war is over. They see the last two weeks as a great victory, and they're forgetting that this is not the end of military action by Azerbaijan. Still, it's evident that the Azeris are demoralised while our mood is upbeat. After all, in the last few weeks we have destroyed forty of their tanks and armoured vehicles. But one of these days they will try again. We must not underestimate their numbers, nor the fact that a military victory against us would boost the careers of many Azeri politicians. When it comes, the attack could be powerful and decisive, and we must be prepared for it. We have only about 6000 troops here, and many of those are Armenian support units not involved in the fighting.'

'What are the chances of a political settlement?'

'Preferable, of course, but unlikely.'

'How well do you get on with your counterparts in Armenia?'

'No problem. I'm also an Armenian deputy minister of defence.'

I asked him about the massacre of Azeri civilians at Kodzhali in March. The Azeris had claimed that a thousand fleeing civilians had been butchered by Armenian troops and although those figures were exaggerated, there was first-hand evidence from independent journalists that many civilians had indeed died. Sarkissian explained that Armenian troops had left a corridor so that civilians could escape from the town. Meanwhile Azeri troops had been firing from houses in the village still inhabited by their owners, and Armenian forces had fired back, inevitably killing civilians as well as soldiers. Moreover, Azeri Grad missiles had landed in the escape corridor, causing many more casualties. He estimated the death toll at about two hundred. He didn't want to deny the possibility that some Karabakh soldiers may have behaved with excessive violence. (Tigran, one of the Karabakh commanders, had a simple explanation. Both Azeri civilians and Azeri troops had been passing through the escape corridor at the same time. When they fired from the corridor at Armenian positions, the Armenians fired back, unaware in the darkness that civilians were among the troops.)

Serge was less apologetic about the burning of Latchin. Latchin was not a village, he said, but a trench. There were three Grad launching sites there. Once the village is razed, Azeri troops will never be able to return. He confirmed that Armenian casualties had been negligible, but couldn't give me Azeri figures.

'They were high, weren't they?'

'High enough.'

I asked whether Russian troops had participated in the recent battles. Sarkissian replied that Russian mercenaries had been hired by the Azeris for up to 3000 roubles a month. Since many Russian soldiers found themselves stranded in the Caucasus, they had little option but to sell their services, and the Karabakh soldiers bore the Russians no grudge. Many Azeri tank crews were Russian, but the instructors at the Grad launching sites, they discovered, were Turks. Turkey later admitted that it had dispatched military 'advisers' to the region.

It was three in the morning. The colonel, who had complained that he hadn't slept for twenty days, was still awake, keeping an eye on Bronson. I headed for the partitioned area where a bunk had been prepared for me, and minutes later I was asleep.

24 The Pincers Tighten

Dimly awake, I stumbled out into a perfect spring morning. I could have mistaken the landscape for Vermont, and the climate too, as the chill of dawn modulated rapidly into the even heat of a cloudless day. After the aridity of Armenia, this freshness and greenness was wonderfully refreshing. The mountains were textured with uninterrupted woodlands mixing conifers and deciduous growths. Farmers came wandering down the road, prodding their cattle gently with long sticks. A stream chirped through the valley and frogs crackled in an adjoining pond. I returned indoors to find the orderly, Mais (after the Armenian name for May, the month of his birth), laying out an abundant breakfast, including mounds of butter and tinned beef from France. No food shortages at military headquarters.

Kamo arrived and introduced me to Tigran, commander of one of the fifty-man units of *fedayeen* volunteers aiding the 1200 men of the Karabakh army. Only thirty-three, Tigran looked older; indeed he looked exhausted, and no doubt was. Unlike the ebullient Kamo, he was taciturn, monosyllabic, crumpled. He had been put at our disposal for the day and could probably think of better ways of spending his Sunday. He drove me into town.

Stepanakert was surprisingly spacious, with long tree-lined avenues and a large square which seemed even larger because of the absence of traffic. Many streets were lined with dreary apartment blocks typical of the most illkempt Soviet design of the past few decades. Their appearance had not been enhanced by the Grad missiles which had smashed into the town all winter. Some buildings were completely wrecked, others ended abruptly where the end of a terrace had been pulverised. No parts of the city had been immune from bombardment, though some districts had survived intact and, for reasons no one could explain, had evidently not been targeted. The roads were dusty but surprisingly clean. With no commercial activity, there was little occasion for litter or debris to accumulate. Some streets still bore the old names – Marx Street and Lenin Prospect – because the city council had been too preoccupied with matters of life and death to get round to changing them.

Shops were boarded up. There were none at all open in Stepanakert, and no market. The bakeries were closed. Even if they'd had sufficient flour, there was no gas to heat the ovens. During the winter natural gas had provided some minimal heat and lighting, but since 8 May there had been no gas in Karabakh. There was no electricity either, and all factories and workshops were closed. The infrastructure had collapsed. Since June 1991 there had been no bus services within Karabakh, both because the roads were vulnerable to Azeri attack and because of the fuel shortage. Twenty per cent of the housing in Stepanakert had been completely destroyed, and half the remaining buildings needed major repairs. In just a few years a city, a region, had reverted to pre-industrial torpor.

In the main square the Supreme Soviet building was only partly serviceable. Panes were missing and the top floor was a wreck. The building next door was roofless and gutted. Around the corner the television centre, hit by three Grads, was a huge pile of rubble. The ground floor of the Central Committee building was being used as a hospital. The main hospital had succumbed to constant bombardment since November and was partly destroyed. Doctors and patients had been moved to the comparative safety of the basement, but conditions had soon become too cramped. Even in this building there was precious little space, a mere twenty-two beds, but now that the shelling had stopped they were planning to move back into what was left of the old hospital. Meanwhile the maternity hospital had been destroyed and its operations transferred to the basement of the Supreme Soviet.

Work schedules had become meaningless. Staff worked as and when they were needed. On 9 May, when the battle for Shushi began, one hundred wounded had arrived in four hours. All the doctors could offer was first aid, and some of the wounded died before they could receive treatment; more serious cases were flown to Yerevan. Fortunately agencies such as the Red Cross and Médecins Sans Frontières (MSF) had kept them well stocked with medical supplies.

'Without those supplies,' said Dr Gukasian, the weary surgeon I was speaking to, 'there would have been disaster here. But since Shushi we have used most of them up, and if there are more battles soon we will be in difficulties. It is quiet in Stepanakert, but in Askeran four people were killed yesterday by Azeri bombardment. We are never without work. The psychological pressure is also very great. Everybody is under stress, everybody has become more aggressive. I have seen complete changes of personality over the years.'

He led me past the bloodstained stretchers propped up in the hallway. In the basement the operating theatre was lit by three bulbs so dim even an Intourist hotel would have been ashamed to use them. Presumably the building's generator had to be used sparingly. The three operating tables were supplemented by a long wooden table also used for surgery during busy periods. Dr Gukasian recalled operating here while the upper storeys of the building were taking direct hits. There had been no electricity, of course, so the surgeons had worked by candlelight and kerosene lamps, assisted by a kind of miner's lamp donated by MSF. He admitted that hygienic conditions were deplorable. In an adjoining room I saw the vats which contained the hospital's water supply. A tiny windowless room with seven bunks provided a rest room for the doctors, and another windowless room, ventilated by a crude air pipe, was a ward for the most serious cases.

'We have no running water, very poor sanitation. We work in dark basements. But in these conditions we have saved hundreds of lives.'

I peered into one of the rooms used as a ward. Two nurses were lifting a heavily bandaged stump and flicking a pile of bloodied dressings on to the floor. This was one of the casualties from Askeran, an Armenian village ten miles away still being bombarded from the Azerbaijani town of Aghdam. A civilian, he had just lost half his leg. He seemed surprisingly cheerful considering the trauma he had just been through, but the grim-faced family members walking slowly down the corridor as I left were stricken and dazed. No wonder Serge Sarkissian had cautioned the population against euphoria. The war was by no means over. In the five months since 1 January 1992, the casualty figures were 534 dead, 836 wounded, 5 missing, and 80 hostages. Civilian casualties outnumbered military by four to one. There was no such thing as an ambulance. The wounded were brought to the hospital by any means possible, in a private car if they were lucky, on the flatbed of a lorry, or on trolleys improvised from boards and bicycle wheels.

'This is our routine.'

In the plaza where a memorial honours the Karabakh warriors who fought in World War II, smaller monuments commemorate two disasters of 1988: the massacre at Sumgait and the earthquake. Here too is the grave of Artur Mkrtchyan, the president of Karabakh who had been killed in April 1992. Initial reports said he had been assassinated, but doubts were soon cast on that account. Tigran told me Mkrtchyan had died accidentally when a gun he was cleaning went off, but the consensus was that he had been the victim of a family squabble. The fact that his family refused to discuss how he had died tended to support this view. It is the Armenian custom for a family to visit the cemetery forty days after a death. Because of Mkrtchyan's status, local dignitaries as well as family friends would call on the bereaved and would then proceed to the plaza, where a small crowd was gathering. The mound of the grave was strewn with yellow tulips and frothy carnations. There was a flurry of activity as a small motorcade drove into the plaza, kicking up a cloud of dust. Mkrtchyan's former deputy and now the president, Giorgi Petrossian, arrived with his entourage. A gaunt man with a short greying beard, he had the only blue eyes I had ever encountered among Armenians. A fat man was introduced to me as the Armenian

Balzac. The family came into view: Mkrtchyan's sobbing widow and his dignified old parents. They headed straight for the grave, and the women flung themselves upon it. The white-haired mother stretched out her arms over the mound and began keening, a high-pitched chanting oration, punctuated with wails of 'Artooor! Artooor!' The dozens of women clustering around the grave were sobbing, Mkrtchyan's father was yelling angrily at the heavens, the widow on her knees dabbed her eyes with a handkerchief. After some minutes the priest took over, intoning his prayers. He was a relative newcomer to the region. The churches were closed down in 1936 and stayed shut until 1989, denying the Christians here access to baptism and other religious rites of passage. Then the Armenian Balzac gave a speech praising the thirty-three-year-old Mkrtchyan. Despite the uncertainty of his death, he said, we should put such matters behind us and concentrate on his achievements.

The speeches were going to continue for some time, so I slipped away. We drove to the fine, stylised monument on the edge of town depicting an old couple of the region in tribute to their (prewar) longevity. On the slopes opposite most of the trees had been cut down for firewood. Tigran then took us to his barracks in a former school, where Vartouhi wanted to take some photographs. This delighted the soldiers, who brought out their finest weapons, most of which they had captured from Azeris, and displayed daggers with scabbards gaudily painted with the word SUVENIR.

Tigran's unit had been founded in 1988 as military support for the Karabakh Movement. These units had been strictly illegal, and captured men from such *fedayeen* militias had usually been dispatched to jails from which they never returned. The youngest of Tigran's men was nineteen, the oldest forty-two. One was a former Russian officer, but he had family connections in the region and was treated as an honorary Armenian. The soldiers, who were enjoying a few days off after the recent battles, were in ebullient mood, but there had been times when they had eaten next to nothing for ten days. Now they had bread and some meat and an admiring female visitor, for whom they posed like mad.

On the steps of the Supreme Soviet Anoush was in dispute with an

American AP reporter who had just arrived from Moscow. The young journalist was evidently weary, and seemed fed up with all sides in the interminable Caucasian disputes that were her beat. Anoush lectured her for being insufficiently interested in the historical background. The journalist replied that she was a reporter who recorded what she saw and let others draw conclusions. Anoush told her that it was no good just ticking off the Armenians for burning Latchin. You had to consider the four-year blockade, the dying babies, the mutilated Armenian soldiers, and so forth. Anoush was right in a way, but she had misjudged the mood. The reporter had just hitch-hiked here from Goris and was not receptive to lectures on her inadequacies. When Anoush grandly said, 'The trouble with the American press is that they don't understand the causes,' the AP reporter tartly replied, 'You're right, that's it, it's all the fault of the American press,' and stalked off. Anoush was amazed that her words had caused such offence.

I was waiting for the prime minister. It was a grand title for the chief minister of a region with the same population as an English market town, but Oleg Yessayan was a tall, impressive man who more than filled the dignity of his office. An economist by profession, he had been appointed to the job in January 1992. He took me up to his office in the Supreme Soviet, and I asked him to describe how badly Karabakh had been affected by the four-year siege.

'It was as much as we could bear. This winter we have been starving. We had so little flour we had to assign one kilo per person each month. That was all. We had the helicopters but they were not enough, since we had to use them for casualties as well as supplies. We are still on the brink of an epidemic here. We have had no industry for two years, and no agriculture either. Because this is a farming region, we are normally close to self-sufficiency. Now we are incapable of supporting ourselves. Without flour we cannot bake bread. Cattle have been stolen, and because there is a lack of feed many animals are dying or have been slaughtered too early. We're talking about the slow strangulation of a people. We tried to solve this problem peacefully. But when our airport was destroyed, we had no option but to use force to reopen the road. We don't think of it as a great victory. It was a necessity. We know it won't lessen the pressure the Azeris will put on us in the future.'

'What preparations are you making for next winter?'

'We're in no position to solve such long-term problems. To get through the winter we need electricity, which we can't be sure of. Our gas comes from Azerbaijan, and for weeks we have had none at all. But the same pipeline also supplies western Azerbaijan and Nakhichevan, so it is not in Azerbaijan's long-term interest to keep the supply shut off. On the other hand the Azeris are working on a new pipeline from Iran, and if that is completed later this year then they will give up using the present line through Stepanakert. We're working on ways to bring gas directly from Armenia to Karabakh. Water is another problem, as wells won't function without electricity. As for bread, we have planted more wheat but we don't know how good the harvest will be. We need 22,000 tonnes each year, but we can only produce half of that this year.'

The population had remained reasonably stable, despite the deportation of five thousand villagers and bursts of emigration from a few districts. More may have wished to leave, but Karabakh's isolation makes any movement difficult. Quite a few people were now returning with their possessions.

The prime minister was sure the Azeris would eventually attempt another offensive; large numbers of troops remained stationed on the borders. Not far from the town of Martouni there was an Azeri village equipped with three tanks, four armoured vehicles, a Grad launcher and five heavy artillery pieces. 'Karabakh doesn't have the resources to cope with such weaponry. And this is not an isolated example. I could give you many others all along the border.'

'What will happen next?'

'There are three possible solutions. First, Karabakh could revert to its former status within Azerbaijan. Second, reunification. Third, independence. The first is impossible – we would become another Nakhichevan, where no Armenians live any longer. If there were reunification, Azerbaijan would probably intensify the war. So in our referendum last December we proposed a compromise:

independence. But this is not a realistic option. The fact is that everyone here wants reunification, though I myself could see some future for us as an independent republic. Unfortunately, the civilised world is indifferent to our problems, even though they could lead to regional war, especially if Turkey becomes involved. Such a war would affect Russia and France and other great powers.'

'It sounds to me like stalemate.'

He shrugged. 'In that case there is no end to the war. Armenia may not win, but imagine what would happen if Karabakh became part of Azerbaijan once again. Either way we would eventually be eliminated.'

Shushi had been visible from the war memorial plaza, a great green hill, one of three lording it over the capital. There had been sounds of rifle fire, but Tigran assured me it was only target practice. At five we left Stepanakert and drove up to the old fortress. The town had been thoroughly trashed, but this was only partly Armenian doing. The civilian population had been moved out six months earlier, and only Azeri troops stayed in the town. The huge Armenian cruciform church had been used as a munitions store and hundreds of empty Grad boxes were strewn outside. A small Armenian tricolour flew from the top of the dome. All the windows were missing but the interior was in reasonable condition. Flowers and candles had been placed on the altar, and men and women were kneeling in prayer. Two women rose to their feet, hugged each other, then wept. Then they stepped outside to take family photographs on the steps.

In Latchin and Zaboukh even more houses were burning than on the previous evening. It was dark by the time we got to Goris and although Tigran was clearly tired he insisted on driving on. At Vajk we stopped for directions. It was midnight, but a man was standing outside the local department store. Apparently the alarm had gone off and he had come to investigate. He urged us to come in and have some coffee, an offer we gladly accepted. Anoush was perplexed: 'The alarm went off? What on earth is there to steal?' Indeed, the total contents of the store consisted of piles of children's knickers and two ghastly nightdresses. Anoush observed that the real reason why the Soviet system had collapsed was because women's clothes were so badly designed.

Further up the road we came to a roadblock. We would have to make a detour. There had been fighting close to the main road along the border with Nakhichevan; one man was dead, others injured. We turned off into the hills and were soon lost. Armen was given the task of hammering on villagers' doors at 3 a. m. to ask for directions. One resident emerged, muttering the following words: 'I have an axe. Don't be afraid.' When Armen explained our predicament, the old man said, 'Any way you want to go, just go,' which was not enormously helpful. The directions he did offer proved inadequate and we had to stop one of the rare passing cars to get further instructions. We were back in Yerevan at five. There was a spare bed in my room, which I offered to Tigran. After shedding his fatigues, supping off wine and cheese, and propping his machine gun against the end of the bed, he fell into a deep and motionless sleep.

In Yerevan it was as though winter had returned. The gas pipeline from Georgia had been mysteriously blocked or severed – reports were vague, some spoke of accident, others of sabotage – and for the rest of my stay there was no heating. Electricity cuts were increased to seven hours a day; trolley buses would come to a halt in mid-run as the power dried up. Without gas to heat the bread ovens, bakeries returned to other methods of heating which pumped black smoke into the blue skies. At one shop I estimated the bread queue at about three hundred. The telephones were working as well as they ever did in Armenia, but the government was not. I had three appointments with ministers which had to be confirmed by me on the morning of the encounters. One appointment materialised; the second foundered because the minister stayed at home that day; the third minister and his secretariat failed to pick up the phone for three hours, and when I turned up in person nobody was there.

In these unpromising circumstances, reforms were continuing. In Georgia, until the new elections of October 1992, government was by decree. Armenia had the advantage of a system of government that was in place, for all its inefficiencies. Reforms talked about but shelved by Gamsakhurdia had been implemented here. By June 1992 80 per cent of the land had been returned to private ownership, with the new owners undertaking to work the land they were given. (A very small percentage of villages voted to retain their land under communal ownership.) The harvest in 1991 had been 50 per cent higher than usual, which, the enthusiasts for privatisation maintained, proved that the new system had demonstrable economic benefits.

Privatisation of state shops had also begun in the spring of 1991 but had ground to a halt as practical difficulties arose. Staff had wanted reassurances that they would not be automatically dismissed by new owners and they had also wanted the opportunity to organise a management buyout. The government had reconsidered the whole matter of private ownership and in the spring of 1992 had placed about sixty new laws before Parliament which would establish the infrastructure for a market economy. Nobody disagreed much on what ought to be done; the arguments were about how it should be done. Private enterprises could be nationalised almost overnight; the reverse process was proving more complicated. I soon learnt the reason why Armenia was full of half-completed factories and roofless apartments. With privatisation on the agenda, there was no incentive for the government to complete these projects. A new law was being formulated to allow incomplete structures to be sold, with the government retaining a proportion of ownership corresponding to its share of construction. That share of ownership would not entitle them to any say in the operation of the completed building, and the new owners would also, in time, be entitled to buy out the government share. Nuts and bolts stuff, but all these matters had to be carefully thought out.

The government had not had an easy time of it, and some of its proposals – affecting the speed of the reform process and the nature of the 'safety net' in a society with diminishing reliance on free public services – had been rejected by Parliament. One senior government official complained, without rancour, that the Parliament elected in 1991 was perhaps ill equipped to deal with detailed legislation. Armenia had adopted a presidential system, with a separation of powers between the executive, headed by President Ter-Petrossian, and the legislature. However, the deputies elected in 1991 had been expected to deal with the great ideological issues: independence, freedom of conscience, the fate of the Communist Party, and so forth. Those crucial matters had been settled relatively quickly and with little dissension; now the debates dealt with less glamorous matters. A veteran of the Karabakh Movement, elected as a reward for steadfastness and courage, might have less interest in working out how apartment blocks were to be maintained after privatisation.

Parliament itself, with 260 seats, was in a somewhat fluid state. The Armenian National Movement no longer enjoyed the parliamentary majority it had secured in 1990, and the governing coalition it had formed was rapidly dissolving. By spring 1992 the ANM, now functioning as a political party, had 56 MPs. The former Communists had split, and there were a number of small parties such as Payrur Hayrikian's Union for National Self-Determination and the National Democratic Union run by the former prime minister Vazgen Manukian. Two diaspora parties, Ramgavar and the Dashnaks, had 25 seats, and still hoped that Armenia's territorial aspirations would one day be recognised; they also opposed closer relations with Turkey. There were arguments too about nuclear power, and about the nature of Armenia's future ties with Russia.

As in Georgia, there was no rush to introduce a new currency, though bills would be printed late in 1992. If the rouble was successfully stabilised, there would be less pressure to introduce an independent currency; were the rouble to become even more worthless, the government would be tempted to proceed. The same was true of the Armenian army. Approved in principle, it was slow to be formed. There was less fervour than in Georgia about throwing out Russian troops.

In Armenia, as in Georgia, it was proving easier to legislate reforms than to implement them. And for the identical reason: a thick skin of bureaucracy remained hostile to change and difficult to shift for lack of a body of competent managers who could replace it. Innovative managers had been appointed as administrators, but soon found themselves hampered by the morass of incompetence and inefficiency around them. Bureaucrats find it easiest to say no, and Yerevan was strewn with frustrated Western businessmen and consultants who had been waiting weeks for appointments. Dossiers were shuffled to distant offices, phone calls not returned. No official ever wanted to take reponsibility for a decision.

Nor had there been much progress towards establishing joint ventures. The Georgians had been more successful than the Armenians in this respect, even though the Armenians would seem to have had an advantage in the form of a vigorous diaspora. Agreements had been signed but most of them came to nothing. For too many Armenian businessmen, a joint venture was essentially a means to travel abroad and acquire hard currency. On the diaspora side, nationalist fervour had overcome business sense. Until the country enjoyed better communications and an adequate transportation system, its entry into the international marketplace was bound to remain slow. The government hopes that Armenians abroad, instead of promoting individual business schemes on a small scale within Armenia, will act as intermediaries between large international companies and indigenous industries, for Armenia is well stocked with factories specialising in electromagnetics, mechanical engineering, textiles, canning and food processing.

The economic revitalisation of Armenia is unlikely to begin, let alone be completed, until the republic resolves the conflicts sapping its energies and clouding its reputation. The Georgians too were keen to end the destabilisation of their country, but for the embattled Armenians the problem was far more serious. Nor was there any resolution in sight. Ceasefires had come to nothing, and the gains made by Karabakh in May 1992 had won the disapproval of a sanctimonious international community. The Armenian government made pious noises about self-determination, but everyone knew that most Armenians longed for reunification. The skirmishing in Nakhichevan, even if no more than a freelance operation by Dashnak-inspired gunmen, was getting out of control.

Azerbaijan would never consent to the transfer of what it regarded as part of its territory to another republic; it would continue to feel justified in resisting secessionist moves on the part of Karabakh. Armenia said it was prepared to listen to any sensible offer made by the Azeris to resolve the dispute, but the only Azeri response was military. The successes of the Karabakh army in May 1992 did not lead to the capitulation of Azerbaijan. In June 1992 Azerbaijan's new foreign minister, Tovig Gasimov, insisted that Karabakh would remain part of Azerbaijan. Nor did the election that month of the Popular Front leader Albufaz Elchibey as president raise hopes for a peaceful solution. The resumption of fierce fighting happened sooner than predicted. By mid-June battles were raging in northern Karabakh, and Azeri and Armenian refugees were streaming out of the region. The Armenians, desperate to maintain the strength of their military forces, forbade able-bodied Karabakh men to leave the enclave. Karabakh volunteer forces were now to be beefed up with conscription. Ironically, the renewed fighting coincided with the resumption of peace talks. It was becoming abundantly clear that optimistic talk of United Nations intervention and peace-keeping forces was chimerical.

By early July 1992, Azeri forces, equipped with 600 tanks, were making serious advances, overrunning Armenian villages within Azerbaijan as well as parts of the region around Martakert in northern Karabakh. Deportations continued, and by mid-August it was estimated that over 500 Armenians had been killed and 50,000 were refugees. About half sought shelter in Stepanakert, which had little to offer, while others made their way to Armenia itself. The road from Armenia was still open, but the Azeri capture of nearby villages made its use extremely dangerous. Stepanakert again became subject to Grad missile attacks and to an even worse threat. Azeri SU.25 fighter-bombers were bombing the capital, and on August 16 alone about forty civilians were killed.

These setbacks had political consequences for the government of Armenia. Dashnak politicians urged the government to become more directly involved in the defense of Karabakh, but Ter-Petrossian stuck to his line, arguing against direct confrontation with Azerbaijan. The pressure became so acute that he threatened to dissolve Parliament and rule by decree. With the world powers and the United Nations understandably preoccupied by the civil wars in Yugoslavia and Somalia, the pulverizing of Nagorno-Karabakh attracted little attention. The faint hopes raised in May had been smashed even sooner than expected. The future for the region had never looked more bleak.

The Armenians, undoubtedly, had been dealt a lousy hand. Their much diminished homeland was largely wilderness. Soviet investment had given them an industrial base without which modern Armenia might have remained in the state of grubby poverty that travellers had noted a century ago – but the blockade had put the brakes on further development. The Ararat valley was fertile, but it was also small. The late 1980s had seen hopes raised and hopes dashed, first by the massacres in Sumgait and Baku and the subsequent displacements of both Azeri and Armenian minorities, and by the horrific earthquake.

Armenia should have benefited from its diaspora, but these communities in exile were proving a mixed blessing, and it could be argued that the diaspora political parties, perpetually aggrieved and immovably distrustful of Turkey, were impeding the republic's movement on to the international stage. The diaspora was also drawing away much of the republic's brightest talent, although there had been traffic in the opposite direction, with two American-Armenians serving as cabinet ministers.

Because the enemies of Armenia had been external, there seemed greater complacency in its halls of power. Georgia, though still divided after the neo-fascist posturing of the Gamsakhurdia régime, was at least chastened. Hard-core nationalists might still yearn for Gamsakhurdia's 'strong' leadership (which in practice had been weak and rudderless) but the vast majority of Georgian politicians knew that sensible and progressive government had to be restored. The presence at the helm of Eduard Shevardnadze would surely prove an incalculable benefit that would hasten Georgia's return from the political wilderness. There were passionate arguments about the kind of democracy the nation required, but no one questioned that democratic structures had to be created and that the reforms initiated by the Sigua government must continue.

The Gamsakhurdia loyalists made their last move in late June 1992, capturing the television tower, only to lose it again to the National Guard after a battle that claimed forty lives. To mark Georgia's admission to the United Nations in early August, the state council proclaimed an amnesty for loyalist prisoners, though not for the ex-president himself. While South Ossetia calmed down, serious ethnic clashes occurred in the northwestern region of Abkhazia. There were fierce battles in Sukhumi, but the better equipped Georgian National Guard soon overcame the Abkhazian nationalist forces. None the less it was a bad omen, distinctly volatile. Ethnic strife, however localised, could only hamper the process of economic recovery planned by Shevardnadze and his ministers.

My eye rests on the simple earthenware bowl given to me by the old woman at the restaurant near Borjomi. It appeals to me infinitely more than the overwrought 'handicrafts' on sale at Georgian souvenir shops. It was handed to me with tears, but filled with that most civilising of liquids – wine. When I think back on my times in the Caucasus I recall Georgia with a warmth that never diminishes. I admired the Armenians as they sought to avert disaster, but I never warmed to this harsh land and its austere people. Of course there were exceptions. I could not think about Aram, the *boulevardier manqué*, without a smile, and Vladimir had a moral rectitude quite alien to the raffish Georgians.

But when the train pulled into Tbilisi, there was always a softness in the air, even in winter. It was Mediterranean in a way that Armenia was not. In Armenia the Middle East is pushing at the door, but Georgia reminded me constantly of Greece, even Italy. Yet Georgia's unique culture – its wild and delicate folk music, its language like breakers swishing across a pebble beach, its sonorous liturgies, its ancient churches – drew me as much as its cousinhood with Europe. These hothouses of the Caucasus, hemmed in by mountains that offered inefficient protection against enemies while allowing indigenous cultures to sink their roots deeply and immovably, were utterly distinctive. Cultural harmony had been fashioned from the most disparate strands; its wilder elements – banditry, seismological uncertainty, chronic political instability – were coherent as well as destructive. There were times when the manipulative Georgians appalled me, but they were charming with it. Emotional and warm-hearted, the conditions of their lives engaged them passionately. They ate and drank with a single-mindedness that would reduce a dietician to stupefaction, and they always gave the impression that life was to be lived to the full.

The future of the Georgians lies in their own hands; their self-destructiveness is worryingly close to the surface. The Armenians are, as ever, at the mercy of their neighbours, their history, their geology. Like the Jews, they have always prospered in their diaspora. Now they must face the difficult task of transforming a homeland into a nation state. Let us hope their neighbours allow them to do so in peace.

Index

Stephen Brook
New York Days, New York Nights £5.99

This is a travel book about one city, for the actual traveller and the armchair traveller. Unfailingly entertaining, it tells you what it is really like to immerse yourself in this inexhaustible place.

'An immensely readable, knowing and funny account of New York life. Brook has supplemented an instinctive feel for the mongrel cadences of the city with some diligent footwork and an unobtrusive willingness to go anywhere. His researches took him from the bowels of the sadomasochistic Mineshaft Club to a distinctly more unpleasant-sounding Third Avenue restaurant; from City Hall to the South Bronx, via subway tunnels, police cars, jogging shoes, trendy SoHo gallery openings, and tacky East Side nightclubs. Brook's jaunty mock self-deprecatory style has more chops than a steakhouse. So read the book, see the city's TIME OUT

Winner Takes All £6.99

Stephen Brook lay bare the contradictions that make Israel both deeply problematic and so fascinating. He has travelled all over this small but extraordinarily varied country, reporting on its diversity, seeking out the widest possible range of Israelis, making sense of this heroic but deeply flawed country, and giving expression to all shades of opinion from Jew and Arab alike.

'His style is breezy and engaging, he is nosey and impertinent. Partly travelogue, his book is rich with colourful descriptions of life. Mr Brook is a perceptive observer' CHAIM BERMANT, THE SUNDAY TELEGRAPH

'Brook's wide-ranging tour through Israel – as much travelogue as political analysis and an ideal companion for the first-time visitor – skilfully captures the neurotic mood of the country's heterogenous society'.
VICTOR MALLET, LONDON REVIEW OF BOOKS

'Elegant, compelling, gripping' JULIA NEUBERGER, THE SUNDAY TIMES

All Pan Books are available at your local bookshop or newsagent, or can be ordered direct from the publisher. Indicate the number of copies required and fill in the form below.

Send to: Pan C. S. Dept
              Macmillan Distribution Ltd
              Houndmills Basingstoke RG21 2XS
or phone: 0256 29242, quoting title, author and Credit Card number.

Please enclose a remittance* to the value of the cover price plus £1.00 for the first book plus 50p per copy for each additional book ordered.

* Payment may be made in sterling by UK personal cheque, postal order, sterling draft or international money order, made payable to Pan Books Ltd.

Alternatively by Barclaycard/Access/Amex/Diners

Card No.

Expiry Date

_____

Signature

Applicable only in the UK and BFPO addresses.

While every effort is made to keep prices low, it is sometimes necessary to increase prices at short notice. Pan Books reserve the right to show on covers and charge new retail prices which may differ from those advertised in the text or elsewhere.

NAME AND ADDRESS IN BLOCK LETTERS PLEASE

....

Name _____

Address_____

_____

_____

_____

3/87